MILL ST

AUTONOMY

Steve Diggle

AUTONOMY

PORTRAIT OF A BUZZCOCK

Steve Diggle
with Simon Goddard

OMNIBUS PRESS

London / New York / Paris / Sydney / Copenhagen / Berlin / Madrid / Tokyo

CONTENTS

'This race and this country and this life produced me . . . I shall express myself as I am.'

JAMES JOYCE
A PORTRAIT OF THE ARTIST AS A YOUNG MAN

PROLOGUE / *SOMETHING'S GONE WRONG AGAIN*

LIFE.

When it's over we measure it in years on headstones. While we're living it we measure it in weeks and days on calendars and planners. We're fooled into thinking life is made of giant blocks of time placed one after the other like train carriages. Birth in Coach A. Death in Coach Z. Or, if you're unlucky, Coach C before you've even got to the buffet car.

But it's not. Life is lived in split seconds, none thicker than a cigarette paper, one fractional moment to the next. And in any one of those moments our lives can stop or start or change so fast we won't even have time to blink.

It's like the Munich air disaster. I was only two when it happened, but my grandad was a devoted Manchester United fan and talked about it a lot when I was growing up. He'd show me the old programmes of the 'Busby Babes', the greatest team of their generation, Duncan Edwards, Tommy Taylor, all brilliant young players with their whole careers ahead of them. Until eight of them were killed when their plane crashed during a take-off.

Because life will do that. One minute you're celebrating knocking Red Star Belgrade out of the European Cup. The next they're dragging your body from the burning wreckage on a German runway.

1

And it's the same for all of us. We wake up every morning believing we've got our day all mapped out and under control, never thinking fate's lightning strike might be coming. But it is. Sometimes it's good lightning, but too often it's bad. And it doesn't have to be as dramatic as a plane crash. It could be as simple as walking round a corner. Opening the front door. Answering a phone.

'RAF'!

The name on my phone screen when the lightning struck.

It was a Thursday afternoon in early December. I was at home in North London, just on my way out to meet my girlfriend. Every year we usually go to a street do down around Shepherd's Market in Mayfair, where they switch on the Christmas lights and hand out free mulled wine and mince pies. But time was getting on and I was running a bit late. So when the phone rang at first I immediately thought that'll be her wondering where I am.

'RAF'!

It wasn't. It was my manager. Raf Edmonds, the great man who'd been taking care of Buzzcocks ever since we got back together at the end of the Eighties. And, god bless him, 30 years later here we were, still going strong, even if now there were only two of us left from that classic line-up. The last original Buzzcocks standing. Me and Pete Shelley.

Me and Pete.

It was *always* me and Pete. From day one, through every incarnation of Buzzcocks, through all the different members down the decades, the one unifying constant was me and Pete. For 42 years, from rehearsing in bedsits to *Top of the Pops*, from Stalybridge to Sunset and Vine, from bathtub speed to Moët & Chandon. Always, me and Pete.

We were born just twenty days apart in 1955: Pete on 17 April; me on 7 May. Aries and Taurus, fire and earth, and as people, polar opposites in so many ways. But, no question, we were brothers. We could laugh like Laurel and Hardy, argue like Steptoe and Son and drink like a couple of Oliver Reeds. Often all three of those in the same afternoon in the same corner of the same pub. But our real magic was always the music. Buzzcocks' music. I needed him to be me just as he needed me to be him. It was the two of us together, that beautiful exchange between

2

our guitars, our different songs, our different voices. Bringing the best out of each other for the whole universe to hear.

And 40-odd years after we first faced an audience the universe was still listening. The Arctic Monkeys' label, Domino Records, were about to re-release our first three studio albums and the early A- and B-sides compilation *Singles Going Steady*. When you've been going as long as we have, after a while you learn to accept that you fall in and out of fashion depending on what other fads and trends are going on in music. But suddenly it felt like our time had come round again. Domino's blessing meant renewed media interest and a busy year of gigging, the cherry on the cake being the following summer when we'd booked the Royal Albert Hall to play the whole of *Singles Going Steady* to mark its 40th anniversary. To think of all those Last Nights of the Proms and bouncing toffs waving flags to 'Land Of Hope And Glory' and now it's our turn to go in there and rattle the organ pipes with 'Orgasm Addict' and 'Oh Shit'. The prospect alone was hilarious.

But all that was to come in the New Year. All we had left in the diary for 2018 was one gig in Arnhem in the Netherlands the following weekend.

'*RAF*'!

So why was Raf ringing? Maybe it was another interview request. With the reissues out in January and the Albert Hall going on sale, me and Pete had spent the past week or so talking to the press, mostly on the phone: me in London, him in Tallinn in Estonia where he'd moved a few years earlier with his second wife, Greta. But if it was, it could wait until tomorrow.

'*RAF*'!

Then again. If it was Raf, it was work.

'*RAF*'!!

I should probably answer.

'*RAF*'!!!

And so I did. I spoke first.

'Hiya, Raf.'

Before he'd even said anything I knew there was something wrong. Something eerie, just in the low humming sound of the phone line.

'Steve . . .'

It was Raf's voice, alright. But he sounded a bit odd.

'Steve . . .'

And then the lightning.

'Steve . . . Pete's dead.'

Pete's dead. One phone call, two words, one second. BANG! And everything my life had been for those last 42 years went up in smoke.

So did time. It was like the world had stopped, like pressing the pause button on a video recorder and the picture freezing in a blur of static. It stunned me in my tracks, like being punched in slow motion. You heard the words, but the force of the blow still hadn't landed. Did he just say what I think he said?

Pete's dead?

Raf told me as much as he knew. That morning Pete had been ill at home in Tallinn and gradually got worse until his wife had to ring an ambulance. A heart attack, basically. They rushed him to hospital and opened him up, but they couldn't save him. He was 63.

I listened as Raf explained all this, but it was like having an out-of-body experience. I was sat with the phone in my hand while my entire world was tipping upside down.

Is this actually happening?

I don't remember what else Raf said or how he hung up, only that the next thing I was alone in my house. As it felt, alone in the cosmos.

Pete's gone. *Pete's gone?*

There's only so many times you can walk up and down your own living room in a state of shock smoking cigarette after cigarette mouthing 'Fuck!' I knew I couldn't go to any Christmas party that night so I must have rung my girlfriend to cancel. I honestly don't remember. All I knew was that at that moment I couldn't face anyone. And I had to get out of the house.

I needed to sit with a pint and try to compute what was happening. Go into that psychological wilderness that death always brings. But I definitely didn't want to talk to anyone, and that wasn't going to be easy. I'm a very sociable drinker in the local pubs near me and know all the regulars. The nearest one was only a few minutes up the hill so my plan was to sneak in, keep my head down, grab a drink and take myself away by myself.

I walked in. And the place was mobbed.

A wake. Would you believe it? I'd just been told Pete was dead and not half an hour later I've walked into a fucking wake.

I knew the bloke too, an actor who also used to drink round and about in the same pubs, so there were a few familiar faces in there who recognised me, giving the odd nod across the room. But I managed to get myself a Guinness without anyone bothering me, took it straight outside and sat on one of the wooden picnic benches off the pavement. The rest were all empty, which is what I needed. Solitude.

I huddled in my coat against the cold, lit a cigarette and sipped my pint. It was dark above with no sign of any stars and teeth-chatteringly freezing. From inside the pub I could still hear the faint laughter from the wake. Friends sharing stories and celebrating the dearly departed. And here I was, still in that raw moment trying to comprehend it all.

Me and Pete. Me and Pete. Me and . . . *Fuck!*

Me. It was just me now. Just me. And the cigarette warming my icy numb fingers. And the pint of Guinness that I could barely taste. And the starless night. And the cars calmly driving past in a world without Pete Shelley. And the one thought screaming through my head over and over again like a stuck record.

'What *the fuck* am I going to do now?'

IT'S A THING THAT'S WORTH HAVING

(1955–1976)

1 / *MANCHESTER RAIN*

THE SOUND OF A GRANDFATHER CLOCK crashing to the ground is the sound of time exploding. Quite literally. All those cogs and weights and pulleys and pendulums smashing to pieces. It's an almighty noise like God stamping a hole through his floorboards and the whole sky falling in. And when you're only 7 years old it sounds like Armageddon.

It was. Complete Armageddon. A few seconds earlier, it had been a normal front room on a terrace street in Manchester. Now it looked like a Holiday Inn after Keith Moon had checked out. The walls were splattered with sandwiches like some sort of dirty protest. The teapot had been tipped up and smashed and the tea leaves trampled into the carpet. Ornaments and plates had been cracked and the bits chucked everywhere. The once vertical grandfather clock was now splayed horizontal making funny whirring noises like it was choking on broken shards of hours and minutes. And standing there amongst it, all giggling so hard they could barely breathe, were the little culprits.

Me and my mates.

Poor Nigel's nan. It was her house. We'd been sat on the front doorstep outside when she had to nip out and put a bet on. Her famous last words: 'You lot just look after the place while I'm gone.'

No sooner was she over the horizon when we invited all the other kids in off the street and trashed the place. It was like a collective madness. Somebody slapped a sandwich on the wall, and the next thing we all went mad. Auto-destruction! The tipping over of the grandfather clock was our grand finale. For a second we all stood there, admiring our crime scene, then upped and legged it round the corner to the labour exchange where we sat on the steps, laughing. Because it didn't feel real. To us the world was a comic strip. This was *Dennis the Menace*, and any minute now the dads were going to come storming down the street, rolling up their sleeves to give us a good hiding. And sure enough, here they were, red-faced and marching towards us. 'Get 'ere, you little bastards!' While we sat there, sniggering, like life was all one big joke.

Why did I do it? I genuinely don't know. It was more than mischief. Maybe it was a latent sense of frustration, even at that age, letting go and testing your limitations. Something primal, a pent-up energy trying to break free. At the time I had no idea what it was. It took me another 14 years or so to find out. Because it was obviously in me, even then, aged 7. Now I look back, I must have been born with it.

Punk rock.

IF JESUS WAS BORN IN BETHLEHEM, punk was born in Manchester. My city. My blood. The first air I breathed. The first sky I saw. The first rain I felt. I was baptised by Manchester rain. And fuck knows there's plenty of it.

Before I was anything else in this world, I was a Mancunian. Before I'm Steve Diggle from Buzzcocks, I'm Steve Diggle from Manchester. I grew up in its streets, each like a sculptor's chisel carving me into the person I am. The streets that taught me to see the poetry of life. Keats saw it in butterflies and nightingales, but then he wasn't a Manc. I learned to see it in cars on bricks and the sound of the bloke over the road beating up his kids when he came home pissed. The beauty and tragedy in the poetry of the streets – streets that are now long gone, obliterated by town planners, whole communities flattened by the fat cats of commerce. But while they tore down the terraces, they couldn't tear up the poetry. Those streets live on, in me and with me, in every breath. It doesn't matter where I live or what stage I'm standing on. I am proudly, and forever, Mancunian.

I, Stephen Eric Diggle.

Stephen was my mam's choice: her name was Janet.

Eric was my dad's choice: his name was also Eric.

I've no idea where the Diggle comes from, other than there's also a village outside Manchester by Saddleworth Moor called Diggle. I've never looked into our family ancestry. At school it was always a bit embarrassing. 'Diggle'. It wasn't your run-of-the-mill Jones or Smith on the class register. It sounded like a joke. *Giggle, jiggle, Stephen Diggle.* But it was Plato who said that if you give something a name, therefore it gives it a meaning. So I've spent my whole life giving meaning to an otherwise silly name.

My first gig was screaming down the delivery room of St Mary's Hospital off Oxford Road. I was born on a Saturday, not a minute old and raring for the weekend. It was also the day of the 1955 FA Cup final. Manchester City v. Newcastle. City lost 3–1. Already, the football gods were warning me I'd be better off supporting United.

The first person to hold me after the midwife was my mam. The second must have been the genie of rock'n'roll. In May '55 it was already out of the bottle. Elvis had made his first four singles for Sun, and by the time I was two weeks old Chuck Berry had recorded 'Maybellene'. It all happened that first year I was alive. Little Richard's 'Tutti Frutti' and 'Long Tall Sally', Johnny Cash's 'Folsom Prison Blues', Chuck's 'Roll Over Beethoven', Carl Perkins' 'Blue Suede Shoes' and Elvis's 'Heartbreak Hotel'. While I was gurgling and soiling nappies in Manchester, thousands of miles across the sea the great gospels of rock'n'roll were being created. My generation, the punk generation, were the chosen ones. The children of rock'n'roll, born in the mid- to late Fifties. The bands that came before us in the Sixties were all war babies. The Beatles, the Stones, all born in the Forties while the Luftwaffe were dropping bombs on their heads. Somewhere between you get generation glam, the Bowies and the Bolans, the baby boomers born into a world where the only pop chart was for sales of sheet music. But my lot, we were the chosen kids of the atomic age. We knew Bill Haley's 'Rock Around The Clock' before we knew any nursery rhymes. We'd never known a world where rock'n'roll didn't exist. It was all ours to inherit. Our birthright.

While they were all rocking in Memphis or wherever else, I was rocking in my cot in Longsight. My first home, Clarence Road. Semi-detached, with a nice garden. Working-class but doing OK.

I was the first child. Contraception not being widely discussed in those days, I was soon joined by three others. Next was my brother, Phil. I became a musician and he became an artist, so together we're probably the two most unconventional idiot sons any parent wouldn't wish for. Maybe that's why they kept going and had my two little sisters, Wendy and Sandra. It must have been some relief that at least they turned out relatively normal.

Dad was a lorry driver, an easy-going man who'd been browbeaten by national service which landed him in the Korean War when he was 18. He never really spoke about it. The fact he didn't meant he must have been through some seriously bad shit. Sometimes he'd come back from the pub with his mate, Brian, a bit of a nutcase who'd been out there with him. They'd be pissed and start singing Frankie Laine songs, 'Rawhide' and 'Mule Train', then Brian would start going on about how he loved kicking the heads off the dead Koreans like footballs. My dad's favourite story was the time they were hiding in a crater together, bullets flying overhead, when he started scraping away at the soil and found a human skull staring back at him. This other young soldier was with them and freaked out so much he dropped his sandwiches. My dad and Brian saw them and went, 'You still gonna eat those or not?' So they lay there, scoffing his sandwiches, next to this skeleton while this poor lad's having a fit. Dad tried to make light of it, but you just knew he must have been scared to death over there. Then, when he came back, the first thing he was told when he stepped off the boat was his own dad had died. 'Welcome home.' So no wonder there was always a distance about him, like something had taken its toll on his spirit. He must have been all of 20 or 21 when he was discharged, so he just kept his head down, got married, had me and started a family. A working man who had to get on and play the game. Yes, sir, no, sir.

Mam had a shop on Stockport Road selling kids' clothes. Before I was old enough for school she'd take me to work with her and leave me with the lovely old woman who lived in the flat upstairs, Mrs Warklin. She was the one who gave me the keys to the kingdom by teaching me to read. Thanks to her, the universe was now all mine to discover, everything from *The Beano* to *Ulysses*. The other great thing about Mam's shop was the backyard, the scene of one of my first sonic epiphanies. It had high brick walls which gave off the most amazing reverb, so I'd spend hours there just bouncing a tennis ball back and forth, listening to this weird echo, completely transfixed. Long before I'd even properly discovered music, I was already becoming fascinated by sound.

Mam's only problem with the shop was she was too bighearted. She was always letting customers buy too much on credit so the books never balanced and, inevitably, in the end the business went under. Too kind for her own good, but that was Mam. She even gave credit to Myra Hindley's mum, who lived not so far away. Weirdly enough, this would have been around the same time my dad got roped into decorating Ian Brady's bedroom. My dad knew his stepdad who told him, 'Eric, this kid's a nightmare, he's just coming out of Borstal.' So because my dad was good at wallpapering he asked if he'd help get Brady's room ready, which he did.

The chilling reality for kids of my age was that the Moors Murderers' Manchester was our Manchester. They plucked their victims from the very streets I grew up in, all to the east and southeast around Gorton, Ancoats and Longsight. So it's not really that surprising that one day I'd end up seeing them with my own eyes.

This was a bit later, when I must have been maybe 8 or 9. It was at a bonfire at the end of our street, and I remember seeing this Teddy Boy-looking bloke with this blonde woman. It was just those two watching us kids run around the bonfire, which even at the time I thought was a bit odd. They were sat on an old broken wardrobe, there to be chucked on the fire, going, 'Come and sit next to Myra.' I never sat with them, and I'm not sure any of the other kids did either. I just remember them being there, and I only mention it because that's how frighteningly easy it must have been for them to do the horrendous things they did. It's one of those weird, creepy memories that only pieces itself together years after the fact. Thinking back and suddenly realising, *Fuck, that was them!* But it happened. Even as us kids danced around the flames, there were real-life monsters watching from the shadows.

WHEN YOU'RE A KID you don't ask, you get told. One day I'm happy playing in our garden in Longsight, the next I'm staring at a brick yard with an outside toilet. After Mam lost the shop we had to up sticks to a terrace in Bradford – part of East Manchester, not the city in Yorkshire – opposite where her parents lived. It must have been a bit of a drop in living standards for them, but I honestly didn't feel any of that at the time. I'd just turned 7, and Bradford became this beautiful crystallisation where I learned to appreciate the real heart and spirit of the post-war generation. It was exactly like the old black-and-white *Coronation Street* which my gran across the road would always watch. Sometimes I'd be over there watching it with her. Odd now I think of it, staring at a TV watching a fictional version of the actual world you lived in. Then you'd switch it off and go outside and there'd be the real-life Ena Sharples in a hairnet shaking her fist at you. Except the one on my street swore a lot more than the one on the telly.

My Coronation Street was Dewar Street, where our family of half a dozen Diggles sardined ourselves into number 17. To start with, the four of us kids shared a room: two beds, boys in one, girls the other, top to tail. If anyone wet the bed, it was a nightmare. Eventually me and my brother moved up to the attic. By that I don't mean a 'loft conversion' like today, just an attic with a window where you could look out and see the woman who lived opposite hanging her bras out on the washing line. There was no central heating, but we did have a bathroom, something of a luxury since not all the neighbours did. Sometimes you'd be sneaking around backyards and see the men in the tin baths in the kitchen like Steptoe with the women in pinnies pouring jugs over their heads. And, like everybody else, we had an outside toilet, which was like being locked in the torture box in *The Bridge on the River Kwai*, except it was usually freezing. All very Dickensian.

The one magical oasis beyond our street was Belle Vue. Say those words to people of a certain age in Manchester and you'll see their eyes light up. Imagine a Lowry painting of factory chimneys and red-brick houses with Disneyland plonked in the middle of it. Well, that was Belle Vue. For grown-ups it was somewhere to go to bet on the dogs, or watch the speedway, or go drinking and dancing. For kids, it had an amusement arcade, a zoo and, if you were a bit older, the Kings Hall where Jimi Hendrix played. The place was already more than psychedelic enough before Jimi arrived. Being a kid from the terrace and suddenly looking at elephants, giraffes, monkeys and all these other exotic animals, you felt you were hallucinating. They even had a 'flea circus', pulling the little chariots. Belle Vue was living proof life wasn't all just cobbles and puddles. Our unique inner-city paradise. And like everything else that was inspiring about old Manchester, the bastards tore it down.

HAVING MY GRAN AND GRANDAD so close over the road was like having an extra set of parents to babysit us when Mam and Dad were at work or when they used to go out, usually somewhere like the Domino club in Openshaw to see Engelbert Humperdinck back when he was still calling himself Gerry Dorsey. Gran was Scottish, and like many great Scots she loved Hogmanay a lot more than Christmas – I've always reckoned I must have got my drinking genes from her side of the family. She was lovely, but if I'd ever done to her living room what I did to Nigel's nan's, I don't think I'd have lived to tell the tale. The only time I came close to trashing it was by accident after I'd made the mistake of joining the boy scouts. I only ever went once or twice as it was all much too regimented for me, walking in circles with a book on your head, learning to tie knots and all that bollocks. But they gave me a banner, a flag on a pole, to march around with. I was dead chuffed so I ran over the road to show my gran. 'Look, Gran! I've got a flag!' Next thing, there's broken glass raining on my head. In my excitement I'd stupidly poked it through the glass lightshade in her ceiling. That put an end to anymore dib-dib-dibbing.

Grandad was a trade union rep who worked out of his front parlour. As a young man he'd been a pretty good footballer who did trials for Preston North End, but they'd told him he was 'too short' to play professionally. Just after they rejected him he was offered a job at an electrical firm, purely so they could use him in the company football team. Instead, he ended up starting a trade union, so they punished him by making him work nights. Then they tried to buy him out, offering him his own office and a new car, but Grandad was having none of it. He told them he'd rather work out of his own front room, which is what he did, surrounded by all these massive ledgers. All the workers would go round his for help, these poor sods with ten kids who'd lost their arms working in the factory with no compensation. Grandad spent his whole life fighting for them. His pride and joy was the certificate up on his wall signed by Aneurin Bevan congratulating him on recruiting his first 150 trade union members. I always remember it hanging next to a photo of his brother, Tommy, a sailor who never came back from the war. There's the spectrum of life right there on one patch of wallpaper. Hope and despair.

He wasn't some bolshy Marxist either. He just believed in a fair day's work for a fair day's pay. He taught me a lot about injustice, which definitely put some fire in my soul, even as a young kid. Grandad was such a gentle bloke in many ways too. He loved his family, he loved the pub, he loved going to the dogs at Belle Vue and he loved Man United, which is why he told me about the Munich air disaster. It still haunted him, the death of all those young players. He'd even kept the old newspaper with the picture of Matt Busby on life support inside an oxygen tent. A fate I'd soon only narrowly avoid myself.

It happened when I was round his house one day. I told Grandad I was popping out to fetch some matches, which I did – seconds before skipping out into the road and straight into the path of a passing taxi. This seemed to be a common occurrence in early Sixties Manchester. No Green Cross Code in those days – kids were always getting ploughed down. The lottery of life. To us, roads were just strips of tarmac to play on, which is why on most streets there'd be more hopscotch grids than actual cars. The same thing happened to my brother. He got run over, and it was touch and go. The school even held special prayers for him, though he luckily pulled through in the end. So in the circumstances I got off lightly. I still don't remember anything about the accident – a total blackout – other than waking up in the hospital and Grandad being there at the bedside. The first thing I said when I woke up was, 'Here's them matches, Grandad.' I'd had my fist clenched the whole time I was out. When I opened it, there were the matches.

Knowing me, I'd probably wanted them to start a bonfire. I don't know why we were so obsessed with them as kids, but we were. Any excuse to set fire to a heap of junk. We used to build them all the time on this patch of waste ground at the end of the street we called the croft (the same bonfire spot where I'd eventually see Hindley and Brady). It was all dust and silt, where back in the war they must have had an air-raid shelter.

It was also where we'd play football, even if most games on the croft, we'd make do with kicking about a tennis ball. I can still see one now in slow motion, sailing through the air and smashing one of the windows in the end houses. Or some bloke running after you threatening to give you a hiding cos you'd just left a dent in his new Ford Corsair. 'Bloody kids!' That's my childhood in two words. Bloody kids. That was us.

At the other end of the street you had the big pub on the corner, the Bradford Hotel. We'd sometimes loiter on the pavement outside waiting for the door to open when there'd be this intoxicating waft of cigarettes and beer. That intense organic hoppy aroma, better than the smell of any perfume. The pub was like a secret adult kingdom, and I was fascinated by all of it: the smell, the sound, peering through the door and seeing the brassy women like Elsie Tanner and the thick clouds of smoke and the old blokes sat playing dominoes. I can still see myself stood there on the kerb, wishing I was old enough to go in and join them. Then, in the evening, you'd hear these toothless hags in the bar wailing Frank Sinatra songs, or there'd be women marching up the street with headscarves like something from *Monty Python* going up to the pub to bring back a jug of beer for their husbands before they got home from their shift.

But all around, the whole community, there seemed to be an openness and a friendliness everywhere. Nobody had anything, but nobody was aspiring to anything either, so there was no one-upmanship of any kind. As a kid, the streets where you live are all you ever know. So for the next seven years Bradford became my entire universe.

My street was *everything*. I quickly made friends with the local kids, and next thing you know, we've got our very own 'street army'. I was General Diggle, obviously. Most of the other street gangs just fought each other. Ours was like the intelligentsia. We were crafty fuckers. The best thing we ever did was steal another street's entire bonfire. In those days serious turf wars were fought every November around Guy Fawkes night. I'd seen some programme about some old battle between the Scots and the English, where one of them had surprised the other by attacking at dawn. So we did the same thing, up and out before the milkman, and nicked all their bonfire wood. We were like ants, passing down all these bits of timber along the backyards, all this firewood they'd been gathering for days before bonfire night. We didn't leave them a stick.

Despite all the mischief, we had a lot of creativity in us. If we didn't have something, we'd go and make it ourselves – an early flash of the punk D.I.Y. spirit. We built a city out of cardboard boxes, our own make-believe Manchester, which we called 'Minichester'. We made a hotel, then a library, then a town hall, like little Billy Liars building our own utopian Ambrosia. Then, once we got bored being gods of Minichester, we started our own street newspaper. We had a John Bull printing set, so we decided we'd make up all these stories about the characters who lived round and about. Real people, but to us they were like something out of *The Dandy* or *The Topper*. There was 'T-Shirt Man', this bloke who always wore a T-shirt, and 'Mr Kind' who was always kind to people. Well, most of the time. Except for the one day me and Nigel were sat out on the step, drinking our sterilised milk, when Mr Kind was walking past and suddenly stopped. He just stared at us, shook his head and said, 'You lads will get nowhere!'

I never forgot him saying that. Mr Cruel To Be Kind. Especially since I ended up on *Top of the Pops* and Nigel ended up becoming a brain surgeon. Whereas one day not long after that, Mr Kind died a hero's death. Sitting on his toilet while having a shit.

'You lads will get nowhere!'

Us lads. To give him his due, it probably did seem like we were going nowhere back then. Daft young scamps always up to trouble, nicking firewood, kicking balls through windows or trashing living rooms just for the fun of it. But a sense of purpose was coming my way fast. The year I moved to Bradford was 1962. The Sixties were about to explode, and so would my head. To the sound of something a lot more harmonious than a crashing grandfather clock.

2 / *AIRWAVES DREAM*

WHEN DID IT START? The mind plays tricks and makes fictions from dead memory, but facts are facts and dates are dates. I was born in 1955, so in late 1962 I'm only 7. The radio's on in the living room with Jimmy Hanley playing all the usual funny children's tunes. Charlie Drake's 'Mr Custer', Rolf Harris's 'Tie Me Kangaroo Down, Sport', all those quirky early George Martin records by Peter Sellers and the Goons. I'm sat half listening, half thinking of whose bonfire to nick, what else to build in Minichester or the next T-Shirt Man scoop in our street newspaper. When suddenly the wail of a mouth organ, a thudding beat and these young male voices singing in harmony.

'Love, love me do'.

That's how I genuinely remember it. Seven years old, and the first time I hear the Beatles it's their first single on the radio. Talk about being born in the right place at the right time.

The radio was the radiogram, this cumbersome monolith that took up half the living room with a massive valve speaker. When you turned it on, it warmed up slowly like a rocket engine preparing for lift-off. I loved playing with the dials, hearing all the hiss and crackling, and then suddenly you'd pick up Radio Oslo and you'd wonder where the hell that was. Even the sound of the static in between sounded amazing. White noise! Years later, when Pete Shelley played me Lou Reed's *Metal Machine Music* I thought, 'Yeah, but I was doing that on our radiogram when I was 7.' One half of this monster was the wireless and the other was the record player where Mam and Dad played their 78s. Their favourite was Nat King Cole, 'When I Fall In Love'. The sound of his voice from that radiogram was like the voice of Moses. You didn't hear him with your ears, you felt him between your ribs. Another 78 they played a lot was Guy Mitchell, 'Singing The Blues', when everyone would whistle along. I just loved looking at all the different labels, the MGM one, which was yellow, and the Capitol one, which was all purple with the silver lettering, like different-coloured sweets.

There was also, already, a rocker in the family. My older teenage cousin, Andy, who lived a few doors down was a Teddy Boy. You'd see him with his mates, all with greased hair, winklepickers, plastic jackets, the lot. Or you'd be playing in the street and suddenly you'd hear 'Awopbopaloomop!' and it'd be him blaring out Little Richard with the windows open, the whole terrace shaking and neighbours banging on his walls. It sounded absolutely *amazing*. So it was all slowly chip-chipping away at my head – the radiogram, my parents' 78s, my rocker cousin Andy – all these different melodies and rhythms bouncing off my ears. But then came my big biblical moment when the clouds parted. A pivotal incident, like the scene in every comic book where something happens to a kid and that's how they get their superpowers. Peter Parker's bitten by a spider and becomes Spiderman. I got bitten by rock'n'roll and became Steve Diggle.

It was all thanks to Ian James, my mate over the road who I used to play cowboys with. He had a big sister, Linda, who must have been getting on 16, with beautiful long blonde hair. I'd have been 7 or 8, and when you're that young and not yet at that fully sexual age, you see a beautiful girl and they're like angels. This day – The Day – we were round his house sat watching her in the corner while she was getting ready to go out. She had a record player, a proper Dansette, not like our radiogram, and she had *albums*. Round ours we were still spinning 78s. And not just any albums. Linda must have been pretty hip, or a bit of a folkie, because she had the first Bob Dylan album. That's the first time I'd ever heard of him. She also had the first Beatles album, *Please Please Me*, the record she was playing that day. So the Beatles are singing and Linda's in the mirror drying her hair . . . with a *hairdryer*! In our house we all dried our hair with a towel, whereas this smooth plastic thing she was wafting about looked like the Russian Sputnik satellite. Real-life science fiction.

So I'm listening to the Beatles, watching this angelic girl drying her blonde hair with this space age machine. And that was it.

ZAP!

I suddenly saw it all. Music, girls, the melodies, the future. A lifestyle awakening. It's like when the Catholic Church make people saints if they see statues of the Madonna crying. I saw Linda James dry her hair to the Beatles. That was my calling.

Linda James wasn't done with me yet either. The first guitar I ever held happened to be hers. She had a little Spanish acoustic which she let me pick up another time I was round their house. I never knew how to hold it properly or what the frets were for, but I just instinctively plucked a string.

'Woooah!'

It was instantaneous. A flutter in my heart, feeling the resonance of that one note. It was an acoustic guitar, but in my little hands its power felt electric, like I'd definitely plugged into *something*. The magic ether of rock'n'roll, maybe. Because even though it would still be many years before I learned to play a guitar, the seed must have been planted there and then. Almost as if I never chose the guitar, more the guitar chose me.

Between the doctrines of Jimmy Hanley and Linda James, the Beatles became my first love. Mine and a million others. Mam bought me my first record from the market, their *Twist And Shout* EP with the cover of them jumping up in the air, which got me leaping up and down all over the backyard trying to recreate the same poses. They'd even earn me a ticking-off after I had my tonsils taken out in Ancoats Hospital. Someone had a radio in the ward, so I was lying in bed recovering when 'Please Please Me' came on and instinctively I started singing along. The matron went berserk. 'Shut up! You've just had your tonsils out! What's wrong with you?' I was completely bewitched by them.

That Christmas, Mam also got me my very own transistor radio, which meant I could lie in bed tuning in to Radio Caroline or Radio Luxembourg and hear all the Beatles I wanted. I was over the moon until the reality of what she'd actually given me dawned. She'd bought it on HP from a shop way over in Gorton, so every two weeks for the next eighteen months I'd have to catch a bus after school to go and make the payments. So that was my real Christmas present: the burden of financial responsibility.

Life was magical enough with four Beatles when suddenly there were five. My dad's last hope of me ever becoming a Man City supporter died on 14 September 1963 when George Best made his debut at Old Trafford. I was already leaning towards United cos of my grandad and the other older kids on my street. Dad had taken me to a few City games too, but every time he did, they lost. Even he must have started thinking I was some sort of jinx. But when Best turned up for United, that was it. Everyone else on the pitch just looked like footballers. Here was a rock'n'roll star. Best wasn't just gifted. He was good-looking, glamorous and cool as fuck. So for the next few years I'd go and watch him play home games, usually with those older kids, there with my wooden rattle going nuts. In a lot of ways he was like the first pop star I ever saw in concert. It felt like a gig, that tribal excitement, the standing terraces, the noise of the crowd reverberating on the metal sheeting they used to have back then which amplified everything even louder. There'd be all the old fellas jeering him cos of his haircut. 'Where's your handbag, Georgie?' But he'd just take the piss, run rings round the defence and score all the time. A proper punk rocker in a pair of shorts. I loved Best, and I'm a red for life, but there eventually came a point when I was maybe 12 or 13 when I had a bit of a realisation. That there's an element to football that's another form of mind control, like giving the plebs something to watch, feeding the Christians to the lions. It was after our little gang graduated to the notorious Stretford End, which meant you were Big Time, but it was also pretty heavy. You'd see all the yobs and the violence, little kids having their scarves nicked by older fans and all sorts of bullying. It was knee-jerk, but I'd suddenly had enough. It was during one match against West Ham. I just left by myself and caught the bus back home in the rain. 'Sod this.' Back to my music where my heart belonged.

By then I was short-circuiting with it. Every time you turned the telly on was like witnessing another revolution. I was 9 when I saw the Stones on *Ready Steady Go!* doing 'Little Red Rooster'. Another massive epiphany, seeing Jagger's face huge on the screen, like he was going to bust out of it and eat the living room. 'Who the hell is *this*?' Incredible.

I'd only just recovered from the Stones and the next thing it's the Kinks, 'You Really Got Me'. *Dah-nah-nah, nah-nah!* It was musical shock treatment, rewiring your whole brain. Suddenly here's the Who with 'My Generation'. KA-BOOM! It was like Hiroshima going off between my ears. Then being at the amusement arcade at Belle Vue and seeing all these older kids in parkas with 'The Who' badly painted on the back. Being only 10, it looked frightening, but at the same time it agitated a strange new excitement deep inside me.

All the kids around me loved pop music too. The key difference was I wasn't only crazy about it, I was also very discerning. I could see there was a massive distinction between what the Beatles and the Stones and the Kinks were doing and what Brian Poole and the Tremeloes were doing. It was an innate hipness, like a sixth sense. You'd see other kids at school quite happy to jig around to Freddie and the Dreamers. Some speccy wanker kicking his legs about to ukulele music on *Blue Peter*? No, thanks! Even when I was 9 or 10 I knew they were meaningless. Same as the Dave Clark Five, 'Bits And Pieces'. Thump! Thump! Thump! It was idiots' music. Whereas Lennon, Jagger, Ray Davies, Townshend, there was *something* there. Something they knew, something they could teach me about life which my parents or teachers couldn't. Which is when I probably decided to stop listening to them. Stick your Pythagoras, I'll stick with John Lennon.

Besides, I now had everything I needed in my little transistor. Lying on my bed in the attic, head on the pillow, blowing my mind to the latest transmissions from Planet Rock'n'Roll. But that was the problem. All this stuff was happening in a different galaxy. The Beatles and the Stones lived in the TV, on the radio and on the turntable. Electric ghosts in the machine. Whereas I lived in Manchester. Wet grey Manchester. The people on my street worked in factories and shops or drove lorries like my dad. That's all anyone ever did round my way. Which meant that's what I was expected to do. Leave school, get a job in a factory, get married, have kids and settle in a terrace with an outside toilet until the day I dropped dead on it like Mr Kind. And I'm only just realising this, I'm only 10 years old, and I'm already feeling like my life can be summed up in the title of the first Beatles LP I ever owned.

Help!

3 / DON'T MESS WITH MY BRAIN

MY EDUCATION can be summed up in one report card.

'He's very perceptive.'

I don't think the rest of it was very good, just that one line. I didn't even know what 'perceptive' meant at the time, but they were right. I had a natural insight. Music had opened my mind up to the universe. Just hearing Dylan's voice on the radio asking, 'How does it feel?' and even though I'm only 10 I'm thinking, *Yeah, how* does *it feel?* There was a new mindfulness bubbling away inside me. As I hit my teens, I started to realise that I wasn't like anyone else I knew, which was scary in a lot of ways. *Why aren't I the same as them?* I was a kid trying to find some magic in life. Only the harder I looked, the less I could see.

I'd been OK up until the end of junior school. We read *The Water Babies* by Charles Kingsley which left a big impression on me, the whole class-consciousness thing, learning that the rich used to send poor kids the same age as us up chimneys. I loved reading, and I even won a Bible there as some class prize, so I can't have been a bad pupil, even if the matron once made me bite a bar of soap for 'telling lies'. I think they call that child abuse today; back then you could make a decent career out of it.

This was Bradford Memorial School, where Bill Tarmey – Jack Duckworth off *Coronation Street* – had been before me. The nearest my class had to a celebrity was the daughter of one of the Swinging Blue Jeans, who

I'd seen on telly doing 'Hippy Hippy Shake'. They were never one of my favourites, but he turned up once to pick her up wearing brushed denim and a suntan. It was a big deal. 'Look! A pop star!' That said, to this day, if you pressed a gun to my head, I still couldn't tell you the bloke's name.

I trod in the footsteps of another infinitely more famous pop star when I moved up to secondary school. My first day at Higher Openshaw, or Varna Street as everyone called it, they gathered us first years in assembly and tried to impress us by preaching about the great former pupils who'd passed through its doors. One was Rifleman John Beeley, some poor sod who'd been killed in the war while taking out the enemy and had been given a posthumous Victoria Cross. The other was Davy Jones from the Monkees. I don't know which felt the more unlikely – that I'd ever be in a situation to do anything heroic or suicidal enough to earn a Victoria Cross, or the chances of me ever getting to America to shake maracas next to Mike Nesmith. Both seemed ludicrous. But I can remember the next time I saw the Monkees on telly, staring at Davy Jones and thinking, 'How the hell did he get *there* from Varna Street?' It should have been an inspiration. All it did was make the already impossible seem even less possible.

The first day, I turned up in my new blazer and satchel, a lamb to the slaughter, being sized up by these terrifying older lads with hobnailed boots and combat jackets with 'Man City' on the back who liked nothing better than flushing first years' heads down the bog. A school of hard knocks if ever there was one. There'd be kids in the playground chucking water bombs at teachers, fights every break and all sorts of vandalism. One assembly, the headmaster held up a toilet seat that had been ripped from its hinges and warned us, 'There's too much destruction in this school!' Maybe that's why they decided to get rid of us all. After about a year, all of us senior kids got kicked out and sent up to another comp, Wright Robinson. Which was even worse.

Worse in the sense it was exactly like *Kes*. I'm sure that's true of anyone who went to any comprehensive in the Sixties, especially in the North. That film just sums it up perfectly, hitting every nail bang on the head – the kids, the teachers, the changing rooms, the strap. That was me, one of the kids outside the headmaster's door, waiting for six of the best. I must have got strapped every other day for doing fuck all. They never needed a reason. My brother Phil followed me there two years later, and they made him stand outside the class just because he was Steve Diggle's brother.

'Sir, what have I done?'

'You're his brother – get out!'

And probably belted him for it while they were at it. The worst was the science teacher who had a paddle, this piece of wood with holes in it, that he named 'Horace'. Every lesson was just another excuse to bring Horace out and thwack some poor bastard's skin off. The only demonstration of physics he ever taught us.

Our games teacher was also just like the one in *Kes*, only even creepier. The first day we turned up for swimming, none of us were prepared so none of us had any trunks. 'That's OK,' he said. 'Just strip off.' He then made us go in the pool naked, swim a length to the other side, come out and walk back along the pool and get in again. All the time he's stood there, eyeing up this procession of naked young boys dripping wet. I knew he definitely wasn't right even before the day he felt up my leg in the changing room. He said, 'You've got a funny pulse.' And I'm thinking, *No wonder! If you don't take your hand away, I'm going to have a fucking heart attack!* His fingers never crept any higher than my thigh, but it was all very dodgy. I dread to think what teachers like him must have got away with.

The only subject I really liked was English. I loved words and always have done since Mrs Warklin taught me to read in Mam's old shop. Maths, I absolutely hated. Geography was nonsense, trying to teach it to kids who hadn't even seen a tree in their lives. And music was a lost cause, mainly because the teacher was having it away with the art teacher so I don't remember any actual tuition. More a case of chucking us a book and leaving us to it while he took her in the store room for a knee trembler. But none of it mattered because, just like Mr Kind, all the teachers had it in their heads we were going nowhere.

Just to hammer the point home, they organised a school trip to Manchester Airport. I can't remember what class it was or the point of the lesson, but when we got there they said, 'You're all going on a plane!' None of us had ever flown before – *nobody* flew back then – so we were all excited, if a bit scared, at the same time wondering, 'Wow! I wonder where we're going?' So they piled us into this little plane and off we went, up into the clouds. The pilot circled around for ten minutes, then took us straight back to Manchester Airport. That was our day trip. Destination: literally fucking nowhere. It was like a metaphor for my entire education, constantly being reminded there was no escape. Try hard as we liked, we were always going to end up exactly where we started. Stuck on the tarmac in Manchester.

What chance did a kid like me have? Absolutely none. But more than anything else, I just felt *apart* from everything. Life was over there and I was over here. The way I saw the outside world was like looking at a train set. Or like Minichester, the make-believe city we built as kids. It was all a surreal joke. These people going about their life in factories and shops and going home to their little houses, just like one big train set. It became my biggest fear. That I'd end up part of the train set, trapped in a clockwork existence I couldn't escape.

It became obvious to me school was only there to wind up the key. You weren't there to be taught, you were there to be programmed so they'd spit you out into the train set. If you were clever, with six O-levels, straight into the nearest bank. If you were thick, with none, into the nearest factory. Either way, you were fucked.

IT'S NOT LIKE I was aspiring to anything or that I thought I was better than everyone else either. I just knew I never wanted any of *that*. All I wanted was freedom, and to be left alone. Alone to think, and to work out who I was. It was like an illness, almost. Before I'd left school I'd already made my mind up that I was going to be a conscientious objector to work. I knew I was never going to have a job, which meant I was never going to have any money, which meant I was never going to go anywhere. That's when my mantra became: 'If I can see the sun and the moon, that's as far as I'm going to travel.'

The worst of it was that, much as I hated school, I also didn't want to leave. While I was there, nobody was expecting anything of me. Once I left, that was me in the firing line. I've a very vivid memory of one day being sat in my gran's outside toilet. It's when you're at your most vulnerable, like Mr Kind, and because of him I've always been a bit careful when I have to go as you never know what's going to happen. So there I was, trousers round me ankles, sat on me gran's toilet, having a shit while also thinking, *Christ,*

I'm leaving school soon – what am I going to do? The two things intertwined in this profound Freudian moment. Fate and faeces. I wasn't scared of the outside world, just worried about it. I knew it wasn't right for me. Not because I wanted an easy life either. I didn't want to be some brainless dosser. I didn't want *anything*. I just knew there had to be *something* else.

My last day at school drew a fittingly undignified curtain on my formal education. As was custom, the term ended with a final assembly where they handed out certificates to all the pupils who were leaving, including myself. But this only took place after an hour or so of speeches and hymns and the geography teacher trying to show off playing 'Kumbaya' or some such bollocks on guitar, more for his ego than anything else. Because it was the final day of term, they relaxed the school uniform rules so you could wear your normal clothes. So I turned up in my cord Wrangler jacket, looking pretty cool, I thought, and there's all my mates with their best gear on. We're outside the gates, about to go in, when suddenly one of us has a brainwave. 'Fuck sitting through the whole assembly. It's our last day . . . let's go to the pub!'

So we did. We were only 15, but the pubs round about Openshaw didn't seem to care – if you had the money, there's your beer, sonny. A couple of pints later, feeling all warm and merry, we decided we'd sneak back into the hall before the end of assembly so we could pick up our certificates. But soon as we were through the front gates a teacher collared us, hauled us into an office and locked us inside. It was next door to the assembly so we could hear it all still going on as they handed out the certificates – 'Jenkins . . . Jones . . .' – announcing all the names one by one, everyone clapping, while we were all trapped in this office, belching and wondering what the hell's happening. Next thing, the door opened and a copper walked in to give us a stiff talking to about the perils of underage drinking. By the time he'd finished, the assembly was over. All the other kids had gone home. Eventually they let us out through the back gates, not one leaving certificate between us. We couldn't have left under a blacker cloud had we tried.

So that was my last day of school. None of your *Goodbye, Mr Chips* and tossing caps in the air, just one last serious bollocking for the road.

But at least I was free. Or so I thought for however long it took for that couple of pints to wear off. Before the next day when I woke up with the worst hangover in the world. The one called reality.

4 / *RUNNING FREE*

SUDDENLY, IT WAS ALL OVER. Education, Bradford and the Sixties. By the time I left school in 1970 we'd moved. Not through choice but the dreaded compulsory purchase order after some architectural genius decided our street and the ones surrounding it were best off being flattened. Some say the Sixties ended with Woodstock or Altamont. For me, they ended when the bastards razed the Manchester of my youth. The street where I'd first heard the Beatles and Bob Dylan, where I'd kicked a ball about dreaming I was George Best, where I first saw the Stones on telly, where we'd all watched England win the World Cup, where my cousins picked me up to take me to the Apollo cinema to see *Help!* and *Zulu*, where I first plucked a string on Linda James' guitar. There's nothing left of it for me to revisit today. Nowhere to go back to. For a long time they left just the pub, the Bradford Hotel, and the old wall where we painted a goalpost. But now even they've gone. Today, there's grass verges where once there were terraced streets. It's still called Bradford, but it's not my Bradford. That one's sunk forever. The lost Atlantis of Manchester.

You read about this sort of stuff in history books. The Highland Clearances, where they scooped up whole communities and told them, 'Right, you lot, fuck off!' then shipped them off to America so they could use their land for grazing sheep. The same thing happened to us. The planners call it 'renovation', but the only thing they're renovating is land, not people's lives, which – the complete opposite – were demolished in the process. Some of the old ladies on our street got packed off to the giant council blocks in Hulme, a grim, horrible place that would soon become notorious for drugs and gangsters. Our lucky dip wasn't much better: Moston, way out in the northeast. It was an estate originally built for the families of miners serving Bradford Colliery, but the pit had long shut by the time we got there. So instead of a bustling working-class haven where everyone had a job and a purpose, it was now a lawless shithole chock-a-block with unemployed alkies, manic depressives and heroin addicts. Every other night you'd hear couples arguing and fights and windows breaking. One bloke on the estate actually upped and ran away to join the Foreign Legion. He must have weighed up the pros and cons of military discipline, heatstroke and sandstorms versus hanging around Moston and decided Moston was worse. And possibly had a point.

While the glass was smashing all around me, I was cocooning myself in music. I now had my own record player so I sawed a hole in the chest of drawers between me and my brother's beds and fitted it in there. My dad nicked me a pair of giant stereo headphones off the back of his van, so I'd lie there, on my bed, often with the lights out, like being in a flotation tank, lost in my own world. One of my favourites was the Simon and Garfunkel album *Sounds Of Silence*. It might sound corny, but I loved lying in the dark with headphones hearing, '*Hello, darkness . . .*' When you're 15 or 16 these songs leave a big impression. Same as 'I Am A Rock', getting into the existential thing of isolation, feeling apart from everyone else, which I already did. The other one that had a big impact was 'Richard Cory', about a factory worker who blows his brains out. If I was already against getting a job before I heard it, I was twice as much afterwards.

That was my thought-wrestling bedroom music, whereas my bovver-booting street music was soul and ska. The number 1 record on my 16th birthday was Dave and Ansel Collins' 'Double Barrel', the start of an amazing avalanche of these cool Jamaican ska records – 'Young, Gifted And Black', 'Long Shot Kick De Bucket', 'Monkey Spanner', 'Return Of Django', I loved them all. Then, in between, you had all this incredible Motown music, the Supremes' 'Up The Ladder To The Roof' and 'Stoned Love' – just the sound of the beginning of that record was like a musical orgasm. In my bedroom, in the dark, I was still listening to rock music, Led Zeppelin, the Stones, the Faces, but tribally I was gravitating somewhere else. This was now the age of the suedehead. I didn't have the haircut, but I had the clothes, the blue mac, the Ben Sherman shirt and the DM boots. Because I was finally old enough to be the type of teenager I'd seen as a young kid at Belle Vue with 'The Who' badly painted on the back of their parka. I was 16 years old. And I, too, was a mod.

I HAD THE MUSIC, I had the clothes, but most important of all I had the scooter. Not just the one either. I started with a Lambretta TV 175. Then I bought another Lambretta, your classic Jimmy from *Quadrophenia* LI 150, off this bloke who was off his head on drink or drugs or a combination of both and let me have it for sixteen quid. Then, like a sign from God, this priest who knew I liked scooters said, 'I've got one if you want to buy it,' and offered me a classic Vespa GS with the old-fashioned flyscreen. Fifteen quid in his collection plate and it was mine. So all of a sudden I've got three scooters. This was many years before I ever started collecting guitars, but it's a similar mentality. A different instrument for a different occasion.

I had mates who were also scooter mods so sometimes we'd drive out to rallies or festivals together, but for me it was about independence. At heart, I've always been a bit of a loner – not in the anti-social sense of pulling away from the crowd, more in the sense that I'm very happy being by myself. So it wasn't about being part of any ten-strong mod armada revving along the seafront to ruck with rockers. Having my own wheels meant I could go off by myself. I was still searching for something, working out who I was and what I wanted to do. I suppose not unlike Jimmy in *Quadrophenia*, except that album hadn't even come out yet, so I was living it while Townshend was still writing it. But just that sensation of being out alone on the road was an exhilarating feeling. Living in the moment. Completely free.

All my teenage stars were now aligning. Scooters, clothes, music . . . and girls.

For most working-class kids, sex isn't a big deal. Your parents never discussed it so you just got on with it. You learned fast, even as a kid. My first brush was maybe when I was 8 or 9, with a doctor's daughter down our street, just fumbling about with each other in her dad's shed. A bit of *Carry On Nurse*. It was all natural, slap and tickle, following instincts, discovering who and what you were about. There were no taboos or hang-ups – we left all that to the poor middle-class kids having nervous breakdowns over it all. Whereas where I grew up, not having much money, people learned to appreciate the simple pleasures in life. Booze, fags, music, sex.

Even at 16 I was still quite shy in a lot of ways, but the scooter gave me a cloak of confidence. I learned all the tricks, riding it side-saddle, all the showing-off stuff, so it didn't take long before I had a girl perched on the back riding pillion with her arms around my waist. The biggest obstacle to sex when you're a teenager is always opportunity, finding somewhere where you won't be disturbed or overheard. That's why most of my teenage sexual initiations took place at night on golf courses and in graveyards. Of the two, morbid as it sounds, I preferred the graveyard. The reason being the flush headstones, the flat ones at grass level, made a hard, if decent, makeshift mattress.

So that was me. Living one day to the next, tinkering in the backyard with my three scooters, listening to music and cruising off to soul clubs picking up girls for a romantic soirée either up the cemetery or in the rough by the eighteenth hole. Just as Mr Kind predicted, I was going nowhere, but having an absolute ball while it lasted. Which, as it turned out, wouldn't be for very long.

I ALWAYS KNEW I was never going to make a very good criminal. I should have trusted my gut instinct and left it at that. But I somehow made a bargain with myself, or with fate. I decided I would commit just one crime in my life, and if I got away with it, then I'd keep on the straight and narrow forever after. That was the deal, straight out of the pages of Dostoyevsky. *Just let me do this one bad thing and I promise I'll be good as gold the rest of me life.*

The one bad thing was nicking a scooter. Yes, I know I had three already, but they kept breaking down and I needed all these different new parts. Or that's how I tried to justify it in my head. This bloke I knew said if I paid him, he could nick the parts for me. My logic was, rather than pay him, why don't I just nick the parts myself? So that's what I did. Stole someone's scooter so I could strip it and fix my own.

STEVE DIGGLE

So far, so good. Only what I didn't know was the bloke who offered to nick it in the first place was part of some criminal gang who'd been stealing so many scooters around Manchester they'd sparked a big police operation to nab them. Which is when they nabbed me instead.

Not long after I'd done the deed, I was driving along on my own when the cops pulled me over. They did the usual 'Is this your scooter?' routine so I showed them my licence. Then they started inspecting it. That's when I started sweating. There were bits from the scooter I nicked with the serial numbers scratched off. If they knew anything about scooters, they'd spot it a mile off. You can guess the rest.

They carted me down to the station in the back of a van. I already knew I was in it up to my neck, but once we got there I realised I was in over my head. Putting two and two together, they'd ingeniously deduced that the young lad in their paddy wagon must be the criminal mastermind behind every scooter theft in Manchester over the last year. I was Mr Big. And now I was in clink, I was going *down*.

They threw me in a cell with a pair of drunken psychopaths, built like brick shithouses and pissed as farts. Tweedledum and Tweedledumber. They'd take turns punching each other out so one of them could get some sleep. I was sat on the cold stone floor watching them, terrified the next punch was coming my way. Luckily, or not, by the Saturday morning they'd moved me into another cell next door with about half a dozen other desperate cases, all stinking of sweat, piss and bad breath. Then, one by one, the cell emptied until it was just me. By now 24 hours had passed. Saturday night, I was alone in a police cell, convinced I was being fitted up to spend the next ten years in Strangeways, feeling pathetically sorry for myself. But it's funny what you find yourself doing in extreme circumstances. Some people might have wept, or screamed the place down, or gone nuts and started bashing their head against the cell door. I turned and faced the wall and had the loneliest wank of my life.

If it all sounds like some depressing Jean Genet play, it was. That grim weekend in jail was a big turning point. My 40 days in the wilderness. I did a lot of thinking, the main thought being: whatever happens after this, there's no fucking way I'm ever going to end up in *here* again. In the end, thank god, they didn't have enough to frame me for all the other thefts. But I was charged and fined and banned from driving and having

33

a scooter licence for two years. That was my one crime, and this was my punishment.

So I was back to square one. No wheels, no prospects, no future. Grounded, in miserable Moston. Wondering just *how bad* could it be in the Foreign Legion?

IN A BIZARRE WAY, for me, crime *did* pay. Losing the scooter meant losing my mobility. Now all I had was the pub, my mates and my music. I knew I needed something to occupy myself the way I used to spend hours stripping down my scooters and fixing them up in the backyard. Something to do with my hands other than stubbing out cigs, raising pint pots and unclasping the occasional bra.

A guitar.

If I hadn't been arrested and lost my licence, I don't know if I'd ever have bothered learning to play one. With hindsight it seems like kismet, even if at the time I was still more pissed off about losing my scooter than I was excited about picking up a guitar. But that's the main reason I did.

King Arthur pulled Excalibur from the stone. I pulled a second-hand Spanish acoustic out of Mazel's by the Mancunian Way. My destiny, and it only cost me six quid.

Mazel's was like a musical Steptoe's yard, floor to ceiling with all sorts of electronics, walkie-talkies, Bakelite valves, things fallen off boats, strange headphones, amps, records, instruments, all manner of rubbish. Sitting amongst it, I saw this guitar and thought, *Yep! She's mine.* I imagined myself serenading girls with it, finger-picking beautiful melodies like Paul Simon. Then I took it home and strummed it. I sounded more like Les Dawson.

It *looked* good, but the bastard was terrible at staying in tune. I even bought some pitch pipes – a little harmonica you blow to make sure every string is the right note – but every time I thought I'd tuned it, a few strums and it started to slide and groan again. But I wouldn't be beaten. I knocked trying to learn chords on the head and started plucking away at single strings instead, up and down the frets. It didn't take me too long to start picking out tunes I knew. That was a eureka moment.

Der-der, der-der, der, der-der-der, der-der, der-der, derrr, der-der!

'Fucking hell! That's Beethoven!'

I'd worked out the 'Ode To Joy' melody from Beethoven's Ninth. That seriously blew my mind: the fact someone like me who couldn't yet play a guitar properly could somehow crack the code and play a tiny bit of Beethoven. From then on, that's mainly what I did, fiddle around with it, picking out these little riffs on different strings. But it was still only something to do in my bedroom. I had no ambition to be a guitar player or be in a band any more than I had being an astronaut. Because I had about as much chance of either.

THIS WASN'T LOST on Mam and Dad. When I left school, they naturally assumed I'd get a job. So did the careers officer who suggested I consider gardening. That pretty much summed up their faith in my intellectual abilities. 'Somebody give that idiot a spade and a pair of wellies.'

I did, briefly, work in a garage because I desperately needed money for scooter parts, but I didn't stick it out beyond a few weeks. It wasn't idleness, it was ideology. Like I say, I was a conscientious objector to work. Just a pity I couldn't get this point across to my poor old grandad.

'Good news, Stephen! I've got you a job.'

My worst nightmare. Grandad genuinely thought he was doing me a favour, probably because he'd had months of Mam grumbling in his ear about me. I was the family problem, so using his trade union connections his solution was to pressgang me into an iron and steel foundry. Anyone else, I would've said no. But I couldn't, not to Grandad.

My first day was like walking into Dante's *Inferno*. Pitch-dark, furnaces, flames, smoke, the stink of sulphurous metal and thunderous clanging and banging. The misery of manual labour, full of hard blokes with blackened faces whose idea of fun was sticking your balls in a vice as an initiation ceremony.

'Welcome to hell!'

As if the shopfloor wasn't scary enough, that same first day we were all summoned up to the club room for a presentation ceremony. Some poor old bloke called Len was retiring. He'd started there at 15 and now he was 65. He looked like a wrinkly little mole and no wonder, 50 years working in the dark and noise, probably blind as a bat and deaf as a post. But this was his big moment, his golden handshake to bid

35

him farewell – a cheap watch and a transistor radio. At that point my arse fell out of my trousers. The thought I might end up like Len, 50 years toiling in the bowels of Hades to be palmed off with some booby prize from *The Generation Game*. But it was the clocking-in-and-out machine that really did it. That sound. CLICK! Like the hammer of a nail in my coffin. Now I *really* understood why Richard Cory pulled the trigger.

I knew I couldn't just leave because Grandad would never forgive me. But I thought, maybe, if I got myself sacked without too much disgrace, I might be able to wriggle my way out of it. For a start I was a dreadful skiver. I'd take half an hour to go for a piss, while most days I'd just walk around the yard in circles carrying a mallet, looking as if I knew where I was going and hoping nobody stopped and asked me where that was. A bit like in the old war films when the POWs are exercising in the prison yard, eyeing up the barbed wire and plotting their escape. My thoughts exactly.

Luckily, the means of tunnelling out found me without having to lift a finger. The foundry had these giant blacksmith hammers that took three people to operate: these frightening big bastard machines that shook the whole street every time they dropped with sparks flying everywhere. If you weren't careful, you could lose an arm in them. You had no idea what these metal pieces they were making were for either; some were round, some were square, they could have been bits of NASA rockets for all we knew. The normal hammers were bad enough, but there was one giant fuck-off hammer used for piecework: the more bits you made, the more you got paid. One day, the gaffer said to me, 'We want you on that.' I took one look at it. *If I go anywhere near that thing, I'm going to get myself killed!* Which is what I told him.

'Sorry, I won't do it.'

That's all it took.

'In that case, laddie, you're sacked. Collect your payslip at the end of the day.'

Hallelujah!

The only bit I was worried about was telling Grandad. Him and my gran had moved to Openshaw, close to the foundry, so I used to go round to his every lunchtime because work never had a canteen. As I'd been sacked in the morning, I still went round his for lunch that day but decided I'd wait till the day was over, go home, break the bad news to Mam and Dad first, then worry about telling him later.

I'd never been so happy walking to work as that afternoon, knowing I only had a few hours left before I'd never have to darken its door again. But as I turned the corner and walked up the street, I could see something was wrong. There was a giant crowd outside the foundry gates. As I got nearer, I recognised it was all the workers, blokes on the shopfloor I knew. Lunch was over, so I didn't understand why they were all standing about outside. So I asked one of them.

'What's all this, then?'

'We're on strike.'

'Strike? Oh, right. What for?'

'Because of you being sacked.'

Could you fucking believe it? 'One out, all out!' They'd downed tools in solidarity and weren't going to pick them up again until I was given my job back. It was just like *I'm All Right Jack*. This Fred Kite trade union bloke, one of my grandad's mates, demanded they reinstate me, which they did. They were all looking at me, winking, as if to say, 'Congratulations, comrade!'

Jesus, this is the last thing I need!

The only positive upshot was now my card was marked by the guvnor. 'That young Diggle, he's a troublemaker.' So he waited all of three weeks, then tried to stick me back on the piecework hammer. Once again I refused, once again he sacked me and once again the trade union bloke went ballistic. 'Don't worry, lad! We'll all strike again!' But this time I told him, 'Don't bother, mate. I just want to go.' He looked crestfallen, like I'd robbed him of the excuse for a good bit of industrial argy-bargy. But that was the ignominious end of it.

Grandad wasn't pleased. Mam and Dad even less so. I was 17, back in my room and back on the dole of my own volition. As far as they or anyone else could see, still going nowhere. All I cared about was not having to go to work and having enough money to go to the pub. That's all I had. A guitar I plucked now and again, my records and my mates down the pub. And I was happy.

Until fate dealt me a lightning bolt that changed everything forever.

5 / *FAST CARS*

RECORDS ARE LIKE PROUSTIAN MEMORIES. A song suddenly comes on the radio and in a matter of notes – BANG! – you've travelled back in time.

'*Nights in white satin . . .*'

BANG! It's 1972, and I'm 17 again, sat drinking in my local pub, the Broadway, where I went pretty much every day to meet my mates. One of those big old Victorian pubs, not a spit and sawdust place but reasonably done up for its day with those typical loud Seventies orange psychedelic carpets. I can still smell the bitter as I bring the glass to my lips and breathe in the dense perfume of cigarettes. The air is smoky, the laughter loud and the banter coarse.

There's Old Joe, the landlord, with elastic bands round his slippers to stop them flopping off his feet. And there's my mate Frank, itching for the next scrap. Some blokes are like that: add alcohol and stir. Frank never needs a reason – it's always over some stupid little incident. Any minute now he'll say something and the tables will flip over like the Wild West. The worst thing being that because he's my mate, the code of pub brotherhood goes that if one of us gets involved, we all get involved. It's horrendous. I hate fighting and always have done. The only thing I've ever wanted to hit is the strings of a guitar. So even when Frank goes off and it all kicks off, my approach to fighting is more psychological than physical, especially when it's some absolute giant who could snap me in half with one hand. I'd sooner try and talk them down than take a swing, like a one-man United Nations. 'Now, come on, it'll be better for everyone if you apologise to my mate!' It usually works. But only *usually*.

A fight night is always a bad night in the Broadway, but whatever the night we always have the jukebox and we always make sure, after the beer and cigarettes, we have enough loose change for it. Sometimes we go to certain pubs *because* of their jukebox, like the old railway inn a bit further down the road. As well as normal records, theirs has these discs of different train noises, so you're sat there with your pint and suddenly on comes the sound of eight carriages being shunted into a siding. This is a typical working man's pub in the Seventies, except you've got all these old blokes swilling bitter and playing dominoes listening to all this clanging and screeching like something by Einstürzende Neubauten.

What makes the Broadway's jukebox so special is the size of the room, so spacious that every record sounds loud and echoey like Phil Spector. The big thing for us is playing the B-sides. So if it's my 10p going in the slot, it'll probably be Hawkwind's 'Seven By Seven', the B-side of 'Silver Machine', or the Sweet's 'Man From Mecca', the B-side of 'Little Willy'. But if it's my best mate, Alan, it'll be the Moody Blues.

'*Nights in white satin . . .*'

A very eerie melancholic record as it is, but coming from that jukebox it sounds twice as ghostly. Maybe that's why that's the one record that takes me right back here. The song of my search for Proust's lost time. Nothing to do with the words, more the sound and the feel of it.

And because it was Alan's song.

IN EVERY GANG OF MATES there's a life and soul of the party. In ours, it was Alan. He was a good three years older than me. I was 17, he was 20 going on 21. He worked in the maintenance department at Agecroft Colliery outside Salford. One of his big interests was trucks. Gardner 180 diesel engines, Foden lorries, all that stuff. He was so enthusiastic he kind of got me into it too, teaching me about all the different makes, which hasn't left me: if I had the parking space for it, I'd still sooner buy myself a Foden truck than an E-type Jag any day.

Apart from trucks, beer and women, like all of us he loved his music. He'd sometimes say, 'Steve, you and me should start a band.' And I'd laugh and go, 'Yeah, we should, one day.' But it was just friends talking down the pub. Much as we both loved music, neither of us were that serious or interested in doing anything about it. We had the pub, we had our mates, we had each other and that was our life. And when you're only 17 and haven't got a care in the world, it's paradise. For as long as it lasts.

Boredom. That's what did it.

There were four of us, me, Alan and a couple of our other mates, in the Broadway as usual one weekday evening. It must have been a bit dead, or maybe we were just restless, but somebody said, 'Let's go into town.' Town being the centre of Manchester, a four-mile bus ride away.

Then another voice piped up. 'I'll drive you.'

He wasn't one of our gang. It was a guy we vaguely knew who sometimes used to go down the pub. A face rather than a proper mate. But he overheard and offered to come with us and give us a lift.

'I've got a car.'

Which he had, but we didn't realise that when he said 'car' he meant a minuscule Hillman Imp. But it was that or the bus. So the next thing, there's five of us squashed into this Noddy car: three of us in the back with our knees in our ears, my mate Alan in the front and this driver we hardly knew.

We made it about halfway down the Oldham Road when we spotted a club and decided to pull over. It wasn't really a nightclub as such, more a pub with a big open space for dancing. We'd had a couple of pints already but we weren't drunk, just a bunch of lads out having a laugh. As we walked in, they were playing 'Starman' by David Bowie, so we all started singing along and waving our arms around, not taking the piss, just enjoying ourselves.

'What do you think you're playing at?'

We hadn't reached the bar when the bloke who must have been the owner shouted at us.

'Sodding get out, the lot of you!'

He must have thought we looked like yobbos come to cause trouble. Maybe they'd had problems with gangs of lads there before. But whatever the reason, that was us barred.

'OUT!'

In hindsight, these are the microscopic fractions of fate you dwell on. The beat of the butterfly wings that cause the tidal wave. *If, if, if.* If we'd only stayed in the Broadway. If we hadn't got in that bloke's car. If we hadn't stopped at that place on Oldham Road. If they hadn't been playing 'Starman'. If they hadn't kicked us out. *If, if, if.* You can torture yourself thinking about these things forever. Or you simply learn to live with what happened.

What happened was that thanks to David Bowie and that narky landlord, we all piled back in the Hillman Imp and headed further into town.

I was cramped in the back on the left-hand side, my two mates beside me. Alan was in front of me in the passenger seat by the door.

We were carrying on along Oldham Road when the driver went to light a cigarette. He had to take his hands off the steering wheel, so Alan reached over to steady it.

It's at this point that the memory gets fuzzy, like a chewed-up video cassette. The scene is in my head, but there's static interference and bits missing. All I can remember is the car suddenly shaking violently, feeling like the wheels must have fallen off. Then my head banging against the car roof. Then careering across the road in front of oncoming traffic. Then thinking, *I'm going to die!* Then suddenly everything coming to a standstill.

When I opened my eyes, the first thing I saw was a petrol pump. We'd crashed into it.

'Fucking hell!'

I thought we were going to go up in flames any second. Then I noticed the passenger door was wide open and the seat was empty. Alan must have run for it already. The three of us were still stuck in the back because there weren't any rear doors and the driver was still behind the wheel. Everyone else was moving or moaning, so at least we were all still alive. I pushed the front seat down and we clambered out over the empty passenger seat, all very stunned and dazed. That's when I saw him.

Alan was face down on the forecourt, like he'd been flung from the car or maybe tried to run and suddenly collapsed. What was weird was in that first instant I didn't think anything of it. I'd seen him in the same position before on odd occasions when he was so drunk he couldn't walk home. For a split second it was, *Oh! There's Alan on the ground, again*. So I staggered over to give him a nudge.

'Alan? You alright, mate?'

The driver was now out of the car. 'I don't think he's gonna wake up,' he said.

I froze.

'Have a look again,' he said.

This time I bent down a bit closer, leaning in so I could see Alan's face. His entire head was split open. You could see all the way inside to his skull, like he'd been hacked by a machete. The impact must have thrown him out of the car at such a speed that he hit something. Blood was pooling – and he wasn't moving.

Alan was dead.

I have no memory of time. It felt like we were stood there forever, petrified like statues, just gawping at our dead mate on the ground. We all must have been white as sheets.

Then the driver started to panic. 'Look, mate,' he said, 'I've got no insurance, no tax, no licence, no nothing.'

We understood. If it happened today, there'd be CCTV everywhere and he'd have been nicked for dangerous driving, manslaughter, who knows. But back then, with no cameras around, nobody was going to grass anyone up. It wasn't like it was anyone's fault. It was a horrible accident.

'Just you run,' I told him. 'We haven't seen you, we don't know anything, just do what you've got to.'

So he drove away in what was left of his battered Hillman Imp, leaving us there until the cops and ambulance turned up. That was the last time I saw him from that day to this.

The police came and took us down the station. We told them what we could, without dobbing the driver in, telling them we'd never met him before and had no idea who he was. There were no charges and none of us were injured. Just scrapes and bruises, including one near my left eye which to this day is still a bit bobbly from that crash. But that was the extent of it. Physically, at least.

Psychologically, it's another story. When you're 17, you're not programmed for death. Your old aunties and uncles, your grandparents, you accept them dying, but not when it's one of your actual mates. One second, there you are in the pub listening to the Moody Blues. The next, he's dead at your feet on a garage forecourt. You don't get over that. Ever. Alan was like the James Dean of the pack, gone too soon. It left me completely numb.

I'd never met his parents until the funeral. They were quite old, a lot older than my parents, and he was an only child. But they wanted me to ride with them in the main car to the crematorium because they said he used to talk about me all the time. They didn't ask too many questions about the accident. I think they just kind of accepted it as one of those things that could have happened to anyone. Again, the memory is hazy. Probably because it's just too unbearably sad to remember. I can still see myself sat with them, having never met them, not really knowing what to say. All of us, completely heartbroken.

Alan's death made the local paper. I cut it out and kept it. I still have it. Just two columns, 17 lines. The headline: 'Crash Kills Passenger'.

> 'Twenty-year-old Alan Hughes of Dean Street, Failsworth, near Manchester, died last night after a car in which he was a passenger went out of control and crashed into a garage petrol pump . . .'

It still puts a chill down my spine. You only live to be 20 and that's your epitaph. One sentence in a tiny story in a local newspaper, just another traffic accident statistic. But there it is, in black and white, which is why I kept it. My best mate. His death.

For about two or three weeks after the accident I walked round in a trance. Today I'd probably have been medically diagnosed with something like post-traumatic shock disorder. Back then, nobody cared – you just had to get on with it. But for me it wasn't so much the emotional impact as the psychological. It was a big moment of realisation, like a headbutt from reality, a harsh wake-up call teaching me that's how quickly life can suddenly go. At any moment. So you've got to *live* every moment. Then it came to me, loud and clear, like a self-made mantra.

Because of Alan, I now know the meaning of death: therefore, I now know the meaning of life.

I BECAME A DIFFERENT PERSON AFTER THAT. My family could see it, my mates could see it, *I* could see it. I reeled myself in and became insular, starting to analyse myself and think internally about the meaning of everything. I'd go to Oxfam and buy books on the history of philosophy, about the Ancient Greeks in Asia Minor, and others about the psychology of suicide – not because I was feeling suicidal but because I wanted to understand the human mind. I retreated to my room and became less sociable. After Alan's death, our old gang of mates fractured, and I stopped going to the Broadway as often. Now and again one of them would bump into me in the street and say, 'Steve! Where the fuck have you been?', like I was some sort of mad hermit they'd not seen in years. I wasn't avoiding them. I wasn't avoiding anyone. I was working on my own state of consciousness. Finding out who I really was and what I wanted to do in life.

Everywhere I looked, everybody else around me was getting married and having kids. I started to think there must be something seriously wrong with me because I didn't want *any* of that. The house, the car, the fridge, the lawn mower, the pram and the two weeks' holiday every summer. To me it was all a mug's game.

So what *did* I want?

Escape. Freedom. And music.

By this point I'd already been banging on the guitar quite a while. But it was only then that I thought, right, the only way out of this mess is to start writing songs and start a band. The very thing me and Alan had spoken about, just laughing down the pub, which still seemed every bit as impossible. Except now it was the only thing that made any sense to me. Because one of us was dead.

'OK, then, Alan,' I said to myself. 'I'll fucking do this band. For you.'

6 / *OPERATOR'S MANUAL*

IF I WAS GOING TO BE IN A BAND, I needed to start getting serious about the guitar. Which meant I had to learn to play one, properly.

The first person I thought of who might be able to help me was a bloke who lived over the road on the estate. His name was Tommy, he played guitar, and the good news was he agreed to teach me some chords. The bad news was Tommy also happened to be a chronic heroin addict. I'd go round his and he'd be trying to show me your basic C and G shapes with all these needle marks up his arms. You'd think a guitarist who liked shooting up as much as he did would want to teach me the Velvet Underground. The funny thing is the first thing Tommy taught me to play was 'Fog On The Tyne' by Lindisfarne. At least it wasn't difficult.

Around the same time I got to know this hippie named Lance. He dressed like he was either going to or coming back from Woodstock – the kaftan, the droopy moustache, the whole 'hey, man!' bit. It turned out he was also well off as his dad owned the Hartley's jam empire and he was the heir to its sugary throne. Presumably, that's why he dropped out, preferring to squander an inheritance built on lemon curd on dope and acid instead. He lived with his mate Arthur, another hippie, the pair of them dossing in a flat in Moston with half a stoned mind between them that they wanted to start a band. Apart from Alan, they were the first people I'd met who'd even suggested the possibility. I don't know if

I believed them, and I don't even know if I believed in myself. All I know is that in the time it took to pass a bong, I'd moved in with them.

I wish I could say for certain exactly how long I stayed, but the concept of time evaporated almost as soon as I'd crossed the threshold. Lance's place was notorious enough to have a local nickname. 'The House of Acid'. From the second I dropped my bags down, my days were no longer measured in hours but microdots.

Drugs. The holy ghost of the rock'n'roll trinity. If I was going to pursue music and sex, it stood to reason sooner or later I was going to dabble with the other. Not making excuses, but I do think my generation was primed for it more than any before or since. It all goes back to the Beatles again. I was 12 when 'Strawberry Fields Forever' came out, and though it's not as if every kid who ever heard it became a drug addict, there was something about the sound of that record and the wordplay of the lyrics that was like an open invitation. Did you want to take whatever John Lennon had taken to make music like this? In my case the answer was a resounding 'Yes!'

They weren't difficult to come by, especially in Moston. I had my first spliff off of a bloke on the estate named Rocky. There was a bit of grass knocking about, but it was mostly resin, the chalky Afghan stuff. I wasn't that big a spliff head because at the time I wasn't really a smoker. I didn't start smoking properly, that is constantly, until I joined Buzzcocks. So whatever the state of my lungs today, I still blame Pete Shelley.

I'd never touched acid before I moved in with Lance, but I was curious about it, partly because of the Beatles, and because by then I'd already read Aldous Huxley's *The Doors of Perception* and *Heaven and Hell*. I was also 17, still messed up in the head over what happened to Alan and willing to try anything to get the fuck away from mundane reality. 'Show me the way to Strawberry Fields, please!'

My first trip was a tab of windowpane acid. There was a bunch of us, Lance and his hippie mates, sat round in the flat, music playing, a few spliffs passing round while one by one he handed us our individual tab. Then we all dropped it together, as one. Very ceremonial, like taking the eucharist. I waited. And waited. Five minutes passed. Nothing. There was still a nice vibe in the room, everyone relaxed and giggly, waiting for the spaceship to land. Then, all of a sudden, it kicked in.

STEVE DIGGLE

I felt as if someone had smashed my brain into tiny pieces and I could see the strings holding the entire universe in place. Visually, it was psychedelically amazing. Mentally, it was fucking terrifying. I imagined it might be all floaty and lovely like watching *Yellow Submarine*, but it was more like having your mind torpedoed by a Nazi U-boat. Being hippies, they mostly listened to prog, so as we were tripping they were playing Arthur Brown's Kingdom Come, a track called 'Time Captives', a weird experimental synthesizer thing. Hearing it on acid felt like you'd been abducted by aliens. I was frozen against the wall, seeing things crawling in the carpet, screwing my eyes closed. *OK, OK, I think I want to get off this bus now! Here's my stop!* But that's the thing about acid. You can't get off. You keep thinking your stop's coming round, but then the bus speeds past it and you're trapped. And so it goes on, round and round, for hours and hours. You take it in the evening, and next thing the sun's come up and you're still crying, begging to be let off the bus. No wonder some people lose their minds and never come back from it. I saw it myself with some of the hippie girls who used to drop by the flat, these middle-class student types who'd drop one hit and the next thing they're in the casualty ward. As that first tab wore off I was thinking, *No way am I doing this madness again!* But when the others came back to earth they all agreed, 'Hey, man, that was a *bad* one.' They were professional acid heads and even *they* said it was a dodgy batch. Just my luck – my first trip and I'd been given the heebie-jeebie stuff.

I took it again, of course. I figured as long as I was going to be living with Lance in the House of Acid it was a when-in-Rome situation. Some aspects of it I did enjoy. Wandering around the park at night, shaking hands with all the trees. A good trip made you see the state of human existence in a different way. It definitely opened up my mind, which is the whole point of taking it. Tuning in, turning on and dropping out. I liked the psychological side of it, staying up all night, figuring out the universe one tab at a time, talking about all 'the normals' outside, while we were supposedly the enlightened ones, off our tits inside. But that was the problem. When it came to trying to make music and start a band, everyone was too wasted. We did, once, hire the local church hall for a practice. That's when it hit home that all Lance and Arthur wanted to do was be in the Edgar Broughton Band circa 1969. They had no ambition, apart from trying to sound like Gong. Whatever they thought they were doing, it wasn't what I was looking for. And for all the nice trips I'd had, acid was never going to be my drug of choice. I liked being out of my mind, but I also liked some guarantee I'd be able to climb back in it again. With LSD, you're locked out and you've lost your keys.

So I did my remaining brain cells a favour by leaving the House of Acid and moving back in with Mam and Dad. Not long afterwards, Lance and the hippies all vanished. I found out they'd all gone off to the Himalayas on some spiritual quest to find some guru who was going to teach them 'the truth'. That was a moment of realisation in itself. How come the guru is always some fat bloke on a hill in India, never some window cleaner in Moss Side? Brainwashed or hoodwinked, it was one or the other. Myself, I've never looked for the truth because I don't actually care what 'the truth' is. Human beings are what they are, and I am what I am. As I was still only just discovering.

THE ONE POSITIVE THING that came out of the House of Acid was Lance deciding he'd enrol at All Saints Adult Education Centre to study the theory of music. As the lessons were on Friday nights I thought it might be a laugh, something for the pair of us to do to kill a few hours before we went out on the lash, so I went along to join up with him. The irony, or inevitability, was that Lance dropped out after a couple of lessons, but I ended up staying the distance, going every week until I eventually made it to Grade 5 in music. I was alright on the theory part, less so on the practical side, mainly because it was all on piano. We could never afford one, let alone make room for it in our house, so the teacher gave me a piece of cardboard with the keys drawn on. I'd be stamping my fingers away in silence. *I know Beethoven was deaf, mate, but this is fucking ridiculous!* The rest of the class was made up of posh women from Cheshire who all had baby grands in their conservatory, and there's me, the pauper in the corner, tapping on my scrap of cardboard. I'd have been better off with comb and paper – at least I'd have made some bloody *noise*. But I did enjoy learning about scales and all the different composers. We also got to try our hands at composition and write our own small pieces of music. The others in the class were saying,

'This is a little bit like Haydn' or 'I wrote this thinking of Brahms'. When it came to my turn, I said, 'Beatles, 1965', half joking, but at the same time this little phrase I'd written was inspired by them, the way they inverted these little melodies all the time. The teacher liked it too, so it gave me a bit of confidence, thinking maybe I could try and write my own songs after all.

In tandem with the music classes I'd also signed up for classical guitar lessons at the same adult college, the proper finger-picking flamenco stuff. The first thing the teacher did was tell me off. 'You hold your hand like a scorpion!' Apparently, you had to imagine you were holding an orange, like the great classical guitar master Andrés Segovia. So I learned to contort my fingers and go to bed every night pretending I was fondling this invisible orange until he was happy. 'Ah! You have a good hand, like Segovia!' He also encouraged me to grow my fingernails, which I wasn't so keen on as it caused obvious problems when it came to copping off with girls. I stuck it out for a while, but then it all became about learning to play from sheet music. I had pages and pages of this stuff. Homework, like being back at school. He said to me, 'Classical guitar is even harder to learn than the piano.' If he meant a cardboard one, he wasn't lying.

The bottom line was, odd as it might sound, I didn't want to *be* a guitar player. I still don't. I've genuinely never regarded myself as a guitar player. I wanted to learn how it worked, and how to use it, but I never wanted to be Mr Virtuoso. To me it was just a piece of wood with strings that made noise. All I wanted was to know enough about it to start making my own noises. Between the theory and the classical guitar lessons I definitely learned some useful stuff, but, ultimately, all any music teacher can do is teach you to play the only way they know. Whereas I wanted to express myself, play my own music my own way without worrying about any rules or anyone breathing down my neck telling me, 'No, no, that's wrong.' I didn't want to learn other people's songs or play in other people's styles. I only wanted to play guitar like Steve Diggle. The only person who could ever teach me that was me.

7 / SITTING ROUND AT HOME

THE FACT I SUDDENLY BECAME a bit of a guitar-strumming bedroom hermit may have had something to do with not wanting to set foot out of my front door anymore. Moston was already a bad area when we first moved there, but every year it seemed to deteriorate more and more. The last straw came one night I didn't go out when a bunch of lads I knew went down the pub as usual, got pissed up and decided to go back to one of my mate's houses. There was a 12-bore shotgun there, so next thing they're all picking it up and playing around with it. Suddenly there's a loud bang and someone's splattered against the wall. Nobody knew the gun was loaded. Any other night I might have been in the pub and gone with them, and it could have been me dead instead of this poor bloke named George Ashcroft. When I heard about it, all I could think of was the Simon and Garfunkel song 'Richard Cory', someone blowing their brains out, even if it wasn't deliberate. Only it was happening for real on my doorstep. I'd been lucky my name wasn't on the bullet that time, but if I hung around Moston much longer, who knew?

Mam and Dad had also had enough by then. There were lads in the houses all around us going to jail, and with my little sisters still at school it was all getting too hairy. Fortunately, they managed to find somewhere in the nick of time, further out in a place called Chadderton, near Oldham, a little house on a hill. The deposit was £25. That was the cost of our ticket out of Dodge.

STEVE DIGGLE

I was now 18, but even in the new house I was still sharing a room with my brother. To say Phil was eccentric would be an understatement. I sometimes wonder if him being run over as a kid did something to his head. Then again, he's always been odd. When we were very young and living in Longsight where we had a garden, our gran used to buy us little Dinky cars. I'd play with mine. Phil would bury his. Every time, every car, he'd go out and bury it in the garden. Conceptual performance art, and he was only a toddler.

Phil always knew he wanted to be an artist. I had the ears, he had the eyes. He'd be out all day around town with pencils and watercolours, coming home with pictures of Manchester Cathedral, filling sketchbook after sketchbook. He was always good at drawing, but then one day he discovered Jackson Pollock and he's never been the same since. From then on, he went all abstract, chucking paint. The thing that pissed our mam off is that he'd chuck it on the walls on his side of our bedroom. He also used to walk about the house all the time in what I used to call his 'spy coat', this big trench coat. Meantime, I'd be sat on my bed working out bits on my guitar. Mam and Dad used to look at us and despair. 'Why can't you two be normal?' My brother used to laugh and say to me, 'Us two, we're the chips that fell through the basket.' But we had this symbiosis because I had the music and he had the art, so we had this constant exchange of ideas and influences. We'd be talking about David Hockney and Ossie Clark one minute, Bowie and Roxy the next. That was unique round our way. The bloke next door just had the telly and the pub. We'd sit and gas about Rothko. It gave us a precious chink of creative light amidst all this working-class drudgery.

The only difference was Phil was always going to go off to art school. Even if he was a headbanger in a spy coat painting abstract expressionism on his bedroom walls, at least Mam and Dad could tell the neighbours he was in further education. My circumstances weren't so easily explained.

Looking at it from their point of view, I was a lost cause. Other young blokes my age were getting engaged and settling down. Mam would always be saying to me, 'Why don't you get married like little Johnny down the road?' She was obviously concerned because I'd only ever brought one girl home for tea. It was like an awkward scene from a Sixties

51

kitchen-sink drama, everyone trying to be polite, chinking teacups and, 'Ooh, would you like some of this boiled ham?' My idea of hell. I never took any more girls home after that.

But the main problem, as they saw it, was having no job. They'd go off to work in the morning with the breakfast dishes piled up by the sink and they'd still be there when they got home. So I'd get it in the neck. 'What the bloody hell have you been doing all day?'

In a word, reading. That's why I loved being on the dole. I may have been lying about on the sofa all day, but it was usually with a book in my hand. I'm a self-taught man, and the dole gave me the freedom to follow my own curriculum. Philosophy, psychology, existentialism, modernism, poetry and literature. My further education was the University of Steve Diggle and I graduated with first class honours.

I've always been a reader. For me, it was all curiosity. I never read anything just so I could show off and bore people with it, like those intellectual snobs who look down their noses at you with complete disdain because you've not read as many Joseph Conrad novels as they have. I felt the same about books as I did about music. Whether you're discovering Bob Dylan or James Joyce, it was all mind expansion. Living at home on the dole, I was on eight quid a week, but the freedom to learn that it afforded me was priceless.

I'd go to the library, though I never bothered getting a card. That was way too much responsibility. You want me to borrow a book and bring it back on time or get fined? Nah, far too risky. Instead, I'd sit there reading stuff off their shelves, bits of poetry by Yeats and Dylan Thomas, or a book about George Gershwin and how he wrote 'Summertime'. It all upped the voltage of the creative electricity in my brain.

I also bought a lot of cheap second-hand paperbacks in Oxfam or junk shops, 10 or 20p a time. Joyce was one of the biggest revelations. Starting off with *A Portrait of the Artist as a Young Man* and then graduating to the monster of *Ulysses*. All that percolation of cinematic imagery and ideas and stream of consciousness was as exciting in its own way as first hearing rock'n'roll. In terms of what he did with words, Joyce was absolutely punk rock, ripping up the rule book. Although he did take it too far with *Finnegans Wake*, which as anyone who's ever gone near it knows is more or less unreadable. I did manage to get through it, but it was like my first bad acid trip. Every page I was weeping, wanting to be let off the bus.*

Those years signing on I was tearing through books every week. Poor restless *Madame Bovary*, existential old Camus, Sartre's *Roads to Freedom* trilogy, bits of Plato and the ancient Greeks, plays by Samuel Beckett, doomy Dostoyevsky, good old Marcel Proust and his madeleines, all the Orwells and his aspidistras, angry young Alan Sillitoe, usual suspects like Kerouac's *On the Road* and turn of the century tragedians like D. H. Lawrence and Thomas Hardy. One of my favourites was Hardy's *Jude the Obscure*, probably one of the most depressing novels ever written, but I identified with a lot of the themes and imagery, especially the little kid being used as a human scarecrow, looking over the hill wondering what was on the other side. I felt the same outsider thing, the stonemason on the fringes looking in. Hardy was also unambiguously anti-marriage, which is why that book landed him in so much shit at the time. If I'd really thought about it, the next time Mam asked me why I wasn't getting hitched like little Johnny down the road I could just have easily told her, 'Read *Jude the Obscure*, Mam!'

All this literature helped me join the dots of who I was and what I wanted to do. Being on the dole taught me the value of time, and even if my parents couldn't see it, I knew I was spending it wisely. Looking back on it now, I can see it as an incubation period. My autodidact years. Consciously or subconsciously, I was mentally preparing myself for something. I had no idea what. But when the time came, I'd be ready.

BETWEEN THE BOOKS, there was still always music. My 18th year, 1973, I'd started going to gigs more regularly. Memories are foggy, but at least I've still got the ticket stubs, all from the Free Trade Hall. The first was Status Quo, in their 'Paper Plane' days, only 65p. Then Strawbs in their 'Part Of The Union' prime, 75p. Then Sha Na Na, who were sort of like the American Showaddywaddy except they looked a lot greasier, only

---

* As soon as I finished *Finnegans Wake* I moved on to a book of short stories by Somerset Maugham. Anyone else suffering after *Finnegans Wake*, I'd recommend this as a good detox.

50p, which pretty much says it all. Then Bowie on his *Aladdin Sane* tour, still only a quid. Then, I'm afraid to say, Yes, a whopping £1.20. But a lot of the time I never actually paid as there was a scam where you'd send a mate in with a ticket but they'd sneak it back out again and pass it on so you'd try and get a whole gang of you in for nothing. Worked almost every time.

For now, watching bands was as close as I ever got to joining one, but at least back in my bedroom my own music had evolved to the point where I'd finally started writing songs and making my own demos. The very first were done with two tape recorders which, like my stereo headphones, my dad had very helpfully nicked off his van for me. I'd record on one, then play it back and sing and play along at the same time while taping it on the other one. Crude three-track recording, all very lo-fi. One of my very first songs was an acoustic thing called 'Fire Down Below', about the fire in your soul. A bit deep and dark, this melancholic tune in A minor, but I was dead chuffed with it, enough to stick it on a tape and send it to Manchester's local Piccadilly Radio. I was naïve enough to think that's how people got discovered. Obviously, they never played it and didn't even return the tape, so I've only a vague memory of how it went. Probably a good thing they didn't, as it's these knockbacks in life that push you on and keep you going. 'Bastards! I'll show 'em!'

Writing songs came out of a love of writing in general. At one point I was even thinking maybe I should try it for a living instead of music, just because I kept a notebook which I used to write little stories in. One of them was called 'The Dead Cauliflower', about a miserable bloke over the road – he was the dead cauliflower. I was always writing bits and bobs, scribbling little attempts at poetry and things, so lyrics were just a natural progression from that.

My big breakthrough was when I upgraded from two tape recorders to this clunky Akai reel-to-reel machine. A big heavy bastard that I managed to hang over my bed after drilling some holes in the wall. A pretty stupid move, looking back, as if it had fallen on my head in the night I'd have had permanent brain damage. But that then became my 'home studio'.

I was now playing electric as I'd saved up money by, very reluctantly, doing a few days' work for my uncle, digging foundations. Him and his mates would all be sat on their arse in the café and leave me out in the rain pushing a wheelbarrow. But then even Christ had to carry his own cross. It was worth it just to get my hands on an Antoria Les Paul copy. It had to be a Les Paul for me as that was The Guitar back then, mainly because of Jimmy Page and Pete Townshend, plus Mick Ronson played one with Bowie. Prior to that, my dad, bless him, had tried to help by nicking me a guitar. I came home one day and he said, 'I've got you one of them guitars you wanted.' I ran upstairs, went in my room and saw leaning against my bed . . . a bass.

I had to explain to him it only had four strings. But the fact I now had one meant having another instrument to mess around with and add to my demos. Owning that Hayman 40/40 bass guitar would also eventually change my life. Even if he did pinch the wrong thing, it was the greatest thing my dad ever did for me. That, and nicking me my first amplifier, a Sound City. Dad never got into trouble either as in those days it was all common perks of the job – the reason the phrase 'fell off the back of a lorry' exists.

Along with my growing collection of guitars I also had a plastic microphone attachment for my stereo. This came in handy one morning when I was lying in bed with a thumping hangover and Mam was hoovering outside the door. I decided to give her a taste of her own medicine by taping her hoovering and then, the moment she stopped, playing it back full blast through my speakers. She jumped out of her skin.

'Now you know what it bloody sounds like!'

That in itself became a strange little turning point, suddenly realising you could tape all these noises and play things backwards and make your own weird avant-garde sound collages like the Beatles' 'Revolution 9'. It was all experimentation, just like playing with the dials on the radiogram as a kid, slowly metamorphosising into Manchester's answer to Stockhausen.

That's pretty much how I spent the final years of my teens and into my twenties. Happily on the dole, sitting round at home, reading books or writing and recording demos. The more I read, the more I learned, and the more I wrote and recorded, the better I got. Until by the time I was 20 I had at least three tunes I was really pleased with. One was

'Fast Cars'. Another was a riff that would one day become 'Promises'. The third was inspired by Krautrock and listening to the likes of Faust and Can. I thought it was funny hearing these German bands singing in English so I made this demo of me, being English, pretending to be a German singing in English. I called it 'Autonomy'.

All these future Buzzcocks songs were created in my bedroom some time in those dole years, from late 1973 to 1975-ish, while Mam and Dad were at work, coming home every night to the same pile of dishes I'd neglected to wash up. The amazing thing was that apart from the odd row they never gave me any ultimatum to get a job or get out of the house. They just accepted I was a hopeless case who wanted to sit in my room taping hoovers and singing to myself. Maybe they were praying that, one day, I'd grow out of it, get a normal job and get married like little Johnny down the road after all. If so, they really should have prayed harder.

8 / PROMISES

ONE DAY AT THE HEIGHT, or maybe depth, of my dole years, Mam went to see a clairvoyant named Mrs Shaughnessy. It was pretty common in those days. Working-class women like my mam would go and see a spiritualist in the same way they'd go out to the bingo, just for a good night out. When she came back I asked her, 'So what did she tell you, Mam?' She said, 'Mrs Shaughnessy told me she could see a spotlight and that one of my sons was going to be famous.' I laughed and said, 'Don't you worry, Mam. I'll be on *Top of the Pops* before you know it.'

I was joking. The weird conundrum was that even though I wanted to be in a band making music, the last thing I wanted was to be on a stage with people staring at me, never mind on telly. The very idea made me feel sick. It was like at school when they used to make kids stand up and read poems at assembly. It happened to me when I was about 13. I stood there, mumbling some poem, burning up bright red, absolutely hating every second of it. So when she said that, I thought it might be my brother, that he could end up being some internationally famous artist like Picasso. I definitely didn't think, *It's a sign!* The only musical progress I was making was in my room, recording demos. Outside, in the real world, my prospects of being in a band were as wretched as they'd ever been.

It was like planets drifting apart. I was over here and rock'n'roll was over there. Musically, there didn't seem to be anything with any life or spark. You had the old guard who I still listened to, the Stones, whose Seventies albums I really loved, everything from *Goat's Head Soup* to *Black And Blue* and beyond, the Who, who I finally managed to see at Belle Vue Kings Hall on the *Who By Numbers* tour, and Led Zeppelin, who'd just brought out *Physical Graffiti*. You had all the exciting American stuff from a few years before that some kids were still listening to, like the Stooges and the New York Dolls. But it felt like that energy had all petered out. You'd watch *The Old Grey Whistle Test* and there'd be ugly hairies with double-neck guitars squealing away with this revolting proggy nonsense. There didn't seem to be anything else.

The nadir, for me, came in April 1975. I can't think what possessed me other than boredom or temporary insanity, but I found myself stood in Manchester's Palace Theatre watching Yes again. The first time I saw them a few years earlier, Rick Wakeman was on keyboards. He'd since been replaced by this ludicrous Swiss bloke, Patrick Moraz. He had so many synthesizers stacked on top of one another it looked like he was playing a telephone exchange. To top it off, being Swiss, he dragged out an alpine horn and started parping away. It honestly couldn't have got any worse if he'd started yodelling. I just remember watching it thinking, *Fucking hell!* Something's *got to change!*

The weird thing was bands would tour and come *to* Manchester, but there didn't seem to be any actual bands *in* Manchester. Not proper bands. The local height of musical ambition was to be the kind of group who'd play the social club where my mam and dad drank. Wing collars and shiny shoes, stood there like farm animals bleating 'Tie A Yellow Ribbon Round The Ole Oak Tree'. That's all anyone I ever met wanted to do. Strap on a guitar and sing cover versions down the pub to impress their mam. You'd meet someone and start chatting about forming a band and they'd say, 'Yeah! We might even get a summer season at Butlin's!'

It made me realise just how hard it is, and how rare it is, to find a kindred rock'n'roll spirit. It's not something you can teach. It's instinct. You either have it or you don't. It's not about snobbery either, it's about a sense of perception. Being tuned in. Not everyone *gets* rock'n'roll. That's why these poor bastards who wanted to play Butlin's and the

Wheeltappers and Shunters clubs existed. They had money to buy guitars and amps and the wherewithal to put the hours in to learn their instruments well enough to play meaningless bollocks like 'Love Grows Where My Rosemary Goes' note-perfect. But they wouldn't have understood rock'n'roll any better had Pete Townshend personally smashed a Rickenbacker over their heads.

The closest I got to anything you might call a group was with these two lads who lived round the corner. Both had proper jobs, so I'd always be waiting for them to come home or take a day off so we could try and rehearse round theirs. We got as far as learning two covers, 'Paranoid' by Black Sabbath and the Stones' 'Brown Sugar'. But I told them that if we were going to be serious, we needed to write our own stuff. I could tell just by the look on their faces that they weren't remotely interested. They'd have been just as happy for us to get together and play the same Stones covers in that front room forever. They just didn't have the hunger, that sense of urgency I felt. For them, it was a laugh. For me, it was a *life*.

In May 1976, Manchester United lost the FA Cup final and I turned 21. Truly, the world was ending. I was still living at home, still on the dole, still going nowhere. That's OK when you're 17, but at 21 you've used up all your excuses. You're not unemployed anymore. You're mentally handicapped.

The sands of time were running out. I was a desperate case, but I still had *some* hope – the last thing at the very bottom of Pandora's Box, so the Greek myth goes. Only by this point things were so drastic I hadn't much left. But I reckon if Pandora had scraped around in her box a bit harder, she'd have discovered, as I did, that underneath hope there was one last tatty copy of the *Manchester Evening News*.

I turned to the back-page classified 'Musicians Wanted' section, ran my finger down the column and stopped at the first one that leaped out at me.

'BASS PLAYER NEEDED.'

I wasn't really a bassist, just the owner of a stolen one. But I thought, *That'll do!* I was willing to try and form a band with absolutely anyone until they said the word 'Butlin's'. So I rang the number.

'Hello?'

The guy picked up straightaway. He sounded decent enough, and keen enough. We spoke a bit about what bands we were into and the sort of things we both wanted to play. I told him I'd written some songs and wanted to do something like the Who – short, sharp three-minute shocks and then smash our guitars. He laughed and said he'd like to meet.

'Are you free tonight?'

'Yeah,' he said.

'OK,' I told him. 'How about we go for a pint in Cox's Bar?'

'Where's that?'

Cox's Bar was one of my favourite pubs in town, on Windmill Street, very central. Maybe it should have rung a bit of an alarm bell that he hadn't even heard of it.

'It's near the Free Trade Hall,' I told him. 'Look, why don't we meet there first and then I'll take you round Cox's?'

'OK. About half seven?'

'Yep, half seven outside the Free Trade Hall. See you there, mate.'

And that's how we left it. Meet outside the Free Trade Hall, then go for a pint and discuss our rock'n'roll future.

My date with destiny. Friday, 4 June 1976.

I WAS THERE ON TIME. Standing, smoking outside the Free Trade Hall on a warm summer evening, waiting for a total stranger to maybe change my life. I was wearing jeans and had longish hair, partly because I couldn't be arsed going to the barbers, but mostly because it was still the mid-Seventies and nobody had told me that if you wanted to join a band you didn't necessarily have to look like one of Led Zeppelin. I checked my watch. Bang on half seven. The Friday night pubs were filling up, and me and this mystery bloke ought to be in one very soon helping to empty the kegs. I twitched and lit another cigarette. Where the hell was he?

'They're in there.'

The voice came from beside me. I looked round and saw a skinny bloke with short curly ginger hair, wearing a two-piece black leather suit, jeans and jacket, just like Elvis in the '68 Comeback Special.

'Sorry?'

'The Sex Pistols,' he said. 'They're in there.'

The Sex Pistols? Wow! What a brilliant name!

Then the penny dropped. There must be a gig that night in the Free Trade Hall and he assumed that's why I was there, to see these Sex Pistols.

'Oh, right,' I said. 'No, I'm actually waiting here for someone. I'm a bass player. I'm meant to be meeting this bloke to start a group.'

'Yeah, I know,' he said. 'He's waiting in here.'

Eh?

Now I was confused. That wasn't the original plan we made on the phone. But then maybe he'd got there before me and decided to have a look at these Sex Pistols instead of going to the pub?

'Come on,' he says, 'I'll take you in.'

It all felt a bit odd, being lured in off the street by some gimpy black-leather bloke. So I asked him what these Sex Pistols sounded like.

Then he said the magic words: 'They do a version of the Who's "Substitute".'

That was good enough for me. Fifty pence? I'm in!

He ushered me inside and up the stairs to a desk where a little chap was sat by the door collecting tickets.

'Here,' the leather bloke said to him. 'I found him outside. This is your new bass player.'

And with these words Malcolm McLaren introduced me to Pete Shelley.

IF THIS WAS A FILM, we'd freeze frame right here, like in *Goodfellas*. The moment I first clap eyes on Pete and he first claps eyes on me. Then you'd hear my voiceover explaining exactly what's happening. You already know why I'm stood there, but the gaps we need to fill in are how, and why, little Pete Shelley got to be sat selling tickets for that first Sex Pistols gig in Manchester.

Firstly, his name's not really Pete Shelley. He's Peter McNeish, from Leigh, near Wigan, which to anyone from Manchester like myself makes him a 'woolly back'. You could tell by his accent. Pretty soon after we met he said to me, 'Name three cinemas in Manchester beginning with T.' I thought for a bit, then shrugged because there aren't any. Then he grinned and told me the answer. 'T'Odeon, T'Apollo, T'ABC.' Typical woolly back humour.

He'd been studying electronics at Bolton Institute of Technology where he'd met an older student from Scunthorpe born Howard Trafford. I'd eventually know him as Howard Devoto. Pete and Howard clicked over a mutual love of Bowie, the Velvet Underground, Captain Beefheart and Roxy Music, the artier glam side of things. Putting this in context, at exactly the same time as I was making demos in my room while trying to form a band in Manchester, fifteen miles up the road in Bolton, Pete and Howard were also trying to get a band together. But they were one sizeable step ahead in that they'd at least found one another while I had nobody. Their only trouble was they couldn't get a decent rhythm section. They got as far as one gig at their college in Bolton playing Bowie and Velvet Underground covers with a drummer who only knew the beat of 'Alright Now' by Free. Which doesn't sound so great when you're actually trying to play 'White Light/White Heat'. The story, as Pete always told me, is that they were so awful somebody pulled the plug before the end. But purely because of that gig, the terrible historical inaccuracy was born that 'Buzzcocks formed in Bolton'. This simply isn't true, and if you finish this book, you'll hopefully understand why.

The real birth of what became Buzzcocks starts in the spring of '76 with the early hype about the Sex Pistols, who'd only ever played in and around London, had yet to be signed and had never been seen or heard on TV or radio. Outside the capital, all anyone knew about them was a tiny handful of early gig reviews in the likes of the *NME* and *Sounds*. One in particular caught the attention of Pete and Howard because it mentioned that the Pistols played a Stooges number. As a pair of devoted Iggy fans, next thing, they'd borrowed a car to drive to London to see the Pistols live for themselves. Which they did, twice in one weekend. They also met their manager, Malcolm McLaren, and began concocting plans to bring the Pistols to the North West. The deal was that if Pete and Howard could find a venue and arrange the gig, then Malcolm would let their own band play as support. And so they ended up hiring the smaller upstairs room in Manchester Free Trade Hall – by name, the Lesser Free

Trade Hall – for Friday, 4 June 1976. Which is why Pete was in the foyer, collecting tickets.

But what made Malcolm think I'd come there to meet Pete?

It was all a glorious mix-up. Proper chance-in-a-billion stuff. That night, as I was standing waiting to meet the guy from the ad in *Manchester Evening News*, unbeknownst to me Pete and Howard had also placed an ad in a local listings mag, the *New Manchester Review*. They still hadn't got a band together in time to support the Pistols as planned, so they were putting the feelers out to find the right people. Malcolm must have known that they were still searching, so when he saw me loitering outside and found out I played bass he naturally assumed I was there to see Pete and Howard. The whole thing was like some Brian Rix farce.

I sometimes wonder what would have happened if the bloke I was supposed to meet had turned up on time? Or if he'd known where Cox's was and we'd met straight there instead? Or chosen to meet somewhere else entirely? Or if Pete and Howard had found somebody else in time for the gig? *If, if, if.* Or maybe fate finally owed me one after Alan's death? All I know is that, for once in my life, I was in the right place at the right time.

'Here's your new bass player.'

That was the lightning strike. One of fate's good ones. Every Buzzcocks song you've ever heard, all roads lead back to that first handshake. The punk rock crackle between the fingers like Michelangelo's *Creation of Adam*. Diggle, meet Shelley: Shelley, meet Diggle.

So there we are. Me and Pete. Now we're up to speed we can unfreeze this image and get on with the film . . .

MALCOLM WENT BACK OUTSIDE to drag more punters in off the street and left us to it. Pete still had to work the door. 'I won't be long here,' he said. 'You go in and I'll see you at the bar.'

Inside, the hall wasn't very busy. To my memory, maybe only 30 or so people there. What I never knew at the time is that those 30-odd people included Mark E. Smith, Bernard and Hooky from New Order and, somewhere lurking in the shadows, a young Morrissey. Then there was me, Pete and Howard, who was doing the lights. If for whatever reason the IRA had decided to bomb the Free Trade Hall that night, then the entire future of Manchester music would have been wiped out in a oner. Apart from Sad Café.

I was at the bar when Pete finally came over. As our first proper conversation began we were still at cross purposes. I was still trying to work out who it was I was supposed to be talking to and he must have been thinking the same thing about me. So we carried on like it was all perfectly normal and this had somehow been prearranged, which it hadn't. But, as we were talking, it became immediately obvious we had a common aim. I told him I'd written some songs of my own, which I think impressed him. Then he told me about him and Howard – who I met only very briefly as he was busy all night hovering around the stage on lighting duty. They'd been writing their own songs as well and had already decided on a band name.

'Buzzcocks,' said Pete.

Buzzcocks?

I loved it. It was funny and rude but still sounded rock'n'roll. Definitely the best band name I'd heard that night after the Sex Pistols. In a roundabout way, it was actually thanks to the Pistols that Pete and Howard came up with it. On that same trip to London, they'd read that week's copy of *Time Out* magazine, which had a feature about the new TV show *Rock Follies*. The headline was a catchphrase from the programme: 'It's the buzz, cock!' A lot of people still think the word Buzzcocks is a euphemism for vibrators. The much less sexy truth is it owes its creation to a London listings mag and an ITV music drama with Rula Lenska.

But this was the magic moment, talking to Pete. The realisation that this little guy was serious. I'd finally found someone who wanted to play original songs. He wasn't talking about doing covers and – *Hallelujah!* – he didn't jinx it by mentioning Butlin's. Pete evidently meant it, the same as I did. Maybe *this* was that kindred rock'n'roll spirit I'd been yearning for all along?

Even if he did look a bit like Ronnie Corbett.

This in itself would have been enough for one night, just the pair of us meeting. But the main event was yet to come.

The Lesser Free Trade Hall wasn't like a typical club or gig venue. It looked like a school-assembly hall, with a high stage at one end and formal rows of chairs laid out on the wooden floor, enough to sit a couple of hundred. Most of them remained empty as the few dozen or so there were all stood waiting down the front. Meanwhile, me and Pete sat on a row near the back where we kept chatting away. Until the Sex Pistols appeared.

If the first major musical epiphany of my life was hearing the Beatles while Linda James dried her hair, this was the second. From the moment they slouched on stage, they were seismic. It wouldn't be entirely true to say they were *nothing* like I'd heard before. I could see Steve Jones was cranking his guitar like the New York Dolls and giving it the Johnny Thunders vibe. But it was the power of it. And the *attitude*. There was Johnny Rotten, with all his teeth, giving it *'I am an antichrist!'* I'd definitely never *seen* anything like them before because they genuinely didn't seem to give a shit about us, the audience. I loved that about them more than anything else. Just seeing somebody on stage venting their spleen like that and getting away with it. And the lack of musicianship hiding in plain sight. The realisation that it didn't matter if you weren't some virtuoso master musician. Even I could get up there and do *that*. The Pistols were the revolution I'd been waiting for all my life.

Their first gig at Manchester Lesser Free Trade Hall on 4 June 1976 has since been mythologised to the point of overkill. But it was all true. That's really how it felt because just look what it did for Manchester. That night the Pistols showed all of us how to storm the Bastille. Because the next thing Mark E. Smith's starting the Fall, Bernard and Hooky are starting Warsaw, who become Joy Division who become New Order, and – give him a few years yet – eventually Morrissey starts the Smiths.

But before any of them, from day one, there was us. At the end of the night me and Pete exchanged phone numbers with a promise to ring the next day and get together for our first rehearsal that weekend round Howard's place in Salford. We were on.

I can't remember much else about going home that night, but I must have been levitating ten feet off the ground all the way. I was buzzing from the euphoria of seeing the Pistols, buzzing from having met somebody serious about forming a band. And buzzing because – as if I knew in my soul – I was already a Buzzcock.

*

SALFORD. Not just the other side of the city, but as every Mancunian and Salfordian knows, technically a different city. To get to where I needed took two buses, carrying my bass guitar in a black bin liner all the way. My destination, number 364 Lower Broughton Road, just round the corner from Man United's training ground, where Howard had a bedsit flat.

I hadn't really met Howard properly at the Pistols gig. So it wasn't until I rang his bell and he opened the door and I saw him in broad daylight that I realised. *He doesn't have any hair!* Well, he had *some*, but his fringe started somewhere halfway round the back of his head. It seemed obvious to me he was trying to model himself on Brian Eno. Then again, god knows what I looked like, stood on his doorstep with hair down to my shoulders and a bass neck sticking out of a binbag. He was probably as alarmed at the prospect of being in a band with me as I was with him.

Luckily for both of us, Pete was already there waiting inside. Howard's flat was very studenty. Sanded floors and tables, the smell of recently boiled brown rice and that day's *Guardian*. I took a quick sneak at his records. As I expected, Eno, Bowie, Lou Reed, but also Dylan, who he absolutely loved; Howard being a man of words, that made total sense. I was also pleased to see he had Silverhead, one of those bands everyone forgets about today that kind of slipped through the net around the time of glam. A bit Stonesy, almost like an early British New York Dolls, they only made two albums then jacked it in; their lead singer Michael Des Barres went off to America to marry the famous groupie Pamela and later become an actor. I didn't think anyone else cared for Silverhead apart from me, so the fact Howard liked them was another good omen.

In contrast, his bookcase was exactly as any later fan of Magazine would expect the sacred bookshelves of Howard Devoto to look like. There's your Samuel Beckett, your Dostoyevsky, your Albert Camus. And there, also, your *Playboy* and *Penthouse*. He had his sex mags carefully arranged on his shelves next to his works by the great intellectuals. I had to admire him for that – it beats shoving them under the bed like the rest of us. Then again, Howard was older than me and Pete. We'd both just turned 21, while he was a wise old 24.

But I hadn't popped round just to admire his collection of centrefolds. This was the make-or-break moment to see if we could actually create anything resembling decent music together as a trio. There was Pete with his guitar, me with my bass, and Howard with a microphone, all three of us plugged into this one amplifier. Pete and Howard had obviously rehearsed a lot before because they'd written a bunch of songs which I now heard for the first time, simultaneously trying to work out the root notes so I could play along. Pete started fuzzing away, I started plodding away on my bass at 90 miles per hour and Howard starts screaming *'I'm gonna breakdown, yes!'* And it sounded . . . ?

Pretty fucking awful, if I'm honest. And yet there was *something* there. Like Yeats said, 'A terrible beauty is born.' A chemistry, an energy, an urgency, the way Howard was spitting his words out like a machine gun. And, to cut us some slack, of course it sounded awful because we were all fighting through the one amp and we didn't have a drummer yet. Bad, yes, but exciting as fuck. And the more we played, the less terrible and the more magical we became. Already, it sounded like a *band*.

It wasn't until a break between songs that I first took proper notice of the big tank in the corner of Howard's room. Like a fish tank with a huge plastic lizard in it. I saw it when I first walked in and thought maybe it was some wacky bohemian student thing. But as we began playing again, in the corner of my eye I thought I could see something moving. I tried to focus on my bass frets and strings, but it was starting to bother me. I quickly peered over again at the tank.

The plastic lizard was staring at me.

Least I'm sure its head wasn't in that position last time I looked? Nah. Can't be. Just ignore it.

But I couldn't help it. I looked over again.

Flick! Flick!

The lizard was flicking its tongue at me.

Flick! Flick!

I thought I was hallucinating. *Don't look, Steve. Just keep your head down and keep playing.*

Flick! Flick!

It did it again. Then the bastard started twitching its horrible feet.

Flick! Flick!

That's when I realised. *It's not plastic, is it? It's fucking real!*

Flick! Flick!

Howard suddenly noticed I was freaking out.

'Oh, don't mind Monica,' he said calmly.

Monica?

'My monitor lizard.'

This is how Buzzcocks properly got going. The three of us in a Salford bedsit, rattling the shelves of neatly stacked Proust and pornography, learning to play 'Orgasm Addict' for the very first time before a captive audience of one hideously ugly monitor lizard.

IT MUST HAVE BEEN about a day or two after that first rehearsal round Howard's when my phone rang.

'Hello?'

'Hi. Look, I'm sorry I missed you outside the Free Trade Hall . . .'

The *Manchester Evening News* guy! He actually bothered to ring back and apologise.

'That's OK,' I told him. 'Actually, listen, I've since met this group, Buzzcocks, and I've started rehearsing with them.'

'Oh . . .'

Shit. The poor bloke sounded really put out.

'. . . Because I was wondering,' he went on, 'if you still wanted to meet . . .'

Well, I couldn't really say no, could I? I must have felt like I owed it to him or something. Or maybe I was keeping my options open just in case it all went to pieces with Pete and Howard. Or having second thoughts about Monica the lizard. But, giving him the benefit of the doubt, we did belatedly meet and go for that drink after all.

Once again, I gave him my usual spiel about how I'd been writing songs and was looking to do gigs playing original material.

'Yeah,' he nodded keenly. 'Yeah. And then halfway through we could do some impressions.'

Uh?

'Like do some comedy routines and that?'

You heard it. He expected us to play 'Fast Cars' and then stick berets on our heads and give it our best Frank Spencer. It was Butlin's syndrome all over again. All I could do was humour him for a pint or two, make my excuses and leave. Because if I hadn't already met Pete and Howard, I'd have probably gone and chucked myself straight in the canal.

9 / *GET ON OUR OWN*

THE AMAZING THING about Pete and Howard was they both had an urgent sense of purpose. They'd got off their arse to go to London and see the Pistols, they'd had the wherewithal to invite them up to Manchester, and even if they couldn't get a band together to support them that time, they weren't going to give up easily. A second Pistols gig was booked just over a month later on 20 July, in the same place, the Lesser Free Trade Hall. This time, Buzzcocks would be up and running. That gave us just six weeks to get ready. And six weeks to find a drummer.

In the meantime, the three of us carried on rehearsing round Howard's flat every chance we could. Him and Pete already had a great first fistful of punk songs, including 'Boredom' and 'Orgasm Addict'. They also threw in a few covers, 'I Can't Control Myself' by the Troggs and, because they were both big Captain Beefheart fans, 'I Love You, You Big Dummy'. We also, briefly, rehearsed Chuck Berry's 'Come On', based on the Stones' version, though that one quickly fell by the wayside.

Around the second time we got together, I politely coughed and said, 'Far be it from me to say, but I've also got this one I've written called "Fast Cars".' I played them my riff and they liked it, though as my original demo was a bit slower we sped it up in keeping with their other stuff. The only problem was I didn't have the words written down on me. My original lyrics, as I'd demoed them, were inspired by a newspaper article about driving in Moscow, how there were only about two makes of car over there, Ladas or Volgas. It started, *'How in Russia do you come by car?'* It was also an anti-car song, or anti-flash-dickhead-in-their-E-type-Jag-driving-it-as-a-cock-substitute song. But because I'd forgotten my lyrics, Pete and Howard took my title to write their own words to my tune – keeping it an anti-car song and namedropping Ralph Nader, the famous American road safety campaigner. So in the end it took the three of us to complete 'Fast Cars', the reason I was more than a bit pissed off when, come our first album, it was credited to just 'Shelley/Devoto'; it wasn't until 1988 that the label belatedly got round to correcting it to 'Shelley/Devoto/Diggle'.

Between all this thrashing and yelling through our one little amp, I was slowly getting to know my two new mates. Howard was both a conspicuous intellectual and a bit of a wry Noël Coward. I had a lot more in common with Pete, but then he was more pub, like I was, whereas Howard was more smoking jacket. Also Pete had a sense of humour, whereas I'm not sure Howard did. He took life *very* seriously and, as I've always said, life is too serious to be taken seriously. No question he was a very intelligent, very philosophical bloke, but I'm not sure it did him a lot of good in the end. He always seemed to be troubled, or a bit self-contained. There was a lot going on upstairs, but maybe too much, like he'd read one Samuel Beckett play too many. Years later, I remember listening to his first solo album and thinking, *Bloody hell, Howard, this is you talking to the psychiatrist now, isn't it?* That aside, I've always liked Howard – those early song lyrics like 'Boredom' were all his, and no question Buzzcocks could never ever have happened without him. Maybe it was because he was that bit older than us, but to me he just never seemed to be able to let go and enjoy it as much as we could.

Pete was a different story. Poles apart as we were in many ways, we just clicked. Being the same age we shared a lot of the same reference points, all the Northern working-class stuff we'd grown up with, everything from *Steptoe and Son* to *Armchair Theatre*, *Play for Today*, Ken Dodd and Morecambe and Wise. As time went on and we became our own double act. I think we both saw ourselves as Morecambe and Wise; the trouble being we both thought we were Eric as neither of us wanted to be the straight man. But the more we saw of each other, the more we bonded, each slowly working out what the other was about. Musically, Pete was big into the Velvet Underground, Bowie, Eno, the arty set, whereas he didn't have much time for the more rock'n'roll side of things I liked, like Zeppelin or what the Stones were currently doing. I realised I'd read a lot more than he had, though he was always more scientific than I was. Pete would watch *Tomorrow's World* and talk about electronics as he'd been studying it at college. 'I could have been a TV repair man.' So it was yin and yang. He was the scientist in the white jacket; I was the bricklayer with a book in his hand.

The big joke was Pete had gone to a clever clogs grammar school in Leigh, whereas I went to a typical Manchester thick kids' comprehensive. So I used to wind him up and say to him, 'You may have gone to grammar school, but you still ended up with me in the end.' It was like the French painters Ingres and Delacroix. Ingres was the fine artist, the golden boy who everyone loved, whereas Delacroix was the bad lad who got into trouble for being too expressive. So Pete was Ingres and I was Delacroix. He had the refinement; I had the feeling. But we both had that dialogue, the exchange of ideas about music and art that I'd only really ever had with my brother up until then. As a band, me, Pete and Howard were three very different individuals, but the magic of Buzzcocks was how we could all tune in and be on the same wavelength. Our big task now was to find a fourth.

One day, maybe the second or third rehearsal, Howard announced he'd found us a drummer. 'A girl,' he said. He probably thought it would look cool in a Moe Tucker from the Velvet Underground kind of fashion. All I could think of was her from the Honeycombs, Honey Lantree, grinning away bashing out 'Have I The Right'. I flinched at the prospect, which I know sounds horribly chauvinist and, being honest, as a 21-year-old bloke from Manchester in the mid-Seventies I would have been. My idea of a drummer was someone like John Bonham or Keith Moon. Punk's sexual revolution of bands like the Slits with Palmolive on drums was still several months round the corner. But whoever our Moe Tucker was, she never turned up. The great mystery woman in the history of Buzzcocks. Howard would say, 'Oh, she's definitely coming over to practise,' but she never did. Maybe she came round his flat once and saw his *Penthouse* collection and got cold feet. I have no idea.

Instead, one day I turned up for rehearsal and there's this schoolkid in a Laurel and Hardy-print shirt sat behind a drum kit. 'This is our drummer,' said Howard, matter-of-factly.

Our drummer. The best ever to come out of Manchester.

The incredible John Maher.

What a godsend. For me, that's the moment Buzzcocks *really* started. John was more than just the missing piece of the jigsaw. It all changed, instantly, from three dreamers strumming and shouting in a bedsit to the most exciting punk band I'd heard besides the Pistols. John was the perfect drummer for Buzzcocks. And, ridiculously, he was only 16.

The exact story of how Howard recruited John is best told by either of them. I think it still had something to do with that invisible girl who never showed and an advert in the back of *Melody Maker*. There was also some parental persuasion involved, as I know Howard had to go round to his house in Old Trafford and reassure Mr and Mrs Maher that their teenage son would be in very safe hands going off to play drums for some weird 24-year-old Eno lookalike shrieking about breakdowns and masturbation. But then Howard could be extremely charming. Whatever he said, it clearly worked, as one day there was John round the flat on Lower Broughton Road, drumsticks in his hand, ready to rock.

For 16, John had a very strong head on his shoulders. He was an intelligent kid who'd just blasted through eight O-levels, and while he wasn't necessarily arty like Pete or Howard, he was very technical. Later on, he'd get into bicycles and cars, learning how to take them apart and fix all the different bits. That's what made him such a natural drummer: he had great precision. He was also very direct and very down to earth. I'm not sure at his age I'd have had the nerve to go off and practise with a load of blokes five to eight years older than I was, but he had a confidence about him. He was so young – he looked *barely* 16 at a push – but he had the fire for it. O-levels is one thing, but there's no substitute for life experience. Joining Buzzcocks at that age, he was like Turner tying himself to the mast to experience the storm. I loved that about John, which is why he became like a little brother to me. After Pete, he was the Buzzcock I had the strongest connection with. And, significantly, unlike Pete and Howard, John was also a Mancunian. There were now two of us in the band.

But at first, all I'm seeing is this kid. *Christ, Howard, is this really the best we can do?* Then he started playing along with us. It was effortless. He had a very simple kit set-up but he could make less sound more. He also used to bang on Howard's coal scuttle which gave off a great metallic clang. As he explained, he'd started off trying to learn guitar but didn't like it so he switched to drums instead.

'Oh, right,' I said. 'So how long have you been playing?'

'I dunno,' sniffed John. 'Maybe six weeks.'

Six weeks! It was ludicrous how good he was. John didn't even seem bothered by Monica the monitor lizard, who was still giving us the tongue-flicking evils in her tank, though luckily not for much longer. Eventually, she got so big Howard had to get rid of her – very humanely, he donated her to the zoo in Belle Vue. But even before he did, not long after John turned up, we shifted from the bedsit to a proper rehearsal space. Howard had wangled a deal with one of his neighbours who was the caretaker of a hall down the road, a youth club adjacent to St Boniface's Church. Now with two amps and a drum kit in a big hall with great acoustics, we could really start making a glorious racket. There was, however, a catch. We were all skint, so none of us could afford to pay the bloke rent. So he let us use it for nothing, on one condition. 'You do a free gig,' he said. 'For the kids.'

He didn't mean kids as in teenagers. He meant kids as in actual kids, the ones from the youth club. Nine-year-olds with snotty faces in Mickey Mouse T-shirts and short trousers. We couldn't exactly say no, so by default we'd managed to get ourselves a second booking at the end of July. Providing, that is, we survived the first.

ONE OF THE BOOKS I'd read during my dole incubation was *The History of Mr Polly* by H. G. Wells. A great story about a bloke who doesn't know what to do with his life and ends up getting trapped in a silly marriage with this woman he can't stand. He tries to get out of it by faking his own suicide in a fire, which goes comically wrong, so in the end he just buggers off and starts a new life and finds peace and contentment with someone else. The moral of the book is that every person must find their place in the world. That really struck me when I read it as I still hadn't found mine yet. But I would.

Tuesday, 20 July 1976, Manchester Lesser Free Trade Hall. Buzzcocks' first gig. The memory is very intense, if very fragmented. There were three bands that night: us, then Slaughter & The Dogs, a bunch of teenage chancers from Wythenshawe trying to be glam, then the Pistols. My first proper meeting with the Pistols was catching them as they fell out of the service lift of the Free Trade Hall, all looking very ragged but glamorous, like the New York Dolls without the make-up. Johnny, Steve, Cookie and Glen were all very friendly to us. Punk was only seconds old so there was no sense of competition or regional rivalry, none of that North/South divide crap, just an instant camaraderie that we were all in this new thing together. They'd brought a crowd up from London with them, including a few journalists, so between that and the local buzz around Manchester following their first gig in June, this second one was always going to have a much bigger audience. This didn't ease my pre-show nerves any, which is when Pete stepped in to help. With a few hours to kill before the gig, he invited me out to dinner.

It sounds weird. It *was* weird, but it was actually a great bonding moment for the pair of us. I've no idea where Howard and John were at this time. Maybe they'd just popped out for a bag of chips and were waiting for us back at the venue. Meanwhile, me and Pete were wining and dining down the road in Pizza Hut.

'Pizza?'

At the age of 21 I'd never eaten a pizza before. This was Manchester in the Seventies, remember. Chips'n'gravy land. My mam or my gran wouldn't have had a clue how to pronounce 'pizza', never mind dish one up for our tea. Not only that, but I'd never eaten in a *restaurant* before. My family never ate in them and I'd never taken any girl out to eat in one. So this was my first ever dinner date. Me and Pete Shelley.

That was one of the great things about Pete, and one of the big differences between us. For a funny little man from Leigh, he was an epicurean. He had a lot of refined aspirations and liked his food, so knew a lot more than I did about where to tuck his napkin.

We sat at a table next to this mural of an Alpine scene painted on the wall. All very exotic. We both had a pizza each – not bad once I tried it – and Pete ordered a carafe of wine to share.

'A what?'

STEVE DIGGLE

This was typical Pete. Apart from a pizza, I'd never seen a carafe before either. When I did, it looked like something my grandad would piss in down the hospital. It was all a mystery to me, Pete talking to the waitress in this foreign language of haute cuisine. But there we were, an hour or so away from being on stage supporting the Pistols, sipping red wine and eating pizza with a knife and fork, all very nice. We must have spoken about the gig that night, but my main memory of our dinner date was talking about the various drugs we'd tried. Pete was very curious about it all. He'd read somewhere that you could get stoned on nutmeg if you eat an absolute ton of it. The only trouble is by the time you *are* stoned, you're half man, half Christmas cake.

At the end, Pete paid for the meal. And never let me forget it. But, as they say, there's no such thing as a free lunch.

The rest of the night is not so much a blur, more a vivid tremor. The noise, the adrenaline, the suddenly being on stage, plugged in, looking out across an audience and thinking, *Fucking hell! This is IT!*

The last time I'd been stood on a stage was when I had to read that poem out in school assembly. That scarred me for life, or so I thought, but this felt very different. For starters, this wasn't 'showbusiness'. If someone had shined a spotlight on me and asked me to play a bass solo like John Entwistle, I'd have crumbled. But the Pistols had shown us the other way. Just get up there, give it all your attitude and who gives a fuck even if you play badly. It wasn't you versus the audience, it was you versus the universe. It was the pure energy of it and the release of it. All that anger and frustration I'd built up for 21 years, all those years of waiting, being on the dole, the few terrible jobs I'd had, the sadness of Alan and the car crash, getting belted by teachers, leaving school under a black cloud, being told by Mr Kind and everyone else 'you'll get nowhere', the smashing of the grandfather clock and the bollocking afterwards. It was like my entire life flashing before my eyes in this intense rush of noise and movement. Stood on that stage, I finally knew who I was and what I was.

We must have played all of 15 minutes, maybe half a dozen songs. At the end Pete was wrestling his cheap Woolworths Audition guitar with Howard and whacking it against his amp. John was so buzzed up he jumped over his kit, out of the hall and into the street. I was so psyched up I ran off the stage, straight to the bar and downed a pint quick as I could. All four of us were effervescing with excitement that we'd actually done it and got away with it. A week later, we got our first review in the music press by Jonh Ingham from *Sounds*. A positive one that mentioned all four of us by name. 'Bassist Steve Diggle, who has a fair resemblance to Johnny Ramone, is equally strong.'

For me, that gig was like being born again. The first time, in St Mary's Hospital, 1955, as Steve Diggle from Manchester. This time, in the Lesser Free Trade Hall, 1976, as Steve Diggle from Buzzcocks.

Just like Mr Polly, I'd finally found my place in the world.

10 / PEOPLE ARE STRANGE MACHINES

OUR SECOND GIG was a lot more casual. A few days after the Free Trade Hall we played our 'thank you' show for the little kids of St Boniface's Church youth club. As an audience they were harder to please than the Pistols crowd, even down to a few heckles. 'You're rubbish, mister!' We also had to negotiate a bit of self-censorship. Howard was careful to change the words of 'Oh Shit' to 'Oh Spit' and I don't think we risked 'Orgasm Addict'. Otherwise it was a hall full of overexcited 10-year-olds going bananas watching Buzzcocks at full pelt. They didn't have a clue what Howard was yelling but they understood the primal energy and chaos of it, which stood to reason. At their age I was smashing up grandfather clocks. This was the musical equivalent.

Some of the St Boniface's kids would also gatecrash Buzzcocks' first official photo session. We thought it'd be funny to get a bag of clothes off the rag-and-bone man and each pick something silly to wear. Steptoe chic! It was all blouses and housecoats and tatty stuff that'd never fit us. I ended up picking this tiny cardigan thing way too small for me. I think Pete and John chose a jumper or shirt each while Howard ended up making a top out of this French shopping bag; typical Howard, ever the existentialist, it would have to be French. We posed by the brick walls near the church, going for a Northern kitchen-sink vibe, me still with my long hair, Howard in his shopping bag, Pete with shades on and lanky young John towering over the lot of us. Then we sat on the church steps when these kids came out of nowhere and started following us around. 'What you doin', mister?' So they ended up being in the group photo which later got used on the back of the *Time's Up* bootleg, the one that looks like a deliberate homage to the Who's *Meaty, Beaty, Big & Bouncy*, even if it was a chance coincidence.

St Boniface's was now Buzzcocks HQ, where we practised as often as we could while waiting for more gigs. If anyone's looking for somewhere to put up a blue plaque for Buzzcocks, that's as deserving a birthplace as any – certainly more deserving than anywhere in Bolton. This is what irks me every time I read 'Buzzcocks formed in Bolton'. *No, we fucking didn't!* We met in Manchester, started rehearsing in Salford, played our first gig in Manchester and made our first record in Manchester. I didn't set foot in Bolton until I was 37! But Bolton still gets the undeserving credit *just* because Howard, born in Scunthorpe, and Pete, born in Leigh, first met there at college. Had Lennon first met McCartney on a boy scouts' trip to Snowdonia, would that mean the Beatles were Welsh? Ludicrous logic, but I digress.

Having the hall to rehearse allowed us to be as noisy as we liked. Pete would sometimes get a bit carried away and start making feedback with his guitar, not the Woolworths one but this other red Starway model that he'd had since his teens. One day, very early on, he got overexcited and smashed it on the ground. He was going for a Pete Townshend but ended up doing something uniquely Pete Shelley. It must have been a perfect splinter in the wood as the top part of the guitar above the strings flew off in a clean break, leaving the rest of it intact. When he picked it up again it still worked except it was now a funny shape, like someone had sliced off the top couple of inches of his guitar the way you'd slice the top off a boiled egg. It not only looked cool, it looked *very* punk rock. A few times I've read people describe Pete's 'sawn-off guitar', but there were no tools involved: it was all a beautiful accident. Howard even kept the top half that flew off as a souvenir. It immediately became both Pete's and one of Buzzcocks' first trademarks. All the early reviewers mentioned it: we were that band with the little bloke with the broken guitar.

Pete had now moved to his own flat a couple of doors down from Howard on Lower Broughton Road, which made things a lot easier for him and the rest of us, rather than him being stuck out miles away in Leigh. I'd go round his and we'd listen to *Diamond Dogs* – both of ours' favourite Bowie album back then – while he ingeniously used to boil up pasta in a coffee percolator. That was Pete the scientist all over. No cooker, so he worked out a way to make pasta using a coffee machine. I think there might have been a tin of tomato soup involved as well as a makeshift sauce.

After our funny little pizza 'date' we'd go out a lot together, just the two of us, usually to the pub. Then one night he invited me to the pictures to see the David Hockney documentary, *A Bigger Splash*. I knew about Hockney through my brother, so I thought it'd be interesting. I also knew Hockney was gay, but I had no reason to start putting two and two together yet. It was only after the film when we went for a pint and Pete started saying, 'Ooh, now you see *him*, over there?' The conversation was starting to get a bit fruity. Then he said, 'Do you want me to walk you to your bus stop?' That was probably the moment the penny dropped. With a deafening clang.

Pete was bisexual. As he explained to me, 'I enjoy the best of both worlds.' People have often asked me if I could tell straightaway whether Pete was 'gay' when I first met him. The answer is no. From the off, I just had him down as a typical Bowie kid. He was arty and sensitive and funny – sometimes, but not always, in a camp way – and obviously not a macho brick shithouse of a bloke, but then it wasn't as if he was mincing around like Larry Grayson either. He was Pete Shelley, his own person, and he wasn't anyone's cliché.

On the road, from what I saw, Pete slept with far more women than he did men. And when I say men, Pete wasn't into butch biker types, he liked boys. Sometimes after a gig he'd say, 'Did you see him in the third row? He was gorgeous!' Or he'd pull some girl after a gig and wink at me – 'I'm really only after her boyfriend.' That was Pete, as promiscuous as he was insecure. The thing is, having known him over 40 years and having tried to psychoanalyse him, he craved affection so he grabbed it wherever he could. Once I got to meet his family, I understood the bigger picture. His dad was a coal miner, and he had a brother who had tattoos and owned a Rolls-Royce who was very much The Bloke, his father's son. Pete, the sensitive scientific kid, was more your archetypal mummy's boy. So I think his childhood locked him in emotionally and created all the insecurities he carried through into adulthood. The sad irony was Pete just wanted to be loved, but at the same time he found it very difficult to give love out. If you listen to his songs, you'd think he was a heart-on-the-sleeve romantic, but he only wrote those lyrics because he couldn't express those same emotions in real life. He wouldn't even give you a hug. The real Pete could be very cold and very detached. He wasn't an easy person to work out. I did, but it took me decades.

When we first became friends I think it was just in Pete's character to be playful and a bit flirty now and again. I don't know if he was testing my boundaries or his own. I'm not saying he *fancied* me either, but I think the kind of person he was, once he developed a strong male bond with someone it was natural for it to cross his mind. 'Shall I put my hand on his knee and see what happens?' Which he did, once or twice, the old Terry Wogan touch. I never took it seriously, and I'm not sure he did either. My attitude, as I told him, was I knew I was straight, so not for me, thanks, but you do what makes you happy. He'd try and tease me. 'How do you know if you've never tried?' I'd say, 'Well, I've not jumped off a cliff either.' But I let him know where my line was, and he knew never to cross it. Our friendship was too important, and Pete wasn't stupid. The funniest thing about all of this was giving my own mam a fright the first time I took Pete home. We'd been out in town drinking so he ended up coming back to crash at mine. It was about 2 a.m. and everyone else was in bed so I told him to kip on the sofa and I'd see him in the morning. The next day, I got up and there's Pete grinning at the kitchen table with a cup of tea and Mam's looking at me in a strange way. 'Is this your new friend?' Bearing in mind I'd only even taken one girl home for tea in my life, I could hear her cogs turning. Pete thought it was hilarious.

He was possibly encouraged in his sexual adventures by his Lower Broughton Road neighbour. His new flat was across the corridor from a guy named Terry who we'd sometimes pop over and visit. The first time he took me round, there's Terry sat up in bed with another bloke. I got the feeling Pete must have known or arranged it on purpose to see how I'd react as he had that classic Pete Shelley smirk on his face, like he half expected me to bolt screaming out of the room. Instead, we sat on the end of their bed talking to Terry and his boyfriend, the pair of them side by side under the same blanket like Laurel and Hardy. I definitely felt awkward but, as with Pete, I never had a problem with anyone being gay or bi or whatever they wanted to call themselves. If I had, I wouldn't have gravitated towards punk in the first place. The way I saw it, sexual experimentation was all part of the anything-goes chaos of it. We were all of us misfits in our own way, united together in this beautiful revolutionary thing we'd created. Whether you were a punk or gay or both, we all shared the common enemy of society's bastards trying to grind us down.

That alliance was made obvious by the fact Gay Manchester and Punk Manchester tended to inhabit the same clubs. There was already a big Bowie and Roxy Music scene in the city, mostly centred round this typical Seventies discotheque called Pip's which had a bespoke 'Roxy Room'. A lot of the first Manchester punks were the same Bowie and Roxy mob who just made subtle adjustments to their hair and clothes. There was also the Ranch Bar, this Wild West-themed basement club where we played one of our earliest gigs. It was owned by the famous drag queen Foo Foo Lamarr, who was like the original Lily Savage. Her real name was Frank Pearson, a local entrepreneur who you'd always see in the papers grinning ear-to-ear with a foot on his Rolls-Royce with its personalised numberplate 'FOO 1', the classic self-made man. To get to the Ranch you had to go through his main club, Foo Foo's Palace, known for being the best place in town to throw a hen night or a stag do. Then, next to it, through this separating corridor, you had the Ranch, which we quickly adopted as a punk hangout. It'd be full of these amazing characters – Bowie clones who'd suddenly started making their own wacky punk clothes, lesbians snogging in the corner, art students, blokes wearing dog collars off their tits on speed, underage drinking, all sorts of funny bohemian goings on. Every now and then a fight would break out and Foo Foo would jump from behind the bar in full wig, lipstick and padded bra, grab the blokes, bang their heads together and toss them out of the place. A sight to behold, and all part of the excitement of that first ignition of punk in Manchester.

The Ranch was one of the few places in the city that would give us a gig, but even then Foo Foo ended up pulling the plug after ten minutes.

'You're too fucking loud!'

That sort of thing used to happen to us a lot in the beginning. Another very early gig was in Stalybridge, not that far out of Manchester but far enough that it felt like enemy territory. This wasn't the city, this was the provinces. They'd never seen a punk band before, as was screamingly bloody obvious the moment we turned up and started unloading our gear. It was a bikers' pub, wall-to-wall long hair, denim cut-offs, Nazi helmets and Maltese crosses, the sort of blokes whose idea of music started and stopped with Black Sabbath. And here's Howard in glittery green socks and carpet slippers and Pete with his little broken guitar giving it 'Boredom'. It was like asking to be lynched. We played our usual set, which lasted about 20 minutes, then came off and were about to pack up when the landlord said, 'OK, have a break and then you're back on at half past.' He expected us to play two sets, like a typical pub band, with a break for the bingo or to serve hot pies in between. The problem was our 20 minutes was pretty much all we had, so that meant playing the same set twice. I'm looking at these bikers thinking, *If we go on again and play the same stuff a second time, they're going to kill us!* But, as fate would have it, we didn't have to. While we were sat waiting having a pint and worrying what the hell we were going to do, the landlord suddenly came over and said, 'Actually, don't bother. Can you just go?'

A typical reaction in those early days, but then it's not really surprising. We were the very first Manchester punk band, going out there like missionaries into the jungle, spreading the gospel. Not everyone was going to be easily converted.

WHILE WE WERE OUT fighting the punk wars in the Lancashire trenches, back in Howard's bedsit a network was slowly building up around the band. Being his mates, they were all unsurprisingly arty intellectual types. It's one of the odd things about punk. On one hand you had us, the bands, the ones who were out there getting gobbed on and punched about, making the connection with the audience, taking it to the kids on the street. On the other, you had the bedsit brigade, the ones who liked to theorise everything, who always had to bang on about situationism and politics in order to prove they were intellectually superior to everyone else. Almost like, much as they wanted to be part of punk, they also wanted everyone to know they were still somehow *above* it.

Howard could be both. He was sticking his neck on the chopping block by standing on stage and yelling 'Orgasm Addict', but at the same time he'd be the first to cross his legs and stroke his chin and pontificate on the existential subtext of it all. His friends weren't dissimilar.

Richard Boon was his boyhood chum from grammar school in Leeds who'd since been at university in Reading. He was like Howard Mk II. When I first met him I thought, *Christ, not another one!* I'm guessing he must have finished university and just decided to come to Manchester because Howard lived there, but for some reason he'd always be the one answering Howard's phone whenever it rang. That's how he got his pseudonym 'Alan Dial', which he used later on when he contributed some lyrics to a couple of Pete's early songs, 'Whatever Happened To?' and 'Just Lust'. One thing led to another, and the next thing Richard became our manager, tasked with trying to book us gigs wherever he could.

A newer acquaintance of Howard's was an exotic girl called Linda who spelled it Linder. He met her at our first gig at the Free Trade Hall; Linder turned up wearing a bin bag. Not long after, they became a couple and she moved into Howard's flat on Lower Broughton Road. Linder was your typical Bowie disciple, red hair and purple lipstick, very arty and sexy. To look at her, you'd never believe she came from Wigan.

Through Linder, we also got to know Malcolm Garrett, a graphics student at Manchester Poly who'd eventually end up designing our record sleeves. A bit later, sometime in '77, a London journalist from *Sounds* called Jon Savage also became part of the extended family. Despite being so posh that to hear him speak you'd think he played croquet for the Young Conservatives, Jon became one of our biggest supporters, bending over backwards to champion us in the press as much as he could. Punk was nothing if not classless. Linder and Jon would end up creating their own fanzine, *The Secret Public*, full of arty collages in the style of Richard Hamilton, which would eventually mutate into Buzzcocks' official fan club magazine.

All these people – Richard, Linder, Malcolm, Jon – would play their part, some bigger than others, in the rise of Buzzcocks. 'The arty lot' – as I'd sometimes refer to them, not because I was by contrast some artless Luddite, but they were all of a different character to myself, and to Pete who was a lot more approachable. Like an intellectual junta, the arbiters of taste in their Ivory Towers. Maybe it's the classic working-class chip on my shoulder, but at their haughtier moments they could bring out the Jude the Obscure in me, making me feel like the unschooled stonemason on the outside looking in. But then some of us fought the punk wars. Others just talked their way through it.

That war was only just breaking out in Manchester, whereas in the capital it had already been raging for several months. So by the late summer of '76, the time had come to offer them some Northern reinforcements. London was about to get its first blast of Buzzcocks.

11 / *SICK CITY SOMETIMES*

I FIRST CAME TO LONDON when I must have been 11 or 12. I had an auntie in Chelmsford, my dad's sister, who we'd sometimes visit in the holidays. One time she had me cleaning her carpet for a bit of extra pocket money, so the next day I spent it on two tickets so me and my brother could daytrip to London. It was only half an hour's train ride away, but pretty mad now I think about it, two young kids going off to the big metropolis by themselves. But that's exactly what we did, me and Phil, off on our little Dick Whittington adventure. We got out at Liverpool Street and then just walked around until we ended up on Fleet Street. It was like being in a film, the red double-decker buses, the black taxis, the buildings, the advertising hoardings, the way everyone was dressed. I'd seen this stuff on TV and record covers, pictures of the Kinks in all their fab Carnaby Street gear posing on a painted Buick Electra, so to suddenly be amongst it all felt like standing at the centre of the known universe, this being maybe 1966 or thereabouts, the Sixties at full swing. Me and Phil must have looked like a couple of street urchins, just wandering about mouths agog at everything. A magical memory. I never thought I'd end up living in London – I never thought I'd ever escape Manchester – but even at that age I knew I had to come back.

Sunday, 29 August 1976, I was back. This time I came by Transit van. We'd driven down overnight straight from Stalybridge after the biker pub fiasco, our destination a fleapit cinema in Islington, the Screen on the Green, where we were booked third on the bill of a punk 'Midnight Special' gig with the Pistols and another new London band. The memory is crystal clear – sharing a bottle of cider in the back of the van as we pulled up, climbing out and unloading our stuff. The first person I saw when I walked through the doors was a skinny bloke in a black jacket with a broken mirror stuck on it. Before I'd time to think whether that was bad luck or not, he spoke to me.

'Wotcha. I'm Mick from the Clash.'

'Hi. I'm Steve from Buzzcocks.'

That was the hands-across-the-water moment. Meeting Mick Jones.

We already knew the Pistols, but suddenly we're in London and here's this other punk band. Now there's *three* of us! Up until that point, though we knew punk was supposedly happening and the Pistols were leading the charge, we didn't know any other punk bands. Because there *weren't* any other punk bands. It's like the *Book of Genesis*. 'And lo! In the beginning, there was the Sex Pistols! Then there was Buzzcocks! Then there was the Clash!' The Screen on the Green was only the Clash's second or third gig. It was our fourth or fifth.

For me that gig was the crystallisation of the whole punk explosion. You had the Pistols, who that night were even more biblical than I'd ever seen them, singing about anarchy; then you had the original five-man Clash with Keith Levene, still very rough around the edges but already you could hear they had their own unique thing going on, singing about London burning with boredom; and then us, singing about nervous breakdowns and *'Admit! You're shit!'* That night, it was like our three bands wrote the script and everyone else who came afterwards just copied it. The Screen on the Green bill cemented the holy trinity of UK punk rock. Pistols, Clash, Buzzcocks. And it only cost a quid to see all three of us.

Enough people have told me over the years what that gig meant to them. Even though the Pistols had played all over by then, it was still a significant moment for punk in London. It also got us another review in *Sounds*, this time by Giovanni Dadomo. Not exactly glowing, mind. 'A boring and highly unimaginative quartet and rougher, as someone remarked to me in the urinal the other night, than a bear's arse.' Anyone who's heard the bootleg might agree his estimation was a little harsh. Giovanni went on to form his own punk group: the aptly named Snivelling Shits.

More than the bands, my strongest memory of that night is of the audience. Just seeing so many kids with dyed hair in Malcom and Vivienne's clothes, the ripped T-shirts and the zips and PVC. It was the first time I'd witnessed the Bromley contingent, including Siouxsie who was dressed like something from *The Rocky Horror Show* in knickers and suspenders with her tits poking out, dancing in front of the stage in her swastika armband. It was sexy and shocking at the same time. We'd never seen *anything* like her in Manchester, since at that point you could still count the actual punks in Manchester on two hands and one foot with a few toes to spare. Here was a whole army of them, and they looked fantastic. That was the point, for me, when it really hit home, that this wasn't just some marginal scene we'd started but a genuine movement. We were going to change *everything*.

HAD HOWARD HAD HIS WAY, everything would have included my name.

'Hmm. Are you sure you *want* to be Steve Diggle?'

I knew where he was coming from. Howard wasn't really called Devoto and Pete wasn't really called Shelley. It probably went back to David Bowie not being born Bowie and the whole punk pseudonym thing with Johnny Rotten and Iggy Pop. He did suggest a few names, which I sadly can't remember, though they would have been pretty weird, like the one Howard later used as his pseudonym on a gig guest list: 'Mole Rothman'. But I was sticking to my birth certificate.

Our appearance was another matter. Apart from Pete, who'd already dyed his hair by then, we must have looked a bit shabby compared with the London crowd. One person described us as looking 'like orphans'. We did. So no sooner were we back in Manchester than Howard also bleached his hair and got himself a pair of leather trousers. It was an overnight transformation. He said 'See ya' one day dressed like a student teacher and 'Hi' the next as this blond leather Nazi with an anarchy patch on his arm.

I finally chopped my hair with a pair of decorating scissors, but I was still clinging to the remnants of my old mod wardrobe, a favourite pinstripe suit from Oxfam and a pair of black cords that were a bit flared, so I had them cut and sewn into tight straight-legs. It was all second-hand and D.I.Y. because we were skint. By then my brother Phil was away at art college in Hull where he used to pick up cheap clothes on Hessle Road. He came home once and gave me a pink shirt that cost him 10p. 'Put that on,' he said. The moment I did, he started ripping the sleeves, then got his brushes out and painted a Co-op stamp and a chimney on it. That was my homemade punk fashion.

This was the real beauty of it all. The *immediacy* of punk. You needed something to wear – get some old rag, rip it and paint it, and suddenly you're a fashion designer. This was the real explosion, not the music but the mindset. You scribble something down in the toilet and the next thing you're a fanzine writer. You nick a camera and suddenly you're a photographer. We could all be anything we wanted and there was no one stopping us. Punk gave us the confidence to do these things. The same as people like Linder: give her a pair of scissors and some magazines to cut up and she's an artist. She summed up the new fearlessness. We weren't waiting for anyone to give us permission or a pat on the head. It was, 'Fuck off, I'm doing *this*.'

I was never 'a musician'. I owned guitars and I knew my way around them, but I'd never have had the chance to get up on stage and make a living out of it had it not been for punk. That was the mental liberation of the whole thing. I own a bass therefore I am a bass player, and fuck anyone who tries to tell me otherwise. When you boil it down, punk rock was just another term for freedom. That's what it was *really* all about and that's what I was looking for. Autonomy and emancipation. It's the only reason I ever wanted to be in a band. To be free, and to be left alone to do what I wanted.

THREE WEEKS LATER, stinking of bleach and sartorially transformed with a razorblade now dangling from Pete's ear, we were back in London for the 100 Club Punk Festival, a two-day event that would also go down in the venue's history as a pivotal moment. Unfortunately for us, most of the history went down on the first day, the Monday, when the Pistols and the Clash played and Siouxsie made her debut with the Banshees featuring Sid Vicious on drums. On the Tuesday, we headlined over the Damned, Chris Spedding and Stinky Toys. Apart from us and the Damned I'm not sure how 'punk' the rest of it was – some bloke from the Wombles and this awful kitsch French band. Everyone who talks about being at the 100 Club Punk Festival only ever talks about the Monday. Tuesday night was more the anticlimax after all the exciting stuff from the day before, as by the time we came on half the audience had gone home, not helped by a nasty incident during the Damned's set when a girl got badly hurt in the face by some idiot throwing a glass (Sid Vicious, as it turned out). Sure enough, the following week's *NME* was all about the Pistols' performance, though we did manage to scrape a mention in Caroline Coon's report in *Melody Maker*, calling us 'pint-sized'. Perhaps more telling, she also picked up on Howard's defensiveness as a frontman. 'He hates being on stage.' I never took any real notice at the time, but with hindsight it now seems obvious. Even then, after only a handful of gigs, the writing was on the wall.

12 / *BREAKDOWN*

FOR NOW, PUNK was still entirely word of mouth and media. You read about it in the music press or the new fanzines that were cropping up like *Sniffin' Glue*, who gave us our first interview, but the only way to properly *see* or *hear* it was to go to the gigs. None of the new bands had made any records yet, and it wasn't until the very end of '76 that any UK punk singles finally arrived: first the Damned's 'New Rose' in late October, then the Pistols' 'Anarchy In The UK' at the end of November. There wasn't anything on the radio or TV either, apart from the Pistols appearance on Tony Wilson's *So It Goes* back in August. But even that was only broadcast late one Saturday night in the Granada region and nobody had a video in those days; most of its target audience, still out in the pubs or clubs, would have missed it.

This was both punk's strength and its weakness. The secret excitement of only being able to experience it live in the flesh in some sweaty club versus the frustration of not being able to take it home and listen to it in your bedroom. Punk was a religion with plenty of hymns but yet to print any hymn books.

If you'd never seen Buzzcocks and judged us purely based on what had been said about us so far in the papers, all you'd know is that we were pint-sized, rough as a bear's arse and that I supposedly looked like Johnny Ramone. Even when the papers did bother to review us, the average hack would usually slag us off because the PA was crap on the night. That was the most annoying thing. If only people could *hear* us properly, they might actually get it.

These must have been the thoughts guiding our feet aboard an orange Selnec bus one dreary Monday in mid-October, dragging our guitars and amps with us, bound for Stockport to make our first demo at 'Revolution Studios'. A fancy name for the loft of a guy named Andy Macpherson who'd converted it into a recording space with a four-track tape machine. A rudimentary set-up – John didn't have to bother lugging his own drums along as they had a kit set up in an airing cupboard – but since none of us had ever been in a studio before it was all rocket science to us.

The idea was to plug in, play and record our entire set. The strange and brilliant thing about it was our naïvety, particularly Howard's. Instead of recording each song, one at a time, he'd got it into his head that we had to play the whole lot, one after the other, but keep deadly silent between them like the gaps between tracks on an album. He must have thought that's how records were made. Even I thought, *Nah, that ain't right.* But nobody argued or told him otherwise, so we just went along with it. We'd play a song, then when it ended Howard put his finger to his lips – 'Shush!' – while we all froze, too scared to move or cough. Then he'd wag his finger and count us into the next one. Andy the engineer never said anything either and god knows he must have been pissing himself. 'These idiots haven't got the foggiest, have they?' But that's how we made what became the *Time's Up* bootleg.

Listening to it today, it sounds so pure and direct. Even though Howard's singing is very affected, at times a bit too much of a Johnny Rotten impression, the words and music were nothing like what the Pistols or the Clash were doing, a lot of which was just fast and heavy rock'n'roll or echoing what the New York Dolls were up to a few years before. Buzzcocks had something else because we didn't have a model. You can hear it. We were trying to find ourselves, using our limitations to our advantage and creating something new. There's a beautiful simplicity to those early songs. Pete's two-note solo in 'Boredom' is probably the best example. What other band would have had the nerve to do that? Steve Jones and Mick Jones both loved showing off and giving it the whole Les-Paul-guitar-hero thing. But even when I offered Pete my Les Paul copy for those early Buzzcocks gigs, he was having none of it. He liked the sound of his cheap broken guitars from Woolies and he could do in two notes what others couldn't do in twenty. *Nee-naw! Nee-naw!* Like Chekhov said, simplicity is everything.

Buzzcocks had that minimalism and discord which had more in common with what the German Krautrock bands were doing than what the American punks like the Dolls and the Stooges or even what the Ramones were doing. It was all instinct. John was making up his own drum parts, Pete was the scientist with a Starway guitar and apart from 'Boredom', which had a bit of a bass run, most of the time I was just pummelling root notes. I could have tried doing my own thing and been a bit fancier but the more minimal, the more powerful it sounded, and I didn't want to ruin the beauty of it. Like Rothko, black and red, it's all you need. Nobody else was as brutalist as we were in those early days. Those demos are like the cave paintings that started modern Manchester music. You hear *Time's Up* and you can hear exactly where Joy Division came from – the minimal guitar, the root note bass, the rolling drums, the urgent vocals, it's all there like the blueprint waiting for others to come along and make their replica.

Apart from anything else, we were oddballs. The London punk bands looked like proper gangs, like a street gang. The Pistols did, so did the Clash and the Damned, whereas we looked like a lost daytrip from the special needs minibus. John was still a gangly schoolboy, you had little Pete in his pink jeans and half his guitar missing, me still wearing waistcoats thinking I'm a mod and Howard up front convinced he's in *Waiting for Godot*. We weren't cool in any way, shape or form, which at the time worried me a bit, the fact that the other punk bands seemed to have more of a rock'n'roll intent, a bit more obvious unity. But now I can see that's what set us apart, that we were much too weird and quirky and strange as individuals to fall into any of the clichés. I don't know if that was being Northern and obstreperous or just the kind of personalities we were. And, in an ironic roundabout way, that's what made Buzzcocks cool in the end.

That, and the fact we had great songs. Had a record company signed us there and then, what you hear on *Time's Up* would have pretty much been our debut album. All those early Shelley/Devoto tunes, the four we'd later redo as *Spiral Scratch* – 'Breakdown', 'Time's Up', 'Boredom' and 'Friends Of Mine' – alongside 'You Tear Me Up', 'Love Battery', 'Lester Sands', 'Don't Mess Me Around', 'Orgasm Addict' and 'Oh Shit', as well as the two covers we always played, the Troggs one and the Beefheart one. The only other early Buzzcocks tunes missing were 'Apollonia's Countdown', which we played live maybe the once, and 'Peking Hooligan', which we did at the Screen on the Green, plus 'Fast Cars', which we'd rehearsed with Howard on vocals. The London bands were singing about the politics of the street. We were singing about the politics of the self. That was another defining thing, and where Howard with his love of literature and existentialism really stood apart on his own. Whether he was writing about his brain turning into porridge or pissing adrenaline or having a wank, you'd never heard lyrics like them before. They were shocking and funny at the same time. Buzzcocks not only had the best songs, but the best jokes.

I've no recollection of why we made the *Time's Up* demo beyond wanting to hear ourselves on tape. Possibly we needed it as a calling card to get more gigs, but it was definitely never intended for public consumption. It was only a couple of years later, once we got signed and started regularly getting in the charts, that the first bootleg came out. It's since been put out officially, now a permanent part of Buzzcocks' legacy. My only regret is that I couldn't have foreseen this at the time: if I had, I might have taken a bit more care tuning my bass.

OFF STAGE, I was still strumming my guitar at home, but I was so happy being in the band I couldn't give a fuck whether I was on bass or bongos. The only dream was to *be* in a band, and I was living it. I never looked at the other punk guitarists with envy, not even Pete. It was exciting enough just playing the gigs and being up there in the eye of the hurricane. But from day one I always knew I wasn't a born bass player. The principles are the same as a guitar – it's a stringed instrument with frets and pick-ups – but though every guitar player *thinks* they can get by fine on bass, it's a whole different board game. The pieces might look the same, but one's draughts and the other's backgammon.

Being stuck on bass didn't bother me nearly as much as wanting to write my own songs. I'd already thrown 'Fast Cars' into the mix, but

I was still a bit shy when it came to letting anyone else hear the other bits I'd been demoing. But then one day I went over to Pete's for my usual bowl of coffee-percolated pasta and took along a tape I'd made of one of my earliest songs called 'I Might Need You'. It was very Beatlesy in a ripped-off moptopish 'She Loves You' kind of way, and the only reason I played it to Pete rather than Howard was because Howard wasn't bothered about the Beatles. He preferred the Stones, and good on him. Whereas me and Pete loved them, sharing stories about going to the pictures to watch *A Hard Day's Night* and the impact that had on us as kids. They became an important bonding musical obsession me and Pete had in common. The words of 'I Might Need You' were pretty bad – *'I want to have my way with you'*, et cetera – but it was more about the melody and the harmonies. Pete obviously liked it because a few days later we were sound-checking for a gig at the Electric Circus when he said to me, 'Play Howard that tune you played me.' It felt a bit awkward, but I strummed and hummed a bit of the melody of 'I Might Need You'. When I was done, Howard, in his typically Howard way, just went 'Hmm'. That pretty much killed it.

But there's a Part Two to this story . . .

THE ELECTRIC CIRCUS was an old cinema waiting to be demolished in Collyhurst, a rough part of Manchester a couple of miles from the city centre. At some point prior to it being a music venue, Bernard Manning ran it as a nightclub. When he left he must have taken most of the fixtures and fittings with him as by 1976 the place was literally a shell falling to bits. So were the people who lived round and about, the hardest of inner-city hard nuts. It was the last place you'd want to go for a night out to see a band, but being the beggars punks were in Manchester in those days, there wasn't a lot of choice. I'm sure anyone who ever got the shit kicked out of them going in or coming out would disagree, but in a strange way its terrible location added to the thrill of the place. For the brief period it existed, the Electric Circus was far and away the most important punk club in Manchester, probably outside London full stop. It put the city on the national punk map for touring bands, also giving Buzzcocks a regular local platform instead of having to scramble around for gigs in out-of-the-way town halls or jazz clubs like Band on the Wall where we weren't wanted. The Electric Circus may have been a shithole, but it was *our* shithole.

We played there three times in the run-up to Christmas, the third time being the most memorable. Thursday, 9 December 1976.

Eight days earlier, the Pistols turned the air blue on Bill Grundy's *Today* programme – the moment the detonator was pressed and punk blew up nationally. The next day it was front page of the tabloids with the famous *Daily Mirror* headline, 'THE FILTH AND THE FURY'. It was as if our mates had publicly declared war on the rest of the country, which in a way they had. Up in Manchester, we were ecstatic. It felt like the storming of the Winter Palace. 'This is it! The revolution!'

The downside for the Pistols was they'd been due to start their Anarchy tour with the Clash, the Damned and Johnny Thunders and the Heartbreakers two days later, but thanks to those few choice swear words on London TV, their gigs were now getting banned by local councils left, right and centre. Luckily, Manchester was one of the very few authorities who didn't ban them – possibly because they were booked to play the Electric Circus, which was in such a state the council maybe hoped the building might collapse while the Pistols were inside, doing everyone a favour. We were planning to go and see them anyway, but then a day or so before, Malcolm got in touch to say he'd kicked the Damned off the tour so we could fill their slot. It felt like perfect timing, setting up a repeat of the same bill as the Screen on the Green three months earlier, only this time on our home turf.

When we met them at the Midland Hotel, the Pistols were already taking the piss out of room service, with trolleys of beer going up and down every five minutes. Malcolm was on the phone most of the time – in the wake of the Grundy incident he now had the whole of Fleet Street on his case – while John was lying on the bed with a bottle of kaolin and morphine cough medicine; popular back then because the kaolin was the chalky stuff, so if you didn't shake it, it'd eventually separate and settle at the bottom so you could just drink the morphine off the top. We also took John, Malcolm, Strummer and a few others to the pub over the road, the legendary Tommy Ducks, which blew their minds. A typical working-class Manchester pub, except it had coffins for tables and women's knickers nailed to the ceiling, all stained with years of cigarette smoke. It would have made an amazing photograph – the Pistols, Clash and Buzzcocks sat together, pints on the coffin lid, under all these dirty panties.

We didn't see much of Johnny Thunders, but then he'd have been on smack o'clock. That was his bag, whereas ours was speed: the go-to punk drug, amphetamine sulphate. The first dab tastes horrendous, like eating scouring powder, but then you educate your tastebuds and you slowly get used to it. Back then nobody could afford cocaine as it was about 60 quid: in 1976 you could have bought a couple of houses in Manchester for that. So cheap speed was our drug, me and Pete's, as well as the odd pill. 'French blues' they called them, these other amphetamines that were a bit nicer than your basic speed. If we had any on us, we'd usually take something before we went on stage to give us a fuel injection. It all added to the arty ramshackleness of it all. Like the French existentialists getting high on absinthe and writing poetry, we'd get wired on speed, then go on and play our version of poetry. *'B'dum, b'dum!'*

That night at the Electric Circus was especially historic for reasons we'd only realise later. The Pistols were their usual amazing selves while, three months after the Screen on the Green, the Clash were like a different band. They'd since got rid of Keith Levene so now it was just the four of them. They were faster, sharper, and Strummer was a lot more aggressive and in-your-face. And then, crucially, you had us, flying the flag for Manchester and the great North/South punk coalition. This was our tenth proper gig, and with the drama and excitement of the whole Grundy furore still raging, it felt like we'd gone over the top with the Pistols together, brothers in arms, fixed bayonets, helping them lead the charge.

The especially historic thing we'd only realise later is this gig would be Howard's last.

THREE DAYS AFTER CHRISTMAS, we were back in a recording studio. This time in the centre of Manchester, Indigo Sound, a proper 16-track facility on Gartside Street. Ever since we made the *Time's Up* tape, the conversation had evolved to trying to make an actual record. That in itself was a testament to the confidence punk had given us and how far we were prepared to go, taking the whole D.I.Y. mentality to its logical extreme. I don't remember any of us discussing actual record companies, which were all London-based anyway. It just seemed obvious. 'We want to make a record. OK, let's do it ourselves.'

We worked out that recording and pressing 1,000 singles would cost somewhere between five and six hundred quid. If we sold them for a quid each, we'd cover the costs and be a few hundred in profit. Young entrepreneurs! It felt like one of those government 'Enterprise Allowance' schemes they used to have, the joke being we were still signing on. But we'd never have been able to do it without the help of Pete's dad, who lent him half the money we needed, an amazing act of kindness and trust.

The rest was scraped together by Howard and Richard Boon, who looked after the logistics of everything, sorting out printers and pressing plants. It was also through their connections with the *New Manchester Review*, the local biweekly equivalent of London's *Time Out*, that we found someone willing to be our producer. The day of recording, we'd arranged a rendezvous in a pub down the street from the studio. We walked in, I looked around and immediately clocked this intense bloke in the corner wrapped in a big thick coat with a bush of curly hair. He looked just like Tom Baker in *Doctor Who*. Our own crazy-as-fuck timelord, Martin Hannett.

On first, very misleading impressions, Martin seemed quite quiet and a bit insular, as if he was more nervous meeting us than we were meeting our producer – although the extent to which he was qualified to justify that job description would soon become hysterically apparent. We spoke a little bit about what we wanted and what records we liked. Martin listened, nodded, finished his pint, and then we all headed over to Indigo. 'To get to work.'

I don't know what we were expecting, but whatever it was, it wasn't Martin. He wasn't a producer. He was a sonic saboteur. At the time he called himself 'Martin Zero', as in zero tolerance for orthodoxy. Martin was as punk rock in his methodology as we were in our playing, the only problem being it's like when two wrongs don't make a right: chaos plus chaos equals absolute carnage. There was an engineer there with him, some poor bloke whose typical day at the office was probably setting the sound levels for Lynsey de Paul. If it wasn't already bad enough with us screaming in his ears, on top of that he's got Martin playing around with the mixing desk like it's a fucking abacus. The moment the engineer would get everything sounding balanced, Martin would be going 'What's this?' and flicking the faders up and down trying to destroy everything. Howard's singing about breakdowns and the engineer's actually having one.

The easiest way to describe Hannett is 'a mad scientist'. He'd studied chemistry and he knew all sorts about technology, but he had a deranged creativity about him. A good thing he never did become a chemist as he'd have been the kind to one day shake up the wrong test tube of nitroglycerine and blow himself and half of Manchester up with it. He did the same with sound. But that was the beauty of Martin. Had anybody else tried to produce *Spiral Scratch*, it might have sounded too clean or nice. He framed it all imperfectly, which itself made him the perfect man for the job. He not only captured our sound, he captured that magic spirit of who we were.

The four songs were chosen democratically, one member, one vote. I don't remember which was mine, but they more or less elected themselves as the ones that went down best live. 'Breakdown' was always a great set opener, 'Time's Up' had that brilliant Howard and Pete call-and-response hook, 'Boredom' was our anthem and 'Friends Of Mine' was a full-on punk charge. Most of them were live first takes with minimal guitar overdubs, exactly as listed on the back sleeve. The whole recording was done and dusted in maybe half an hour. That's as much as we could afford.

For a front cover, we went to Piccadilly Gardens in the centre of town with Pete's new Polaroid camera he'd been given for Christmas. We had a few statues to choose from – Queen Victoria, Robert Peel – but in the end we settled on the steps beneath the Duke of Wellington. The Polaroid film cartridges were expensive and you only got about ten exposures a time, so because Pete had already been messing about with it, there were only two shots left. This put extra pressure on Richard Boon, the finger on the button, not to fuck it up. The first exposure, Howard blinked.

'Bollocks. We can't use *that*.'

Now we only had one left.

'Shit! Nobody blink! Nobody blink!'

Nobody blinked. The second one, the last Polaroid on the film, came out just as you see it on *Spiral Scratch*: John and Howard to the fore, both looking incredibly calm, with me and Pete poking our heads behind them. *Hey, hey, we're the Buzzcocks!*

Richard had already been using 'New Hormones' as a name for our management company, so that became our record label, with the *New Manchester Review* letting us use their office on Oxford Road as a contact address. We left all that side of it to Richard, who went ahead and gave it the catalogue number ORG1, as in 'orgone', some clever in-joke to do with Reichian theory. Whatever made him happy.

The physical release of *Spiral Scratch* was all a bit of a jigsaw. The sleeves were printed in Manchester while the actual discs were pressed up in London. We drove down to pick them up from an industrial estate, then Howard's living room became the assembly line to put it all together. It took forever, all four of us sticking a thousand records into a thousand sleeves, having to check every disc for faults. After the first ten, I'd had enough. It was like working in a biscuit factory. 'Hang on, this ain't rock'n'roll!' I suddenly had a flashback to being back in the foundry, thinking of ways I could skive. In the end, me and Pete dashed off to the pub down the road for some respite. It all felt too much like manual labour.

I wish I could say the first time I played *Spiral Scratch* and heard myself through a record player was a life-defining moment. Sadly, I genuinely don't have any snapshot memory beyond the obvious excitement and pride that we'd actually done it. Personally, I'd no idea how the hell we were going to flog them, or even if they'd sell, but then in the first stroke of January 1977, record distribution wasn't my problem. I had a far, far bigger one.

HE WAS SO CASUAL ABOUT IT. That's the weird thing. There was no drama, no big summons to a band meeting, no forewarning of any imminent catastrophe. Me and Pete just turned up at Howard's one day, the three of us all sat in the same room where we'd had our first practice, and he said it as matter-of-factly as someone saying they'd bought a new kettle.

'Oh, by the way, I'm leaving.'

Pete was as shocked as I was.

'EH?'

That was our reaction. Utter disbelief.

'The band,' said Howard. 'I've achieved everything I wanted to do. I've made a record. So I'm leaving.'

For a long, horrible moment I fell into a black hole, my thoughts tumbling one after the other like dominoes. Howard's leaving the band equals the band's finished equals I'm fucked and back to square one.

This was my big, big problem on the first stroke of January 1977. And it must have lasted all of two seconds.

'OK. We'll carry on.'

Pete. He was instantaneous.

I turned and looked at him.

'Won't we?' he said.

If ever in my life I could have kissed Pete Shelley, it was there and then.

'Yeah,' I nodded. 'We'll carry on.'

It was that simple, that instinctive. Neither of us wanted to quit, nor did John. Even Howard seemed genuinely pleased me and Pete wanted to keep it going. It was all completely amicable, as he'd still remain closely involved in our management for most of the next year until he went off to focus on his next group, Magazine.

But that was that. The end of an era. Buzzcocks Mk I lasted all of six months, from our first gig at the Lesser Free Trade Hall in July '76 to Howard leaving at the beginning of '77. In total he only ever played ten gigs with us. For him, *Spiral Scratch* was the climax. For me and Pete, it was only the prelude.

'We'll carry on.'

When I think about those lightning strikes of fate, that was one of the greatest things ever to happen to me. By leaving Buzzcocks, Howard changed my life, and Pete's. It radically altered the group chemistry, allowing Pete to switch over to lead vocals and me to switch from bass to guitar. And he was completely right. The *Spiral Scratch* Buzzcocks could only ever have gone so far. What we'd achieved in those first six months was phenomenal in itself. We came from nowhere and put Manchester on the map as the first non-London punk group. It's why I always say 'punk was born in Manchester' because it was a purely London thing until we started Buzzcocks: the Pistols were the box of matches, but we were the touchpaper that set the whole country alight by proving anyone could do it. And we made the first independent punk single. So punk's not even over and we've already created indie. Had it all ended with Howard, people would still be talking about Buzzcocks today as an influential underground cult.

'Just a pity they only ever made that one EP.'

Fortunately, we didn't. Mine and Pete's philosophy was, 'Man down? We'll keep going!' We loved it much too much to stop. Brilliant as *Spiral Scratch* was, we had so much more to give. And, besides, thanks to dear old Mrs Shaughnessy, I'd still a promise to keep.

'Don't you worry, Mam. I'll be on *Top of the Pops* before you know it.'

POSTSCRIPT. That 'I Might Need You' story, Part Two.

It's the start of '77. Howard's just left, and me and Pete are discussing how we have to change the group around, working out the new dynamics of what it is we need to do. Then he tells me he's already got one new song.

'Great! Let's hear it.'

So he plugs in his guitar and sings it to me.

By the first chorus, I'm gobsmacked. It's nothing like I expected because it's nothing like what Buzzcocks have been playing with Howard. It sounds *just* like an early Beatles song. Not the same as my 'I Might Need You' but a similar poppy melody with typical moptop *'oh-oh'* harmonies. Almost as if he'd secretly been looking to do something a bit Lennon and McCartney and the moment he heard my demo he thought, *A-ha!*

I'm listening to him, amused, and a bit taken aback, but I'm not pissed off. How could I be? Because this is the moment that feeling hits me. The feeling that I now know what me and Pete's new Buzzcocks are all about.

'What do I get? Oh-ooooh, what do I get?'

The feeling this is going to be amazing . . .

BUYS YOU YOUR LIFE, SIR

(1977–2022)

13 / *FRIENDS OF MINE*

VOCALS, GUITAR, BASS AND DRUMS. That was the simple formula of Buzzcocks Mk I. But now Pete was going to sing lead and I was going to switch to guitar, that'd give us a lot more power: vocals (Pete), two guitars (me and Pete), bass (?) and drums (John). Finding the (?) was our new problem. Pete stuck a 'Wanted: Bass Player' ad on the noticeboard of Virgin Records in town, but we didn't have much time to waste as we'd just been booked to support the Clash in London. That's when Garth's name cropped up.

He was one of Pete's old grammar-school friends from Leigh. He did have a surname – Davies – but to us, and to punk history, he was just 'Garth'. Like Sting and Prince, some people only need one syllable to get them through life. I've never met anyone else called Garth, and probably just as well. One Garth was already Garth enough for this world to contend with.

Apart from Pete's school connection, Garth had also played his part in the conspiracy theory to erroneously credit Bolton as the birthplace of Buzzcocks. In April 1976 he'd been the bassist for Pete and Howard's lone college gig there playing Bowie and Velvet Underground covers. By process of elimination, and a bit of desperation, that made him the most likely candidate.

As an ice-breaker audition, Pete invited him round to Howard's flat. We sat there waiting, three in a row like a panel of talent show judges, when in walked this massive bloke in a kipper tie and a three-piece suit. The sort of suit maybe a mod might wear, except Garth didn't have the body of a mod: he had the body of the Pillsbury Doughboy. As one reviewer later said, he looked 'more like a butcher than a musician'. His actual day job was something to do with installing computers, not that it made any difference. He was the most un-rock'n'roll-looking bloke you'd seen in your life. I couldn't imagine him playing bass except maybe 'Save Your Kisses For Me' with those farm animals down the social clubs. Punk rock obviously hadn't touched Garth yet in the way it had touched the rest of us, and I'm not sure it ever did. The first time I saw him anywhere near a pub jukebox, he put on a Conway Twitty record.

So on first impressions, and without having heard him pluck a note, I wasn't convinced. I'd grown up poring over pictures of bands like Small Faces who *looked* like bands. The three of us were all young and skinny, but now suddenly here's this giant bookend of a bloke at the side of the stage.

But then we took him for a pint in the pub down the road, the Old Priory. That audition he passed. Much like myself, Garth loved a drink. I'm not sure if the drink loved him as much back in return, but as friends I realised we were going to get on famously. Probably too famously. After every rehearsal, Garth would say, 'Fancy a drink?' Every time I'd say, 'Oh, go on, then,' and every time it took me three days to get home. We brought out the beer monster in one another something terrible. There's a picture that our mate, the photographer Kevin Cummins, took of me being carried out of the Ranch Bar with Garth, some time during '77. That photo says it all. We wouldn't go out 'for a drink', we'd go out 'to get drunk'. The object of the evening was total mental annihilation, and me and Garth were spectacularly good at it.

The problem of Garth's appearance was soon fixed thanks to a classic Devoto sartorial makeover. Howard tried the same with me to begin with when he suggested I play our first gig supporting the Pistols wearing this three-quarter-length kimono and no trousers – basically, trying to make me look ambisexual like David Bowie. I told him, 'Nah, I'm alright with me jeans, thanks.' But Garth was a lot more susceptible. It was a bit like an episode of *Mr Benn*: one day Howard took him aside into another room, shut the door, then five minutes later out walked Garth wearing a boiler suit looking like something from *A Clockwork Orange*. To give Howard his due, at least he got him out of his kipper tie into something slightly more 'punk'. Even if he still looked like a butcher.

By the time Garth joined, we'd shifted our rehearsal space from St Boniface's in Salford to the centre of Manchester. The chronology gets a bit convoluted, but basically there were two. One, just briefly, was a local help centre for Manchester drug addicts called Lifeline; we'd be practising in one room while they'd be queuing up for their methadone in the other. But the main one was a warehouse called TJ's on – fittingly enough – Little Peter Street. It was the same place Joy Division later used, which you can see in the video for 'Love Will Tear Us Apart'. That room was where we wrote most of our early hits – so not only did Joy Division nick their sound off early Buzzcocks, they also nicked our bloody rehearsal space. In fact, we even gave them their first gig supporting us at the Electric Circus when they were still deciding whether to call themselves Stiff Kittens or Warsaw, dressed in shirts and ties like Hitler Youth. Only their moustaches weren't so much Adolf, more door-to-door insurance salesman.

A typical day at Lifeline or TJ's would start around lunchtime, one o'clock, and go on until five when the pubs reopened. I think that's the bit Garth liked best, not so much being in a band but the lifestyle of every day rehearsing then going on the lash. As a bass player he got the hang of our stuff fairly quickly, though he didn't so much play the bass as punch it. He had a very aggressive style, but then when drink got the better of him he could be a very aggressive bloke.

Unfortunately, so could Pete. He had a heart of gold, but the shy sensitive guy you hear on his records wasn't the same guy in the pub. Pete was sharp and hard underneath. People who saw him as some little camp chappie couldn't have been more wrong. He was a hard-drinking son of a Scotsman who could put away more pints than you'd ever believe possible for a bloke of his height. Music soothes the savage beast, so without the music, and with one drink too many, the drunk Pete Shelley could be an absolute nightmare. This was the ticking timebomb of the whole situation with Garth and the band dynamic. Him and Pete had known each other since they were kids, so there was not only a history there but a strange antagonism. We'd all go out for a band drink, then a few pints in they'd start nipping at each other, petty things that probably went back to grammar school. Next thing you know, they're rolling around on the floor brawling with each other. They looked ridiculous. Garth being his size and Pete being his, it was like David and

Goliath. So we might have found ourselves an OK bass player, but in the process we'd introduced this mad dysfunctional volatility to the group.

It was only *after* he joined that Pete took great pleasure in filling me in on some of Garth's many peculiarities. Apparently, he had an odd phobia about fish fingers being too greasy, so every time he cooked them he had to dry each one with toilet roll before he could eat it. He also had some very bizarre speech hang-ups. Pete told me Garth used to work in a shoe shop but found it very difficult because he couldn't say the word 'feet' – a pretty bloody severe handicap when your entire job revolves around footwear. It wasn't a stammer but some sort of psychological block. He could only say 'them things on the end of your legs'.

I'd soon witness first-hand evidence of Garth's speech difficulties when we drove down to London for that first gig with him, supporting the Clash at this funny cinema up in Harlesden that specialised in kung fu films. Once we'd arrived and set up our gear we went to a local café for a pre-show tea and ordered bangers and mash. When the waitress brought Garth's plate over, his face froze.

'I didn't ask for those.'

'Ask for what?'

'Them.'

'What?'

'Them little green things!'

There were some peas dished up next to his mashed potato, but Garth couldn't say the word 'peas'. I'm staring at him. *Is he for real?* Meanwhile John's trying his best not to piss himself and Pete's trying to catch my eye with his devilish little 'told you so' twinkle.

Poor old Garth. I really, *really* liked him as a mate, and here we were not even having played our first gig with him. But, already, I knew. He had to go.

THE HARLESDEN GIG was the public unveiling of Buzzcocks Mk II. We found ourselves in an odd situation where *Spiral Scratch* had just been released, the reviews had been amazing (we even squeezed a 'terrific' out of *Melody Maker*'s Caroline Coon, who'd since decided she loved us), John Peel was playing tracks from it on his nighttime Radio 1 show and, as a result, we'd made our money back and were pressing up several thousand more copies to keep up with the demand. The trouble was all this praise and attention was being lavished on a version of Buzzcocks which had ceased to exist. For those first few months, some slowcoaches would be coming to our gigs still expecting Howard on stage screaming 'Breakdown'. Instead, they got little Pete Shelley singing 'What Do I Get?' It was still Buzzcocks, but to them it was like we'd broken the Trade Descriptions Act.

As it was, we were still playing a lot of the old Howard material – the *Spiral Scratch* numbers, 'Orgasm Addict', 'You Tear Me Up' and 'Love Battery'. We dispensed with the Troggs cover, but Pete adapted the Beefheart one into a new song of his own. The way we'd been playing 'I Love You, You Big Dummy' sounded nothing like the original anyway, so he just kept the military rhythm and chords, added lyrics and created 'Sixteen'. He also now had 'What Do I Get?' and a couple of others – 'Get On Our Own', 'No Reply' – that were a lot more melodic and sing-songy than the old stuff and a sign of things to come. And my own 'Fast Cars' was now a regular part of the set.

I could already see a change in Pete – a healthy one. Now Howard was gone, and it was just me, John and Garth he had to deal with, he seemed a bit more relaxed and levelled out, like he could drop some of the artier pretensions he perhaps felt he'd had to live up to before. We'd never have played a song like 'What Do I Get?' with Howard in the band, so that in itself was a major breakthrough. The easiest thing for Pete to have done would have been to get up on stage and do a bad Devoto impersonation to try and kid everyone we were the same *Spiral Scratch* band. The fact he didn't, that he went up there and made it his own thing, took a lot of balls. It's one of the many, many things I loved about Pete. He was far tougher than he looked. Even the way he dealt with hecklers and the whole punk spitting nonsense. 'It's soggy enough up here without you lot adding to it!' 'Don't gob at me! You wouldn't gob on your record player!' Like some Northern club comedian, he never took any shit off the audience.

Musically, the new two-guitar Buzzcocks clicked from our very first practice – even with Garth using his bass as a punchbag, or rather my bass as I lent him the same Hayman 40/40 I'd been using, the one my dad nicked off his van. But as soon as me and Pete plugged our guitars in together, there was a spark there, a magical symbiosis that we'd slowly hone and perfect into something unique. Pete was the chords man, whereas I was more riffs. Whenever he'd play us a new song he'd usually just sing it over strummed chords. Then I'd learn it and work out any gaps where I could embellish any little riffs or harmonies. It all goes back to that first cheap Spanish guitar and working out how to play Beethoven's Ninth. That mentality, finding these simple melodies on a couple of strings, set me up for the rest of my life in Buzzcocks. A good example is 'I Don't Mind'. It's Pete's song – and it's a *great* song – but the guitar riff in the *'when you call me'* bit is something I came up with when we first rehearsed it. That's often how we did it: he'd make the cake, I'd do the fancy icing. Those early days, we were very casual when it came to the writing credits. Basically, whoever came up with the chords, it was always their song. Since it was more often Pete coming up with the words and the basic chord pattern, there are a lot of 'Shelley' songs where the signature guitar hook is actually one of mine. I'm not saying this to take anything away from Pete – the beauty of his songwriting speaks for itself – just to explain how we worked together as a band.

The Harlesden gig was like a dry run for what became the White Riot tour a few months later: the Clash, us, Subway Sect and the Slits. My main memory of that night, apart from the Peasgate episode in the café with Garth, is the shirts we wore. It had been decided, probably by Richard Boon, that we should make an effort to stand out against the usual punk fashions by adopting an 'arty' image with the help of one of his university mates, this girl called Janey. She made us these shirts based on Mondrian paintings with big blocks of colour and criss-crossing black stripes. For some reason which should have rung alarm bells, Pete was the only one who didn't wear his. So he was in the middle, all cool dressed in black, while me and Garth and John were up there sweating in our fancy new pop-art gear. But it was only when we came offstage and peeled off our clothes that we realised the worst of it. Whatever colouring Janey had used to make those shirts had soaked right through, dyeing our skin. The three of us standing there, half naked, we looked like a packet of Opal Fruits.

THE WHITE RIOT TOUR was our glorious breakout moment. Prior to that we'd only ever played locally in and around Manchester or odd gigs in London, usually on the invite of the Pistols or the Clash. Now, here was our chance to take Buzzcocks to the masses all over the country. It was the same 'punk package' concept as the Anarchy tour, only, being a lot less notorious, the Clash evaded the local council bans that scuppered the Pistols. So it became less like a tour than a crusade. All these kids stuck in the back of beyond – Swansea, Middlesbrough, Aberdeen, Dunstable – who'd never seen a punk gig were about to have their lives changed forever. That's not an overstatement. We'd ride into town like gunslingers, shoot the place up and ride out again knowing that as soon as we'd gone there'd be half a dozen local punk bands forming and as many kids in their bedrooms starting their own fanzines. This was our message. 'YOU can do this! YOU can be part of this!' The White Riot tour really felt like The Revolution. Or, like in one of my favourite films, *Rocky II*, when Rocky's running through the streets and all the kids start running behind him like the Pied Piper. That was us: we were Rocky, leading all the kids to the top of the steps, pogoing with joy. Over the years I've met so many people from famous bands who've told me the reason they first started was because they caught the White Riot tour in Edinburgh Playhouse, or Eric's in Liverpool, or wherever else. Even at the time, amidst all the chaos and the noise and the aggro and the gobbing and the ripping up seats and the fights breaking out in the crowd, standing on the stage and looking out over all this raw young humanity being let off its leash was electric. Lost in that moment, you genuinely felt this was something that was going to change the world. And even if it didn't change *the* world, it changed ours.

A proud moment was an early homecoming in Manchester at the Electric Circus. Strummer even insisted we take him back to Tommy Ducks (those tobacco-stained knickers on the ceiling clearly left a big impression). For some reason, that night Joe asked if he could borrow my guitar for the Clash's set. Of course I said yes. He customised it, Clash-style, by glueing newspaper headlines to the front of it. They were still stuck on when he gave it back. Afterwards, as we were travelling down south in our own van I realised he'd also broken one of the machine heads: the cogs at the top of the neck that tune the strings. The next day we were all due at the Rainbow in Finsbury Park, so as soon as we arrived I bolted up to the dressing room to find Joe. 'Fucking hell, man! You've bust my guitar!' He just smiled and very calmly stuck his hand in his pocket and pulled out a spare machine head. 'Sorry, Steve,' he said, 'try this one.' Most guitar players only ever carry spare plectrums around with them. Only someone as cool as Strummer would carry spare machine heads. So thanks to him, and Pete with his nail file, I fixed it just in time for the Rainbow gig. I've still got that guitar with its five cheap gold machine heads, plus the white one Strummer gave me. Impossible not to think of him every time I play it.

MEANWHILE, THE RELATIONSHIP between Pete and Garth was growing ever more fractious. So fractious it was threatening to cost me my life.

At some point between gigs, they were both back in Leigh visiting their families, so I'd borrowed my dad's car to drive over for a night out. My brother Phil was also with us, so after the pub I offered to take everyone home. I'm ashamed to say I was horribly over the limit – you'd think I'd have known better after what happened to my mate Alan – but it turned out I wasn't the biggest liability. As I was taking Pete back to his parents' house, he was in the passenger seat beside me while Garth was in the back with Phil. Like clockwork, suddenly Pete and Garth started snapping at each other. Next thing, there were hands slapping across the seats while I was doing my best to keep focused on the road. I turned round for one second to look at them. 'Pack it in, you pair!' And in the same breath smashed into the side of a van at a crossroads.

The car bonnet concertinaed. Everyone jolted.

'SHIIIIIT!'

Garth must have legged it out of the car, as one minute he was there, the next he was gone. All I remember is somehow screeching away and chugging the remaining three of us down the road as far as Pete's house. 'Look,' I said to him, 'I'm well over the limit, here. Just let me park up in your dad's drive till the morning?' But he wouldn't. Pete wanted nothing to do with it. He just ran off into his house and slammed the door. Instead, me and Phil had to crawl round in our dad's newly fucked car to some back entry and hide the night there, shivering, hoping the cops didn't find us. I was a friend in desperate need, but Pete left me high and dry to save his own skin.

This was a new side to Pete I'd never experienced. A strange cold unempathetic side. And, sadly, not the last time I'd be on the wrong end of it.

*

STEVE DIGGLE

THAT JUBILEE SUMMER OF '77 marked Buzzcocks' first birthday. When we'd formed the previous June, we were one of barely half a dozen punk bands in the country. Now there were hundreds of them. Every time we played a gig it seemed there were always a couple of new chancers on the bill with us, enough to keep clubs like the Electric Circus ticking over nicely week on week. Being brutally honest, most of them were shocking. There was a massive difference between bands like us, the Pistols, the Clash or the Damned going out there to inspire and connect with the audience, and these diabolical clods in the wrong bondage trousers gurning the worst kind of 'I hate you!' pogoing nonsense with no insight or meaning. They were farm animals, no different to the crap social club bands. But there were some notable exceptions.

The Jam joined us at the Rainbow on the White Riot tour, and they were fantastic. Apart from Weller's whole energy and attitude, their mod-punk R&B crossover was totally up my street. I still bump into Weller occasionally, and it's always nice catching up, the same when I see Steve, Cookie, Glen, Mick, Paul, Captain, anyone from those first few original bands who led the charge. There's an affinity and kinship, an unspoken look in our eyes, like retired old soldiers on Remembrance Day with our medals from the punk wars. Last of the Strummer Wine.

Another band that sticks out is X-Ray Spex, who supported us the only time we ever played the Roxy in Covent Garden. Poly Styrene was magical. Seeing her up on stage giving it 'Oh Bondage Up Yours!' – now *that* was punk rock. I can still picture her in my mind, standing at the front watching our set, this funny little chubby woman in a khaki army hat and goggles. She was one of those rare original one-off characters punk shook to the surface. You couldn't fake being a Poly Styrene or a Paul Weller any more than a Johnny Rotten or a Pete Shelley. They were the real deal amongst an ever-growing sea of fakes and bullshitters.

The upside of the national punk epidemic was the overnight record company gold rush. Suddenly the Jam were on *Top of the Pops*, the Clash's album had gone Top 20 and the Pistols' 'God Save The Queen' broke number 1, even if the BBC weren't allowed to mention it on air. Punk was now money, and the major labels were pretty indiscriminate about who they chucked it at. So long as they could package it as 'punk', the cheque books were open. All any band had to do was sign on the dotted line where it said they owned your arse for the rest of your life and then kiss creative freedom goodbye.

That's why Buzzcocks played the long game. It was a classic tortoise-and-the-hare situation. Every band was rushing to get signed, rushing out a single, rushing out an album, only to be used up and spat out six months later. We had the faith to hold out until the right offer came along. Everyone thought we were mad. As early as the Anarchy tour, Malcolm said to us, 'Why haven't you got a deal yet? You're leaving it too long! If you don't sign soon, it'll be too late.' But we weren't fools.

For us the only deal breaker was artistic control. At one point we had Maurice Oberstein from CBS ringing Richard Boon's phone off its hook, offering us the Earth. We didn't want the Earth. We just didn't want any suits bossing us around telling us what we could and couldn't do – everything the Clash, the ones who *had* signed to CBS, would soon be warning us about in 'Complete Control'. More than anything else, we wanted someone who genuinely gave a shit about the band, who didn't just treat us like the next packet of cornflakes on their company sales chart. Luckily, such a person existed.

Andrew Lauder looked like your typical Seventies A&R man. Moustache, receding hair, thick specs, his top shirt buttons undone just enough to let his chest hairs poke out and a pair of bullhorns hanging on the wall of his office at United Artists, just off Oxford Street. He was also the only A&R man who bothered his arse to come up from London to Manchester and see us play, wine and dine us on his hotel bill and talk to us about what *we* wanted. Other labels probably offered us more money – at one point we had six of them banging on the door – but Andrew was the only one with the right empathy. He was our guy.

It said it all that he didn't force us to come cap-doffing down to London but brought the contract up to Manchester himself. The deed was done on the beer-stained bar of the Electric Circus straight after we played a gig. The date was 16 August 1977. We'd just heard the news Elvis had snuffed it when in a few strokes of a pen we, too, were now recording artists. The passing of the rock'n'roll baton. The King was dead – long live Buzzcocks.

14 / *NOISE ANNOYS*

YOU SIGN A RECORD CONTRACT. The ink dries. You wake up the next morning. You're still living in a box bedroom at your mam and dad's. There's no Rolls-Royce waiting outside the door. You get up and pull your trousers on and check the pockets. You're still skint. That's the reality.

At least as a new 'employee' of United Artists I was finally off the dole. So was Pete, who'd had his stopped a few months earlier after we made our TV debut playing 'Boredom' on Tony Wilson's *Granada Reports*. Tragically, the episode's been wiped from the archives: a landmark piece of punk history, gone forever. Albert Finney was also in the studio being interviewed. Having grown up as a fan watching him in *Saturday Night and Sunday Morning*, suddenly there's *the* Arthur Seaton sat in front of me. Talk about punk being born in Manchester? That's the original Johnny Rotten right there. 'Whatever anyone says I am, that's what I'm not!' There was also a bloke showing off this eagle strapped to his arm that started pissing and shitting everywhere, classic chaotic live TV. Finney was amazing, though. At the end he said, 'Love that song "Boredom", lads.' Coming from him, that's as great a compliment as we ever had. But Pete being on local telly, looking so unmistakably Pete Shelley, some guttersnipe from the DHSS saw it, grassed him up and stopped his giro.

Being newly signed to a label is a strange situation. You're doing alright, still playing the gigs, the hotels are paid for, there's food and beer laid on, but you stick your hands back in your pockets and you're still cash poor. There was an initial chunk of money advanced to us on the condition we had to spend it all on new gear immediately, which we did, buying guitars and amps. That in itself was pretty surreal, walking around Manchester city centre with a grand in your pocket. *Fuck! I've got to get rid of this quickly!* We hurried down to A1, the main music shop in town, where me and Pete both saw this Gordon Smith guitar we liked. We thought it might look good having one each on stage, matching guitars, but as they only had the one Pete bagsied it. They also tried to advise us to buy big Marshall stacks, but we preferred these cool little square H/H amps which had amazing reverb. If you picked them up and moved them, they'd make this great noise. *KCHHHHAAANG!* Because I'd just been reading Isaac Asimov's *I, Robot*, I started calling them robots, and the name stuck. From then on these H/H amps were 'the robots'.

I ended up spending my own share of the gear money in London at the Orange shop on Shaftesbury Avenue where I found this 1959 Gibson Les Paul Junior. It was bright yellow, known as a 'TV model' because back in the Fifties and Sixties it showed up high contrast black-and-white on old tellies (it's the one I'm holding on the cover of *Singles Going Steady*). The odd thing was the bloke who sold it to me told me it used to belong to Tony Hicks from the Hollies, also from Manchester, as if some mystical sixth sense must have drawn me towards it.

If it wasn't for this drip-feed record company cash flow situation, Buzzcocks may never have originated our soon-to-be-notorious backstage rider demand. The catalyst was when we played a club in Blackpool called Mr Jenks. It sticks out in my mind because we were staying in the same hotel as Derek Batey, the host of *Mr & Mrs*, which me and Pete found hilarious. We saw him in the bar and started laughing to ourselves doing our own Derek Batey impressions. 'Ooh! Now, does he go to bed with his socks on? Does he *not* wear socks in bed? Or are you not really bothered?' In *Mr & Mrs* it was always the same: every third choice was a 'not really bothered'.

As usual this hotel was all paid for, but we'd been grumbling for a while about waiting for the money to come through. So me and Pete went, 'Fuck it! Let's get a load of bottles of champagne and stick it on the bill.' Just taking the piss since the record company were picking up the tab, and as a bit of a passive protest over the fact our cash hadn't come through yet. But then as we're sat there drinking it, we're looking at each other going, 'It's alright this champagne, isn't it?' We both developed a taste for it. And so a precedent was set.

The next gig, there it was on the rider. Not just any champagne.

'Moët & Chandon.'

At first, venues would pretend to ignore it. We'd get there and go, 'Er, where's the champagne?'

They'd look at us funny. 'Champagne? Look, lads, you've got all your beer in there. Nobody has champagne.'

So we'd have to tell them. 'Well, no, it's on our rider. See? Moët & Chandon.'

They still wouldn't get it. '*Champagne?!* You're supposed to be a punk band!'

'So?'

'So the Damned don't ask for fucking champagne!'

'That's their problem. We're Buzzcocks and we've asked for champagne. You agreed to provide us with champagne. It's there, in our contract. Moët & Chandon. Otherwise we're not going on.'

Which is how I coined our infamous catchphrase.

'Listen, mate, it's like this. No Moët – no show-ay. No Chandon – no band on.'

That's how it started. Every gig, it had to be Moët. And we genuinely refused to go on if we didn't get it.

There was a very practical reason for it too. In the early days, we'd go to the pub round the corner, neck a few pints, then race back for the gig. But as we got bigger and more recognised by fans it was less hassle to stay in the dressing room before the show. So we'd drink champagne by the pint, like rocket fuel, before we went on. Me and Pete would request four bottles each. We'd have one apiece before the gig, then I'd always have one with me to drink on stage. The others were for afterwards, inviting people back for a drink. 'Fancy some champagne, darling?'

Also, we could only ever drink it out of plastic pint glasses. In the early days, the venues would sometimes give us proper flutes –

a complete waste of time. You go on stage and rest a fiddly champagne flute on top of your amp, it's just going to tip over and spill all down the insides and blow the valves. Which actually happened once or twice. That's why only flat-bottomed pints would do, so we could neck it by the gallon.

Me and Pete only chose Moët because it was famously posh and expensive, but once we stuck to it we refused any other brand. Sometimes we'd arrive backstage and there'd be a case of Bollinger or Taittinger waiting for us.

'Oi! What the fuck's this?'

'That's your champagne.'

'It's not Moët.'

'But it's the same thing.'

'It's not what we asked for.'

'This is all we could get.'

'It's the wrong stuff.'

'But won't it do?'

'No. You get us what we asked for or we're not going on, simple as that. No Moët – no show-ay.'

'Are you serious?'

'Fucking deadly. No Chandon – no band on.'

And so it went on. Hilarious scenes. We never let anyone off the hook either. Sometimes, especially when we played anywhere in France, they'd think they were doing us a favour by getting us some really ridiculous fancy local stuff. Special anniversary edition, all boxed up in wood, with hand-engraved commemorative crystal flute glasses. We'd look at it and go, 'Thanks, that all looks very nice. Now where's our Moët & Chandon?'

Their faces would drop. 'Pardon, monsieur?'

'You know. Moët & Chandon. The stuff we stipulated. Otherwise we're not going on.'

And if ever any venue argued, we always had the ace answer up our sleeve.

'No, mate, you don't understand. It has to be Moët because of the size of the bubbles. You know, for the throat, to help singing. This stuff you're giving us, the bubbles are the wrong size.'

In the grand scheme of diva rock'n'roll riders it really wasn't a lot to ask for. One crate of specified-brand bubbly. It's not like we were demanding live puppies or bowls of Smarties with the brown ones taken out. Over the years it would earn Buzzcocks a reputation for being 'champagne punks', but even that didn't bother me. My response was: 'Well, Orwell was a champagne socialist, so what's wrong with that? He went to Eton, but I'm from Manchester, mate. If champagne's good enough for him, it's fucking good enough for me.'

WHILE WE WERE BUSY guzzling their profits, United Artists were eager to make good on their new investment as quickly as possible. Because Andrew had already had punk chart success with the Stranglers, he thought the obvious move was to put us in the same shithole studio in Fulham where they'd made their first album with the same producer. On paper, it should never have worked. Martin Rushent fancied himself as a bit of a flash Jack-the-Lad type. He'd cut his teeth engineering sessions for Shirley Bassey, he liked the ladies, drove a Jaguar and made no secret of the fact he voted Conservative. He was also the best thing that could have happened to Buzzcocks.

From one Martin to another, Rushent was the calm we needed after the storm of Hannett. He didn't try and change us or mess around with the songs. He just let us plug in and get on with it while he did his magic and made us sound amazing – a miracle in itself considering the limitations of this tacky TW Studios in Fulham. As a band/producer relationship, his methods complemented ours perfectly. You'd hear tales about other groups having nightmares trying to get it to sound right, getting frustrated, the producer screaming threats to bring in session musicians, everyone having hissy fits and storming out. Not with Martin Rushent. He made making records seem ridiculously easy. Because he was ridiculously brilliant at it.

Our first session with him was to rush out a single before Christmas. Even though we'd been signed by a major we never had any delusions about having a hit or getting on *Top of the Pops*. If we had, there's no way we'd have chosen 'Orgasm Addict' as our major label debut. A song about wanking with the line *'Johnny want fuckie'* was never going to be Tony Blackburn's Record of the Week. Not surprisingly, the BBC banned it.

It was one of our oldest and could have very easily made it onto *Spiral Scratch*. Personally, I'm glad we waited. When Howard sang 'Orgasm Addict' it was always quite spiky and nasty-sounding. When Pete sang it, without losing any of its edge, just the tone of his voice made it a lot cheekier and funnier. And naughtier.

Incredibly, the label suits didn't protest, though their pressing plant did. It was delayed for three weeks because they said it was pornographic filth. Our reply was, 'You mean to say none of you lot have ever had an *orgasm* before?' But after a bit of industrial to-ing and fro-ing it finally came out that November in our first Malcolm Garrett sleeve, based around Linder's now-famous collage of a naked woman with a steam iron for a head. The back featured a band photo of the four of us standing in a bus stop taken by Kevin Cummins. Unlike me, Pete and John, it was the first record Garth had ever made. And, before it hit the shops, it would already be his last.

THE ACCIDENT WAITING TO HAPPEN finally happened on stage in Coventry. We now had a tour manager, Pete Monks, who'd pick us all up and drive us to gigs. The day of reckoning, when we turned up to collect Garth at his mum's house in Leigh she told us he'd gone to the pub. Sure enough, as we were driving around trying to find him, here came Garth walking down the street swinging a carry-out. We bundled him into the car, where the rest of us were trying to get this ghetto blaster working. It was low on batteries, so the first garage we saw, for some ridiculous reason we sent Garth in to buy new ones. It was only as we were driving away again that we realised he'd bought the wrong size. We needed DDs and he'd bought these giant U2 jobs. Only Garth didn't seem to understand. He was trying to ram them in this ghetto blaster, becoming increasingly agitated.

'These fookin' things won't fit!'

We were all laughing, apart from Pete who took it as his cue to start ripping into Garth. But Garth was adamant.

'Are you sure they're not the ones? This one's a bit fookin' tight!'

YOUNG, GIFTED AND MANC: Me, aged 22, backstage at the Marquee,
London on 4 August 1977 (© *Kevin Cummins/Getty*).

LEFT: The Glummer Twins – me and Pete, November '77 (© Sheila Rock/Shutterstock).
ABOVE: Marc Bolan bangs the gong for our *Spiral Scratch* EP – less than four weeks after this picture was taken he'd be dead (© Kevin Cummins/Getty).

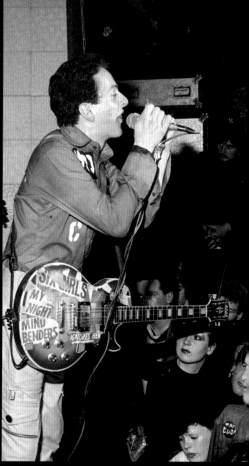

ABOVE: Our first gig with Garth and those dreaded Mondrian shirts, Harlesden, 11 March 1977 (© Ian Dickson/Shutterstock).

RIGHT: Me enjoying a typically quiet night out at Manchester's legendary Ranch Bar, July '77 (© Kevin Cummins/Getty).

OVERLEAF: Pick 'n' mix punks – (left to right) John Maher, Steve 'Paddy' Garvey, Pete and myself outside Woolies, Manchester Piccadilly, May 1978 (© Fin Costello/Getty).

OPPOSITE: My Antoria Les Paul before and after Strummer. **Far left:** playing it at Eric's in Liverpool on the White Riot tour, 5 May '77. **Left:** three days later the same guitar gets a Clash makeover when I lend it to Joe at Manchester's Electric Circus (both images © Kevin Cummins/Getty).

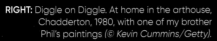

OPPOSITE: Och aye the brew – taking a dip at the Loch Lomond Rock Festival, 27 May 1979 (© *Adrian Boot*).

RIGHT: Diggle on Diggle. At home in the arthouse, Chadderton, 1980, with one of my brother Phil's paintings (© *Kevin Cummins/Getty*).

BELOW: Manchester reunited. Me and Pete together again on stage at the Ardwick Apollo, May 2012 (© *John Bentley/Shutterstock*).

SOUL SURVIVOR: Life, rock'n'roll and Buzzcocks goes on – aged 68, on stage and on fire at Koko, Camden, 22 March 2024 (© Perry Smylie/Mirrorpix).

And so it went on, swearing and bickering all the way to Coventry.

The omens were fairly bleak before we'd even got there. Unsurprisingly, the gig was a shambles. As it began, I could hear Garth's bass OK through my monitors, but then it suddenly stopped. I looked over and he'd chucked his instrument on the floor, mid-song. Then he screamed something at Pete and wandered off. Half a song or so later, he came back, played a bit more, then threw it down again like he was trying to smash it. Meanwhile, I was trying to carry on as normal, wondering what the hell was going on when Pete came up and shouted in my ear.

'Turn your treble down!'

At first I didn't know what he meant. There was desperation in his eyes. 'Can you make your guitar sound more bassy?'

I looked over again and realised it was now only the three of us left on stage. Pete wanted me to compensate for the gap in the sound by making mine sound like a bass. Garth had fucked off.

That was the bitter end for poor Garth. Him and Pete were no longer speaking, and after the gig he drove home separately with the roadies. A day or so later, he called me up to apologise. 'Look, I've been to the doctor's,' he said, blaming it on the drink, 'and I'm going to get help.' I really did feel genuinely sorry for him, but by then, between the car crash and a few other silly incidents at other gigs when we'd had to restrain him, I'd definitely had enough. If it carried on the way it was going, the next time someone might actually be murdered – most likely me in the Pete v. Garth crossfire. I don't know who did the actual sacking. I doubt Pete did. He'd heckle you in a drunken argument but he could never handle actual confrontation. It must have been left to Richard Boon as I remember him ringing me to discuss it. I told him straight. 'Garth's got to go, man.' And he did.

All said and done, hypocritical as it may sound, I've very fond memories of Garth. We were great drinking buddies, we had some seriously mad, happy times together those few months he was in the band, and it should never be forgotten he helped keep Buzzcocks afloat during a critical period of transition. But it was never going to work, not him and Pete being in each other's company 24/7 and with all the added pressure heaping on us now we'd actually been signed and had an album to make.

Which left me, Pete and John exactly where we were when Howard left nine months earlier. Scratching our heads and pinning cards on notice boards.

'Wanted: Bass Player.'

IN OCTOBER 1977 they were harder to find in Manchester than you'd think. In the short term we borrowed Barry Adamson from Howard's new band, Magazine, who was kind enough to fill in for a few gigs we'd otherwise have had to cancel, but that was only ever going to be temporary.

The formal audition process was painful beyond belief, not for lack of applicants but because of the cavalcade of jokers who turned up. The most un-punk-looking blokes with their basses strapped so high they could rest their chins over the top of them. One guy even had the audacity to say, 'Well, it's OK doing *your* songs, but I've got some really great tunes we can do.' *Unbelievable.* We spent an entire day in this village hall in Chorlton, ploughing through one after the other.

'Next!'

At the end, having seen nobody we liked, me and Pete ran into the toilet and shut ourselves in a cubicle. Now that the major label money was coming through, we could finally afford the major drugs. Cocaine. We snorted a fat line each, then looked at each other, both near-hysterical crying laughing, wondering what the hell we were going to do. Even I was starting to think, *Jesus! Was Garth really* that *bad?*

A day or so later, still feeling fairly pessimistic, we were back in Chorlton, this time at the home of one of Hannett's mates, a lovely bloke called Paul Roberts. He'd converted the basement of his semi-detached house into a cool little studio – Drone Studios – where we'd arranged to audition two last candidates. Two last straws to clutch at.

The first was some guy who played with a jug band, which didn't sound very promising, but he was actually OK. The second was this 19-year-old kid from Prestwich who told us he was friends with the Fall. He sounded good, and he looked good, but he was very quiet, and we didn't get a sense of any big personality. As the Prestwich kid got up to leave, John said, 'Hang on, I'm off to the shop. I'll walk you down the road.' So off they went, leaving me and Pete wondering whether we should just toss a coin. It could have gone either way. When John came back, we still hadn't decided. So we asked him who he thought was the better of the two.

'I liked that last guy,' said John.

'OK. Why's that?'

'Just now, in the shop. He bought me a Mars bar.'

Which is how Steve Garvey became a Buzzcock.

HE SAID HIS FRIENDS called him 'Paddy', so since having two Steves in the band was going to be confusing, he was henceforth Steve 'Paddy' Garvey.*

Everyone should know there's no 'the' before Buzzcocks, but once Paddy joined we became *the* Buzzcocks. The Fab Four.

As a bass player, he was perfect. It helped that he was already a fan who'd seen us play, so unlike those other donkeys who auditioned for us driven by pure ego, Paddy was driven by passion. He didn't want to be in any old band, he specifically wanted to be in Buzzcocks. Just as well, since that winter of '77 he hit the ground running on our first headline UK tour, and by Christmas we had him in the studio with Rushent recording our next single.

'What Do I Get?' was the first chapter of Buzzcocks' New Testament. Everything before that – *Time's Up*, *Spiral Scratch*, even 'Orgasm Addict' – was strictly Old Testament. Psalms from the Book of Howard. Whereas this was the Gospel According to Pete Shelley.

People call it 'a love song', but it was always much more than that. Like all of our songs, it's about the human condition, trying to cope with the reality of life and basic emotional needs. Existential in a very universal way. What do any of us get? And Pete's (mostly) two-note guitar solo – that's the beauty of simplicity right there. Not less is more but less is fucking magnificent. Some songs are just great songs, the kind anyone

* Good old Steve Garvey has always been just 'Steve' to me. But for the purposes of this book, and because others did at the time, I'll call him Paddy.

could sing, whether Pete Shelley or Frank Sinatra. 'What Do I Get?' is one of those songs.

Musically, and as a band, it marked the end of our Pistols era and the beginning of our Beatles era. By the end of '77 punk was already on its last legs. The epitaph was *Never Mind The Bollocks*, the Pistols' debut album which came out one week before 'Orgasm Addict' and pulled the glorious final curtain on it all. It wasn't so much that punk was dead, more its spirit had flown. The only groups who survived kept its energy and flew away with it into something new. Like we did.

So Paddy came along just in time. He not only gelled as a bassist, he looked the part. Aesthetically, he was everything Garth wasn't: young, skinny and good-looking. The teeny pop mags loved him – he even ended up on the cover of *My Guy* – so once he showed up, a lot more girls started coming to our gigs. Everything finally fell into place. Now we all had similar-length dark hair, similar heights and similar waistlines. On stage and on camera, for the first time ever, we looked like a *group*. Best of all, having the Prestwich kid join our gang had finally tipped the scales. Buzzcocks were now three quarters from Manchester to just one quarter from Leigh. And, for the record, still not one Bolton-born bone between us.

15 / MOVING AWAY FROM THE PULSEBEAT

IT WAS EVERYTHING I thought I ever wanted. Sex and drugs and rock'n'roll. Actually, that's not true. Rock'n'roll. That's all I ever wanted. The first two are just the byproducts of the third. The splashes from the stone thrown in the pond. Rock'n'roll is the stone. Rock'n'roll means escape and freedom, and that was my only dream. Sex and drugs is just the carpe diem stuff. Orgasms and adrenaline, lived in the moment and lost as soon as that moment's passed. You can't hold on to them afterwards like you can a record. All that's left is empty wraps and stained sheets and a hollow nothingness. Until the next one.

I know because I've lived it. And I've no shame in saying I've loved it. Being on the road, after every gig, booze, cocaine, women, the sexual freedom of it all. Pete was the same. He was an artist and he was brutal like myself. We both embraced the hedonism and intensity of the lifestyle full-on, straight from the pages of *Hammer of the Gods*. John and Paddy liked a drink and a party, but they knew where to draw the line. The only line me and Pete knew was the next one chopping out under our noses. The same when it came to sex. We were the two massive tarts. He'd swing either way, but some nights there'd be the farcical situation of the pair of us trying to pull the same woman backstage like something from a *Carry On* film. I think a lot of the women Pete attracted wanted to mother him, or possibly 'cure' him, but he certainly didn't bat them away.

It wasn't just sex either. In those early days we'd invite fans back to our gaff and end up *talking* all night. All part of the social ideology of punk, breaking down the barriers between the band and the audience. I've lost count of the nights I ended up in hotel rooms sat like a counsellor listening to kids spill their life stories. They'd just been kicked out of their flat, their boy/girlfriend had just dumped them, they hated their job or their parents, they were desperate to get out of their town. The nature of our songs and Pete's lyrics attracted that sort of fan. We were the ones asking the questions – it's just that we didn't have the answers. That's what these kids wanted from us. I say 'kids', but a lot of them were our age, late teens and early twenties. We were still trying to figure out the world as much as they were, only they expected us to have the magic solution. It was all an eye-opener, gaining insight from these complete strangers about the reality of their existence in Dundee or Doncaster, these far-flung towns that hope forgot and where every day was another battle just to stay sane. Punk rock was our equivalent social media, bringing us together. There was no computer technology, no algorithms involved. Just music, possibilities and human beings.

So, yes, on tour I enjoyed the constant supply of drink and drugs and the constant opportunities for no-strings sex. Given the chance, what 22-year-old bloke who'd come from fuck all wouldn't? But even at the time I always knew self-gratification for its own sake was a pointless existence. Pablo Picasso must have shagged more women in his life than any punk band, but that's not why he picked up a paintbrush. It's not the reason I picked up a guitar either. I was looking for self-enlightenment.

IF I'D FOUND MY PLACE in the world in Buzzcocks, I found my place in the *London A–Z* the first time I stepped into Olympic Studios. Until then, we'd been living in Punkland. The Roxy, the Marquee, the Vortex, the crappy studio in Fulham where we made 'Orgasm Addict'. Olympic was like walking through the cinema screen into *Rock'N'Roll: The Movie*. It was the strangest feeling of déjà vu because without ever having been there before in my life it was immediately familiar. *Hang on. I know* *this!* The orange sound screens, the high ceilings, the carpets. As a kid I'd sat in my bedroom studying it all on the sleeves of Stones albums. I'd seen the Jean-Luc Godard film of them recording 'Sympathy For The Devil' here. *Jesus! Jagger was over there. Keith sat over there. And now I'm fucking stood over here!* It was like an out-of-body experience. To suddenly become part of the same lineage as them – Hendrix, Zeppelin, the Who, even Bowie, who made *Diamond Dogs* there and which I'm sure wasn't lost on Pete. And now Buzzcocks had barricaded ourselves into that very golden citadel of rock'n'roll history.

All the stars aligned. The right place, the right people, the right time. Us in Olympic Studios with Martin Rushent and his right-hand man, a great engineer called Doug Bennett. That was the dream team. We worked hard and we worked fast and we always put in a proper shift. Lay down three backing tracks, pick the best one, do the vocals and guitar overdubs, then onto the next. The genius of Rushent was he let Buzzcocks be Buzzcocks. What you see is what you get. Bang, bang, bang, just get it down live, then mix everything. We'd start at midday, finish by 7 p.m. and be in the Red Lion round the corner by five past. I used to love the whole routine of waking up in the hotel every day then jumping in a black cab to the studio. It all felt so romantic and glamorous. This was the dream I'd always been chasing as a kid. To be sat in the back of a cab, the streets of London scrolling by like a film, on my way to a recording studio. That defined the freedom of rock'n'roll to me more than any sex or drugs.

We started our first album in the last week of 1977: by weird coincidence, 28 December, a year to the day we made *Spiral Scratch*. It was very much a record of two halves. The first side is like a goodbye to old Buzzcocks, mopping up the last of the early songs we'd yet to record properly: a few hangovers from the Howard days, 'You Tear Me Up' and 'Love Battery', my own 'Fast Cars' with Pete and Howard's lyrics, plus Pete's 'No Reply', 'Get On Our Own' and 'Sixteen'. In concert, the breakdown in 'Sixteen' used to be this freeform discord chaos, with everybody making noises and doing their own thing, so in the studio we mucked around putting weird sounds on top, backwards tracks, odd little effects. Pete always said he got the idea for the laser zaps after Jon Savage took us to the pictures to see *Star Wars*. I remember Jon taking us but I don't remember much of *Star Wars*. I fell asleep.

But, for me, the first album is all about the second side. It set a template for future Buzzcocks albums in that side one was the pop side, whereas apart from 'I Don't Mind' – the best pop song on there – side two was the more experimental side. The side of us I always preferred.

'Fiction Romance' was another Pete song where I added my own extra sparkle. The original riff when he first played it to us was pretty linear.

Dun-dun-dun-dun-dun! (Silence.) *Dun-dun-dun-dun-dun!* (Silence.)

When we began rehearsing it, I started playing around until I added two high notes in the gap.

Dun-dun-dun-dun-dun! Dur-nur! *Dun-dun-dun-dun-dun!* Dur-nur!

So I gave 'Fiction Romance' its magic Dur-nur! Like a blip on a heart monitor, the song would have been too flat without it.

My big moment was the first purely solo Diggle Buzzcocks tune, 'Autonomy'. I'd had the riff up my sleeve for a few years and the lyrical idea of singing like a German Krautrock band singing English. Basically a young bloke in Manchester trying to sound like Can. The words are a sort of pidgin English call-and-response. Autonomy was something I was still trying to find in my life when I wrote it. It's fundamental to all of us, the human desire to live a free, autonomous existence. So the song poses a psychological question.

The descending chord riff at the start came out of me just messing around, freethinking. I was looking at the fret markers, the dots going up the guitar neck, and in a moment of inspiration thought, *What'd happen if I just strummed down them really fast?*

Diddle-um, diddle-um, diddle-um, diddle-um, diddle-um, diddle-ummm!

Simple as that. The chorus riff is similar, quite mechanical-sounding, very clean repeated notes this time moving up the scale, but very powerful and melodic. Johnny Marr said the first time he heard 'Autonomy' it marked a new day for guitar playing, like hearing the sound of new Manchester. A beautiful compliment, especially coming from him.* The

---

* I've had conversations with Noel Gallagher about Johnny's guitar playing, the pair of us laughing going: 'How the *fuck* does he do it?' The man's a wizard. I sometimes call him 'the *other* John Maher' – he was born with the same name as our drummer, which is why he changed the spelling.

ironic thing about that is 'Autonomy' was actually played on the sound of *old* Manchester, the Les Paul Junior that used to belong to Tony Hicks from the Hollies. The weirdest thing about that being the first day or so we were in Olympic, I was crouching on the studio carpet, taking that guitar out of its case, when I heard someone shout.

'Hey!'

When I looked over, there were two heads poking round the door. One of them was Kenny Lynch, the funny guy you used to see on *Celebrity Squares* who wrote songs for Cilla Black and Small Faces. The other was his mate, Tony Hicks. He was looking at my new Les Paul.

'Hey! I think that's *my* guitar.'

Immediately the suspicious Manc mentality kicked in.

Shit! I know it is *his - and now he's gonna tell me it's fucking nicked!*

But he just wanted a play on it for old times' sake. 'Man,' he said, 'I wish I'd never sold that, now.' You can hear the richness of its tone on 'Autonomy'. The combination of that guitar through our little robot amp, the H/H, in that giant room at Olympic was the secret technological formula for the Buzzcocks sound.

'I Need' was something we wrote after coming back from the pub during a break in rehearsal. After a couple of pints I was feeling energised, thinking, *We could do with something fast, furious and frenzied.* So I instinctively came up with the punchy riff. As we were getting into the surge of it, Pete started singing *'I need'* over and over and then, later, came up with the rest of the words. Pretty automatic. Sex! Love! Drink! Drugs! Like Maslow's hierarchy of needs set to music.

The finale, which between ourselves we always simply called 'Pulse Beat', was the best of all four of us. Pete had the frame of the song, then I put some weird chords on top and spontaneously started the riffy solo bits in the breaks. I've no idea where they came from. They're almost Indian raga-sounding, these strange exotic melodies. By then it had got to the stage where Pete would come up with a song, then I'd begin to play off him and our guitars were like two grindstones sparking off one another. 'Pulse Beat' is a great example, all those harmonics and harmonies, almost like a cut-and-thrust 'Dueling Banjos' situation, Pete doing his bit, then me fencing back at him in response. *En garde! Touché!* But it would still be nothing without John's drums. The song had a standard Bo Diddley rhythm, but John did his own tribal twist on it, almost conversational, each drum fill responding to the previous one. No other drummer would have done what he did. And then with Paddy finding his own beautiful bass groove between our guitars it all slotted in just perfect. What you hear on 'Pulse Beat' is a unique telekinetic chemistry between the four of us.

That's why I'm so proud of that second side, 'Autonomy' and 'Pulse Beat' in particular, because it shows off the strange avant-garde streak we always had. Even those weird rising tones at the end, one of Pete's ideas, a thing called pataphysics, where it sounds like the notes are constantly going up even though every repetition it starts from the bottom again. It was all spontaneous experimentation, trying things out and making it up as we went along. So it was never a straightforward 'punk' album. The whole running order, starting with the little intro blast of 'Boredom', a nod back to where we'd started with *Spiral Scratch*, then into 'Fast Cars', all the way through to the end of 'Pulse Beat', is like the journey from punk to post-punk. There's a very good argument to be had that punk ends on side one of the first Buzzcocks album and post-punk begins on side two. We mapped out that entire musical evolution over a single record.

The title was a Linderism. *Another Music In A Different Kitchen* was the name of one of her collages, or certainly something that came via her, Howard and Richard Boon. It was always left to the arty lot when it came to Buzzcocks branding. But it did suit the album. It *was* another music, and it *was* different.

I was always cool with the title, less so the original sleeve. One day as we were finishing, Malcolm Garrett came down the studio with his design. 'Here's your record cover.' Silver and orange, nice lettering, all sharp and clean and modern except there was this big square in the middle with a collage of a salad bowl with eyes and teeth sticking out between the lettuce leaves. It was another Linderism, same as the sleeve of 'Orgasm Addict'. Except her steam iron-headed nude worked because it was a powerful, shocking image, perfect for a punk single. This was crap.

The others didn't seem to have any strong opinion on it. Pete liked it, but then Pete would have gone with whatever Richard or Howard wanted. I was the only one who put my foot down.

'Malcolm, there's no fucking way I'm having *that* on the cover of our first album.'

So the two of us entered a long, gruelling debate over it. I asked why there couldn't be a picture of us on the cover. Like Rembrandt, a face tells a thousand things. I wanted the people who bought it to be able to relate to the band, the way they did when we played live. It was about that communication and interaction between us and them. Not them and a plate of fucking eyeball salad. So I was being the awkward one, going against the flow, but I knew that collage was completely wrong. It wasn't anything against Linder either. I just didn't like the idea of our records, our music, being hijacked by other people, using it as a platform for themselves. My attitude was: 'You've done a collage? Great, go and hang it in a gallery. That's your art, but this is mine, so go stick your pictures somewhere else.' I wasn't going to let this one go.

Anyone who's seen the cover of the first Buzzcocks album will know I won the argument. Malcolm climbed down, and the salad collage was replaced by a band photo I chose taken by Jill Furmanovsky from *Sounds* of the four of us against the sound screens in Olympic, all wearing black shirts; the same photo session also produced the cover of *Singles Going Steady*. In the shot on the sleeve of *Kitchen*, I'm actually out of focus, but it was such a good group portrait I told him, 'That's the one.' The fact you can't see me properly was me taking a hit for the team. If being blurred was the price I had to pay for getting rid of that horrible bloody lettuce, so be it.

ONE YEAR EARLIER, we'd been scrambling for reviews in the music papers for our debut EP. Now we were launching our debut album with the help of the *Daily Mirror*. That's how stupidly far and fast we'd come in twelve months.

Since we were already touring the week *Kitchen* came out, we were roped into some daft promotional gimmick through their *Mirror* Pop Club where we'd release 2,500 helium balloons over the course of the week outside different Virgin Megastores. 'The Great Buzzcocks Balloon Hunt'. Each balloon had an orange tag attached to it, like a postcard. The idea was any kid who found a balloon could write their name and address on the card, send it to our label in London and they'd get a free copy of the album plus a poster and badge and the usual bits and pieces. We did a few of these launch events, Manchester, London, Leeds, Newcastle, but the one I remember most is Liverpool. There we were, stood outside the record shop holding these balloons, waiting for the countdown to let them go. They held a lot of gas so it took all your effort clinging on to these things to stop them drifting off. As we're waiting, straining on these balloons, we're surrounded by a gang of cheeky little Liverpudlian kids – 'Ay, mate!' – all crowding tightly around us. When the time came, we let the balloons go, everyone cheered and the kids suddenly all ran away. Maybe a minute later, I put my hand in my jacket pocket. I'd had fifty quid in it before the balloon launch. Now it was empty. While I was setting them off, I'd been robbed by some 8-year-old Scouser. They'd even nicked me fags.

From that point onwards, pretty much as soon as we were signed, we were always on the road. It was the old cliché that bands always moan about: make album, tour, make single, tour, make another album, tour, ad infinitum. Some bands liken it to a treadmill. It was never ever a treadmill to me. This was the only job I wanted. I was still living at home, so if I wasn't on the road or in the studio I was back in my tiny bedroom at my mam's listening to her hoovering, same as when I was 17. I'd much rather be recording in Olympic, sweating on stage in Bristol or glugging Moët & Chandon backstage in Swindon waiting for the coke to arrive. I wasn't suffering for a second. I never wanted any of it to end.

During that first album tour we had just one free day between gigs set aside to make a new single. Since Rushent couldn't get Olympic this particular day he booked us into Abbey Road instead. It's not as if I took these things for granted; it was just our runaway train was going so fast I didn't have time to question it. 'OK, so yesterday was Chelmsford, tomorrow is Sheffield, but today we're making a record in the same place where the Beatles made practically everything they ever put out? Fine! Let's get on with it.' I'm not even sure Abbey Road had allowed any punk band through its doors before us. We could well have been the first.

Studio 2, the Beatles' old room, is an old-fashioned set-up with the George Martin control booth at the top, like a ship's cabin, then a staircase leading outside down to the live room below on the lower deck. Anyone who records there probably sheds a good half stone as you're constantly up and down the bloody stairs. It's a bit like that Stan Freberg cartoon of 'The Banana Boat Song' with Speedy Gonzales running back and forth behind the glass. '*Day-O!*' 'Too loud, man!' That was us.

Because we'd just exhausted pretty much all the repertoire we had on *Kitchen*, our stock of new material was fairly thin, apart from 'Noise Annoys' which became the B-side. It had a lovely bit of destructive chaos in the middle where we overdubbed our own sound effects with the four of us crowding into the drum booth and picking bits of kit up, chucking it everywhere. Crash! Bang! Wallop! Another nice bit of experimental craziness, carrying on from the one in 'Sixteen'. Again, that was a Pete song where I stitched some of my own little riffy bits through the middle eight. Always a blast to play live, as we did on Peter Cook's TV show, *Revolver*. Cook was hilarious and, true to form, pissed. He came into the dressing room where we were having make-up put on us, like you're supposed to have on telly, and started winding up these poor make-up girls. 'He doesn't need all that bloody nonsense on his face! He's a Buzzcock for fuck's sake! Leave him alone!'

The A-side was an old one of Pete's, amongst a handful he'd been storing up his sleeve since long before Buzzcocks. 'Love You More' was over and out in less than two minutes. Wham! Bam! A short sharp shock of a song. I loved the sting in its tail: Pete fools you into thinking it's a straightforward love song and then in the last line he whips out the razorblade. That abrupt ending was one of Pete's more majestic moments of inspiration. No fade out, no ringing last chord, just cut it dead.

By that single we'd really mastered the *'oh-oh!'* backing harmonies which were becoming another trademark. The fans loved them as they could sing their hearts out at gigs. It always sounded amazing, having a whole venue roaring back at you, *'OH-OH!'* Nearly all those early Buzzcocks hits, there's an *'oh-oh!'* in there somewhere. It even got to the point where we'd cut a single and someone would go, 'Hang about! Where's the *"oh-oh!"*s? It's not a Buzzcocks record without an *"oh-oh!"*!' Even if 'Love You More' wasn't necessarily our best single, in terms of our finest *'oh-oh!'*s it's up there as a contender.

*

PUNK HAD GIVEN US AN EXTENDED FAMILY, bound by adversity, phlegm and cheap speed. That first album tour we invited the Slits as support. They'd been our friends since the White Riot tour and they still didn't have a record deal – probably because even at this stage they sounded like a car crash. Musically they were rough and raucous, but that's what made them exciting, plus within the maelstrom of chaos they had this cool punky reggae thing going on. More than anything else they were fearless. They must have had more showers of gob and beer cans raining down on them than any of the male bands. Bearing in mind Ari Up was still only a teenager, the Slits always stood their ground. The very act of those four girls standing on stage being themselves was a powerful fuck off in itself.

After the last night of the tour in Croydon, we all ended up having a party together back in London at the house of Ari's mum, Nora. I never twigged at the time, but the fact Rotten was there, they must have already been an item; he'd later marry Nora, the great love of his life. It was the first time we'd seen him since the Pistols had disintegrated in the US a few weeks earlier. In between he'd taken time out in Jamaica to decompress, and you could see he was already metamorphosising from Rotten to Lydon. The whole time he wore this black Mad Hatter's top hat, like Bolan on the cover of *The Slider*, which he never took off. John was always great with us, and to us. Years later, I read him being interviewed about which other punk bands he rated. He said, 'Buzzcocks were fantastic.' The feeling's mutual, John.

Beyond our punk family, we still had our real families. As we got bigger and grew out of the sketchier clubs, whenever we played Manchester they'd want to come and see us. Part of me used to cringe because suddenly you had to be on your best behaviour. The night before, after the gig I'd have probably been up all night off me head on champagne and drugs, maybe having a bunk up with a fan who I knew I'd never be seeing again after breakfast. Now I've got all our mams and dads and sisters and aunties and god knows who else wanting to pop backstage going 'coo-ee!' The ultimate style cramper. But it took me a while to appreciate how much it really meant, not just to them but to me. God knows I must have let Mam and Dad down so many times in my life, getting sacked, getting nicked, being on the dole all those years, hiding in my room with my guitar, giving them all the ammunition anyone needed to rubberstamp me as a useless fuck-up. Yet without trying to, just by following my own path in life, I'd finally done something to make them proud of me.

The most touching moment was one of the last gigs of that tour, a few nights before Croydon. We played the Civic Hall in Middleton, just outside Manchester, where only a few years earlier I used to go to sign on. Because he told me years later, I know Mani from the Stone Roses saw us there that night. More importantly for me, so did my grandad. After the gig, as the roadies were clearing everything away, I led him up onto the stage. Poor Grandad was getting on. He was a short overweight old bloke and now needed a walking stick, but he hobbled out and stood where we'd been playing, under the lights, looking out over the empty venue. There were still a few fans milling about, asking for our autographs and chatting to us. I could see him watching all of this, a massive smile on his face, the pride bursting out of him. To a Manchester-born-and-bred trade union bloke it must have all seemed so exotic, seeing his grandson up on a stage singing 'Autonomy' (not to mention Pete singing 'Orgasm Addict' and 'Oh Shit'). But even if he wouldn't have understood a lot of the music, I could tell by his eyes he understood what it meant – to me and to our audience. It's why I've always treasured that moment, me and Grandad with his little walking stick, standing there together on the stage of Middleton Civic Hall. No generation gap that night. Young and old, we were as one.

16 / *LOVE IS LIES*

I FINALLY MADE GOOD on my promise to Mam on Thursday, 27 April 1978. That night she and anyone else switching over to BBC One any time after 7.20 would have seen Buzzcocks on *Top of the Pops*. I don't remember Mrs Shaughnessy's prophecy featuring anything more than spotlights. Or if she also had a vision of Jimmy Savile introducing us, she never told Mam.

Over the next year and a bit, through every single from 'I Don't Mind' to 'Harmony In My Head', we appeared in the studio seven times. There was meant to be a stigma with punk bands and *Top of the Pops*, mainly because the Clash famously refused to go on. But apart from them, pretty much everyone else did. We did, so did the Jam, the Damned, X-Ray Spex, the Banshees, Generation X, any of us who ever had a single in the charts, even Lydon with Public Image Ltd. It seemed a bit silly and hypocritical not to. We'd all grown up wanting to be in bands because we'd seen Bowie, Bolan, the Who, the Stones, et cetera, on *Top of the Pops*. The fact the rest of the programme might be shit – which was the Clash's problem with it – was even more of an incentive to appear. There'd be kids at home grimacing through Leo Sayer and the bloody Smurfs and then suddenly here's Buzzcocks. We were the Trojan horse in the living room. Also, if you didn't go on, and you didn't have a substitute promo film, there was always the danger you'd end up as a dance routine by Legs & Co. This was the Clash's price for not showing up.

It all looked very glamorous on TV, but the reality of *Top of the Pops* was a studio of boring old blokes in jumpers and ties shouting at kids, 'Don't stand there! Go over there!' Like a PE lesson, all very strict and regimented.

Being invited on meant every time we had to go through the motions of their whole Musicians' Union farce. The BBC had made some silly agreement with the MU that every band who appeared had to re-record their song specially for the programme from scratch. It meant you had to waste a day in a studio, usually somewhere like AIR above Oxford Circus, pretending to do another version under the eye of a clock-watching MU representative. Every act went through the same charade. You'd make sure they saw you in the live room, all plugged in to your amps with your headphones on, checking the sound levels. Maybe you'd bother to do one run through of the song, just to make it extra convincing. Then you'd chuck them a tenner and say, 'Tell you what, mate, why don't you nip out for a few pints and come back in an hour or so.' Few refused. Or you'd take them out to lunch and get them so pissed they'd fall asleep in the corner. Either way, the moment they were out of the door or unconscious you'd switch the tapes to the same version as the proper single. They'd come back or wake up, still drunk, listen to the tape and say, 'Nice one, lads, sounds great', then everyone could go home or, better still, back to the pub. Occasionally there'd be some poor naïve idiots who didn't realise the scam and who'd actually bother to record a new version which, without fail, always sounded fucking dreadful. Did they seriously expect Queen to come in and knock out a brand-new 'Bohemian Rhapsody' in the time it took some MU bloke to neck a couple of pints? It was laughable.

The show itself was always pre-recorded on a Wednesday to air the following Thursday night. Once, we were driving back from London to Manchester on the Thursday after filming our slot when we stopped off in Stoke for a pint. There was a TV in the bar, and it must have been just around 7.30 as no sooner had we ordered than *Top of the Pops* came on and there's us on the screen. The landlord was double-taking. 'Wait! What? Is that . . . no? Can't be!' He couldn't work it out. Like a lot of people he believed it was always broadcast live.

Filming day was always a boring long slog with hours of hanging around and being bossed about by those same grumpy men in jumpers and ties. First a camera rehearsal. Then a dress rehearsal in your stage clothes. (Usually what we were already wearing anyway, unlike Showaddywaddy: one time they were on the same show as us and did their first run through in plain T-shirts and jeans, looking like a gang of builders.) Then the main recording once they'd frogmarched the audience in, by which time we were usually pissed, having spent the rest of the afternoon up in the subsidised BBC rooftop bar getting smashed on Pernod and lemonade. We were only miming after all.

The most surreal thing about it was the unlikely paths you'd cross. One show I was stood during the rehearsal watching Dean Friedman when this little fella with an afro in a silver suit sidles up to me.

'Steve? Hi! I'm a big Buzzcocks fan.'

It was Bobby Farrell – the bloke from Boney M who used to do all the Cossack dancing to *'Ra-Ra-Rasputin!'* My new showbiz buddy.

Our only moment of controversy, if you can call it that, was the second time we did 'Everybody's Happy Nowadays'. Me and Pete had been discussing money and how we felt about it now that we were making enough of it to live reasonably well. I told him my attitude hadn't changed from when I was skint. Other than allowing me to live more freely, it didn't mean anything to me. Never has. There was also the niggling punk hang-up that if you were making money you'd somehow sold out and become a slave to capitalism. I didn't believe that, but I told Pete to prove I wasn't I'd love to fill a wheelbarrow full of cash, take it to Albert Square in the centre of Manchester and set fire to it, just as a symbol of my contempt for money. Our chat obviously kicked off a train of thought in him as the next time we came to do *Top of the Pops* he decided to wear a fancy jacket with a fiver and three pound notes very prominently fanning out of his top pocket as an ironic ostentatious display of wealth. All eight quid of it – the same as I used to get every week on the dole. We were taking the piss but also asking questions of the viewer at home: did money have any real meaning or was it just a flash accessory? Incidentally, that performance aired between Legs & Co flashing their knickers to some disco number and the video for

Village People's 'In The Navy'. We rested our case. This is why *Top of the Pops* needed Buzzcocks.

NINETEEN SEVENTY-EIGHT, we worked our arses off. Three UK tours, plus dates in Ireland and Europe, five singles and two albums. And yet I somehow still found the time to cultivate a serious relationship.

It's been one of the big conundrums of my life. Growing up, I conditioned myself so far against all the conventions of being in a normal couple, getting engaged and settling down with a wife and kids that I ran in search of the complete opposite. It wasn't all Thomas Hardy's doing. I'd seen all my uncles get married and every one of them looked like they'd been sentenced to the electric chair. Then the awful reception afterwards with all the curly sandwiches and the sour-faced in-laws. It was death to me. I was against the whole concept of security, be it material or emotional. It's why being in a band suited me. The itinerant sexual freedom. But then you come home off tour, and you realise you need, or want, somebody there. Rock'n'roll has its own fucked-up moralities. It's easy to judge, but it's hard to understand it unless you're in it, living it. So I knew I was never going to change my ways for anyone. The thing is, I also knew I wanted to be with Judith.

She was an art and design student, still living at home in Worsley, outside Salford. Her family were Quakers, famously good at furniture, which is what Judith later specialised in. I got to know them as very kind and caring people, despite a rocky beginning. The first time she invited me over for a family meal was like a bad scene from a Victorian drama where the workhouse pauper is taken to tea in the posh house. Her mum offered me a choice of desserts.

'Would you like the pavlova or the gooseberry fool?'

Me being me, I had to get Wolfie Smith about it.

'I don't eat sweets, they're too middle-class.'

The whole table froze. So I think I muttered something about George Orwell to ease the tension, hiding behind books as usual. Silly of me, really, as over the years I learned a lot from them, even going to a couple of Quaker meetings to see what it was all about. I really appreciated a lot of it, especially the pacificism and the fact Quakers were conscientious objectors during the war.

Judith was beautiful, smart, very creative and had great taste in music, including reggae, Culture's *Two Sevens Clash*, all sorts of cool stuff. But even at the outset I had the wherewithal to warn her I wasn't exactly the most eligible bachelor in terms of prospects. The band was only just taking off and I had no idea how long it was going to last. We'd earned a bit of money after the first album so I'd just bought myself a little terraced two-up two-down near my mum's in Chadderton. As I didn't have a car then, I bought the first house I found that I could walk to from hers. Beyond that, I had zero security. I told her, in all seriousness, she'd be better off going out with a lawyer or an accountant, someone she knew was going to be able to support her in life. I was a big risk. God help her, she was willing to take it.

It must have been serious because when I first got together with Judith I took my eye off the ball when it came to songwriting. I should have been working on ideas for our second album. As it was, I only finished one song. 'Love Is Lies' was similar to the things I'd been demoing at home years earlier, an acoustic Bob Dylan-style thing. Something fans would never have expected on one of our records, which is another reason I was really pleased with how it turned out, even if I chose to sing it in a slightly unnatural voice. But vocally I was still finding my way. The words were a deliberate devil's advocate, the antithesis of what Pete would normally sing about. His lyrics were about wanting someone to love him. Mine were about rejecting it all as an illusion. Maybe it was some twisted subconscious double bluff because I'd finally got myself a steady girlfriend. My way of protesting, to the world, to myself, that I didn't care if anyone loved me or not because it's all a load of lies anyway. Maybe I was protesting too much.

But then I wasn't alone. Love was in the air for all of us that summer of '78. Everyone was falling, even Pete. With someone he shouldn't't've.

HIS NAME WAS FRANCIS. He played drums in Pete's new side project, the Tiller Boys. This was in '78, when Buzzcocks had finally made it, and for some reason Pete suddenly began pissing around with this wacky experimental music group. Maybe he felt straitjacketed by what we were doing to some extent, but I could never understand it. 'Erm, so what's wrong with *our* band?' I thought we should stay exclusive to what we were doing. We had a great group, great songs, and I wanted to keep that pure and precious. We could be experimental *within* Buzzcocks without having to waste time farting about on the side with other stuff that was never going to be as good. So the Tiller Boys felt like a tiny splinter in the band's side that, over time, became a wedge. The very slow beginning of the end.

Francis became Pete's flatmate and – as was always implied but never really discussed – his boyfriend. I've no idea how Pete dealt with the same moral issues I did when it came to shielding Judith from the gory details of my antics on tour. But being with Francis never changed Pete either, not when it came to boys *or* girls on the road. He still had plenty to shield.

Pete's personal life was his business, and so long as he was happy I didn't care who he had a relationship with. He'd never discuss it and neither of us ever broached the subject with the other. But 'Pete' and 'happy' were becoming two words used less and less frequently in the same sentence. You only needed to listen to the lyrics he was coming up with to gauge that one. But then had he not met Francis, he might not have written *that* song.

My thoughts on 'Ever Fallen In Love (With Someone You Shouldn't've)' haven't changed since Pete first played it to me. The moment we heard it, we all knew it was a very good song. I still feel the same. It's a very good song. All that's changed is having to live with its disproportionate status as the greatest thing Buzzcocks ever recorded. It's the one tune people who don't know Buzzcocks probably know because they've heard it on a compilation, or a cover version. Tokenist Buzzcocks for fly-by-nights. I've never had a problem with 'Ever Fallen In Love' as a song. I still like it, fans still love it and I still play it. It's the fucking albatross of what it's become that's my problem. The implication that it's The One, better than everything else we did. Seriously? I don't even think it's *Pete's* best song. But for better or worse I've had to learn to live with, and under, its shadow.

Pete's muse for the song was Francis. He never told us, and we never asked. It wasn't in us to ever say, 'So who's that about, then?' (But it became obvious and, later, Pete confirmed it.) It's why it's sometimes held up as a 'gay love song', even if like all the best Buzzcocks songs – now that we've established it's not *the* best – its power is universal. Anyone who's never fallen in love with someone they shouldn't've hasn't lived properly. That's the element I appreciated: that Pete had written an *anti-love* love song, like I'd done myself with 'Love Is Lies'.

The other significant factor in its popularity is purely statistical. It became our highest charting single, reaching number 12. So, purely on a technicality, 'Ever Fallen In Love' *is* our bloody 'biggest hit' after all. But I'm OK with it. If I'm honest, even I can see why it's the one that sums up Buzzcocks in a lot of people's eyes. It typifies Pete Shelley doing what Pete Shelley was always brilliant at. Writing punchy pop songs about nobody loving him.

JUST SEVEN MONTHS separated the first day of work on our debut album and the first day of work on our second, *Love Bites*. If bands had to record to the same schedules today, they'd be getting anxiety counselling. We just said, 'OK, then,' and hailed the next cab back to Olympic.

Between being with Judith and running around partying, my head was elsewhere that summer, so all credit to Pete who carried most of the can on that album. As with 'Love You More', a lot of his songs were things he'd written years before the band – 'Real World', 'Nostalgia' and 'Sixteen Again' (Pete always used to enjoy telling people that he wrote 'Sixteen Again', on our second album, before he wrote 'Sixteen', on our first). 'Ever Fallen In Love' was new, as was 'Operator's Manual', another great song, very simple and very clever, writing about love like it's hi-fi instructions. That was quintessential Pete, the scientific wrestling with the emotional. Only in real life, the scientific usually won.

Echoing our first album, the second side of *Love Bites* is where the most interesting stuff happens and where we all pulled our weight. I had 'Love Is Lies', while Paddy brought his own instrumental, 'Walking Distance'. I'd been talking to him about different bass styles, showing him Stanley Clarke's *School Days*, which I think may have been the trigger. The next band rehearsal he came in and said, 'What do you think of this?', then played this cool little melody. The great thing in those days was it was all very open for anyone to bring their own bits in and let the rest of us knock it into shape. John was especially instinctive. I'd start playing a riff and say, 'It goes like . . .' He'd usually cut me off. 'Don't worry, I know.'

Even the spectre of Garth would leave his mark on *Love Bites*. He was never credited for it, but the descending riff for 'Nothing Left' is something Garth used to play around with in rehearsal. I don't know if it was deliberate or subconscious on Pete's part, but he took it lock, stock and barrel for his own. Musically, 'Nothing Left' was a bit of a 'Fiction Romance Part II', with the same *dun-dun-dun* chugging guitar tempo (but no magic *dur-nur!* this time). The long instrumental breakdown lent itself to me and Pete having another of our back-and-forth guitar volleys, especially when we played it live and improvised, like the only time we appeared on *The Old Grey Whistle Test* where Pete dropped in a bit of 'Strangers In The Night'. (You can see I'm very sulky in that performance. I wasn't happy about our song choices, 'Sixteen Again' and 'Nothing Left'. I can't remember which alternatives I was arguing for, but I was outvoted, so come the taping I just kept my head down and stood strumming, looking all moody and miserable.)

My two favourites on that album are probably the last two. I loved 'ESP', not just as a song but as something to play, which I could happily all day till the cows come home. I think it's one of Pete's best and I'd take it over 'Ever Fallen In Love' any day of the week. So magical, that same riff repeating over and over while the different chords of the song swirl around it. You had to adopt this strange state of zen concentration to play that riff again and again without mucking it up, just empty your mind and get into this meditative zone where you weren't playing the riff, it was playing you. Then Rushent, giving it the epic fade out, like it's moving away but really, really, *really* slowly, which is why it ended up so long. For me, 'ESP', is Buzzcocks defined. Melody meets avant-garde.

The same applies to 'Late For The Train', which had the working title 'Doner Kebab' as the syllables matched the rhythm – *dun-dun dun-dun*. It's like a futurist sound sculpture, no lyrics, just the four of our instruments creating this savage locomotive grind. John could, and did, play the beat live, but for the purposes of the track and to keep it extra tight and mechanical-sounding we used a tape loop. These days it would be a piece of piss on a computer, just cut and paste. Back in the good old analogue era, Rushent had to meticulously chop the precise bit of John he wanted out of the reel, then run it through the tape heads in a seamless loop, effectively turning John into a drum machine, which is what it sounds like: a piece of industrial machinery hammering out a robotic tempo. The basic tune came from Pete, who only had two chords, but just that interchange between them was enough. It's what I loved about Buzzcocks back then: our brutal minimalism, those endless variations on simple repetition. Once we had the basic track, Rushent played around and added his own little tricks, like the fade and return to make it sound like the train disappearing into a tunnel and blasting out of the other side again, and the *'Wooooooh!'* at the end, the only 'vocals' as such, howled by all four of us round one microphone. 'Late For The Train' was a sonic work of art.

I was never convinced about the sleeve of *Love Bites*. Malcolm Garrett had gone for a white design based around a circle with René Magritte-style handwritten lettering. 'Ceci n'est pas une pipe.' Ceci n'est pas une Buzzcocks sleeve if you ask me. All a bit twee and sweet shop for my tastes. But at least there was a band photo on the front, so I couldn't really complain this time around. It certainly didn't do it any harm as it ended up our most successful album, reaching number 13. And I'm sure having *that* song on it helped.

FROM FIRST TAKE TO FINAL MIX, *Love Bites* only took us two weeks. That's not including the extra single we recorded that same fortnight to stockpile for the winter. 'Promises', the tune I'd written and demoed years ago at home, would be my first Buzzcocks A-side. Or *almost.* Stupidly, or lazily, I'd never finished the words for the verses. I only had a theme and a rough chorus.

> *'All of the children let it down (down!)*
> *All of the children let it down (down!)*
> *With promises (oh-oh!)*
> *With promises (oh-oh-oh!)'*

It was always going to be a political song about the promises governments make and never keep. By 1978, the political landscape of Britain was dire. Labour were on their arse and Thatcher was racing towards Number 10. 'Promises' would end up being released during the notorious Winter of Discontent when the country was crippled by industrial action. So the timing was perfect for Buzzcocks to finally make their Great Political Statement. Or would have been had I finished the bloody words.

Instead, we made a rough demo of it first up in Manchester with me '*la-la-la*'-ing and sticking in random placeholder lyrics. *'Doo doo doo, doo doo, I'll make a cup of tea on my own.'* Gibberish, but even the Beatles used to do it, like when McCartney came up with the tune of 'Yesterday' and started singing the first thing he could think of: 'Scrambled eggs'. So, apart from the choruses, my original 'Promises' was all scrambled eggs. Until Pete came along and turned it into an omelette.

He'd been watching me through the glass from behind the mixing desk. As I was still singing away, he'd been scribbling things down. 'I think I've got some verses,' he said. We tried them, they fitted, they stayed. And so 'Promises' became yet another broken-hearted Pete Shelley song. The final credit was 'Diggle/Shelley'. It's as close as we ever came to writing eyeball-to-eyeball.

The B-side was Pete's 'Lipstick', based around a great riff Howard had already asked to borrow for 'Shot By Both Sides', his debut single with Magazine. Pete very generously said yes. Just a pity he never saved it for us as Magazine's came out long before ours, and while it didn't take anything away from it, by the time anyone heard 'Lipstick' it unavoidably sounded a bit second-hand.

Ending our boom year of '78 with a bang, 'Promises' charted that December, seeing us back in the BBC bar getting slaughtered before another *Top of the Pops*. Our unintended Christmas single, not that we had much chance getting to number 1. That year Boney M had it all sewn up with 'Mary's Boy Child'. My new mate Bobby. Good for him.

17 / *WHY CAN'T I TOUCH IT?*

I WASN'T FAMOUS and I never wanted to be. Even though by the end of '78 I'd been on TV tons of times and had my face on the cover of music magazines, that wasn't 'fame'. I was known by fans of the band. I'd get recognised out and about as 'Steve from Buzzcocks'. Kids would stop and chat to me, maybe ask me to sign something – a record, if they had it on them, if not bus tickets, till receipts, any old scraps of paper – but that didn't make me a celebrity. I was only famous in *their* world. Buzzcocksworld. Once, when I was still living at home, some girls tracked me down and knocked on our door. It was the night after a gig so I was knackered, sleeping it off. Mam woke me up. 'There's some fans outside. You've got to go down and see them.' I told her to leave me alone. She kept on at me. 'Haven't you got a poster or something you can give them?' I leaned out of bed, picked up my dirty socks off the floor and said, 'Here, give 'em these.' She didn't think it was funny. 'You must be nice to your fans! If it wasn't for them, you wouldn't be anywhere!'

Of course, she was right, but she didn't understand that it wasn't about all that. Fame and ego and autographs. That was disgusting to me. I never wanted my name in lights because I wasn't doing this to be loved, probably more to be hated, or to pose a question. The ethos of punk was that we were no different from our audience. The moment anyone asks for your autograph they're subjugating themselves. It's like saying, 'You have more worth than I do.' I only wanted to be appreciated, not worshipped. It's why, to this day, I'll talk to anyone. I live in Real Street, not Fame Street. I still take the bus and the tube everywhere. (Even after Buzzcocks supported Iggy Pop at Crystal Palace in 2023, I went home on the Overground.) I've never been a member of the Groucho Club or any of that elitist bollocks, because it *is* exactly that. Bollocks. I'm a pub man and always have been. So if you're stalking Steve Diggle, you've a better chance of finding me in the Dog & Duck than you ever have in Soho House.

The only reason I ever do sign stuff and pose for photos with fans is because I know it means something to *them*. I get that, and I've learned to get over my own embarrassment and awkwardness. They just want their personal memento. But it's the meeting and talking to them, human to human, that matters. It's always a two-way communication. They're not just meeting me, I'm meeting them. Have my autograph by all means, but remember, I'm no better than you are.

But then it was relatively easy for me. I wasn't the bloke on stage standing in the middle. I was the one to the left in the white jeans on *The Old Grey Whistle Test*, or to the right in the white jeans on *Top of the Pops*. (I only had the one pair, which I must have worn on practically every TV show we ever did. Not the comfiest either – very tight around the crotch.) I wasn't the member all the journalists wanted to interview. If it was all four of us round the tape recorder, I might chip in with the odd quote. Once or twice I did do feature interviews by myself, but it wasn't exactly, 'Hold the front page! We've got a Steve Diggle exclusive!' I was never going to be The Scoop.

It was different for Pete. All eyes on him. All TV cameras zooming in on him. All microphones poking up his nose. All photo sessions, asked to take two steps forward from the rest of us. To begin with, if ever anyone put Buzzcocks on their front cover, it would be a group shot. Over the course of '78 that changed. A Buzzcocks cover of *NME* or *Record Mirror* was now just a photo of Pete. The curse of lead singer syndrome. We were the band, but he was the star. God help him, he *was* famous.

It couldn't have happened to a worse-suited person, never mind a worst-dressed person. Pete never had any fashion sense, which is why he'd sometimes borrow clothes from the rest of us for TV, like the white shirt with black stripes he's wearing on *Top of the Pops* for 'Ever Fallen In Love'. That was one of mine.

But then very few people *are* cut out for fame. Pete definitely wasn't. He wanted to be loved, but fame is a false love. A cruel conditional love. It magnifies people's insecurities, and Pete had plenty. Obviously, he had an ego – everyone who does anything creative has to have some ego just as a means of motivation – but he was never about shoving it in anyone's face. It was the ego of the artist. He liked to create, make music, write songs, experiment with noises. He had the confidence and self-belief to stand on stage and be on TV and have journalists cross-examine him about his songs and his sexuality every five minutes. But that didn't mean he enjoyed it. On top of that, partly because of the Shelley surname, critics were starting to hail him as 'a poet'. All it did was increase the pressure and make him even more self-conscious. He was Pete Shelley, the little guy from Leigh who wrote 'Love You More'. Now he had this mantle of Wordsworthian genius to live up to. It was too much.

The cleverer you are, the worse fame is. Thick people must be great at being famous. Take it all on the chin, everyone loves me, isn't it all marvellous. But if you're smart sensitive Pete Shelley, it fucks with your entire sense of self. I could see it in him. I could *hear* it. Starting to question it all. 'Why am I doing this? What's the point of it all? Is this what I really want out of life?' He was ever so slowly cracking up. Perhaps because of all this media scrutiny Pete was starting to take a lot of acid (he obviously enjoyed not being able to get off the bus a lot more than I ever did). He also had the whole Francis drama going on at home – which, if the lyrics to 'Ever Fallen In Love' were anything to go by, clearly wasn't plain sailing – mixed with the madness of Buzzcocks on the road. Every tour brought more drink, more drugs, more womanising, and bloke-ising in his case. I was happy to dive into the storm and be tossed about in the insane hurly-burly of it all. Pete was in danger of being smashed on the rocks. Ultimately, it was less about fame than being cut out for rock'n'roll. I was born for it. Pete just wasn't.

FOR ME, IT WAS ALL STILL AN ADVENTURE. I took the rough with the smooth. The rough, when it came, being pretty fucking rough at the best of times.

The bands who survived punk, us included, had all moved on musically, but a lot of the audiences hadn't. It was worse for us now that we'd become a chart band. We'd attract young teenage fans to our gigs, including a lot of girls, who'd find themselves hemmed in between bovver-booted skinheads and beered-up idiots gobbing and chucking pint glasses. Touring the country in '78 and '79 was like a Russian roulette of aggro. Some towns you'd have an amazing crowd. Scottish audiences were amongst our best, especially Glasgow. The only trouble I had up there was the accent when it came to signing autographs after the gig. 'Can you sign this, ken?' It was like a *Two Ronnies* sketch where every fan I met introduced themselves as Ken. I'm thinking, 'Who's this Ken they're all talking about?' So I'd be writing 'To Ken' all the time, not realising 'ken' is a common Scottish figure of speech like 'y'know'. Newcastle City Hall was also great, the Geordies being every bit as bonkers about us as the Scots, so bonkers one fan even brought their pet tortoise backstage and asked us all to autograph its shell. And Liverpool Empire, scene of a genuine *Hard Day's Night* moment where we had so many fans besieging the stage door after the gig we had to be smuggled out in a police car. These were the gigs you lived and breathed for. But every now and then, on a bad night, you'd get a Brighton Top Rank.

As was so often the case, what began as lairy misplaced affection quickly spiralled out of control. All through the gig there'd been a shower of empty cans and plastic cups. Obviously, everyone there had come to see Buzzcocks so it's not like they were trying to boo us off. It was meant as a roundabout compliment, like spitting. 'Love you guys!' DOOF! A plastic cup bouncing off your head. But by the end of this Brighton gig these 'missiles of love' were getting a bit much. Someone had to say something, so I did. As we were leaving the stage to go off before the encore, I told the crowd, 'Calm down! If you don't stop throwing things, we're not coming back on.' I felt a bit ridiculous, like a teacher who can't control the class telling everyone to behave. Probably why nobody took any notice.

Backstage, we were all asking each other, 'What do we do?' I was all for going back on. 'If we don't,' I said, 'the way that lot are acting, there'll be a fucking riot.' But Pete was against it, as was John. Meantime, our roadies were getting battered with more crap being thrown at them while they were setting up for the encore. So, not for the first time, I was outvoted. We didn't go back on. And, just as I predicted, the shit hit the fan.

For safety we were told to lock ourselves in the dressing room. It was situated right behind the stage which had a giant metallic oyster-shell design on its back wall. The sound of several hundred cans and cups raining against this metal oyster shell was like a hail of bullets. That's how it felt sat in the dressing room, being under machine-gun fire. We never physically saw what happened, only heard the St Valentine's Day massacre raging through the wall. The crew described it to us later. People stormed the stage and started wrecking the gear, smashing things and punching each other. Some nutter picked up an amp head and chucked it, hitting someone in the crowd, which could easily have killed them. It was a bloodbath, but there was no hope of us going out and trying to stop it once it kicked off – we'd be lynched. We just had to sit and sweat it out till the riot was over.

The dumbest thing about it was *we* got the blame. The following week, letters in the music press slagged us off as 'uncaring'. The violence was supposedly all our fault for not playing an encore. I especially got it in the neck because I'd spoken to some fans after the gig and said that we'd probably get banned from the Top Rank venue chain after this. By the time my comment made print it was twisted along the lines of 'Brighton's a shithole and we'll never play here again', or words to that effect, which I never said. It pissed me off enough to write a letter of clarification to the *NME*. They printed it.

> Picture this . . . a group leaves a stage, hoping to return. Roadies mill around, adjusting mics, as roadies will. Immediately, one gets a can in the balls. The others retreat under a shower of glass. Sadly, the group decides not to return for an encore. Is this reasonable? One might think so . . .
>
> As to Brighton, we told some kids that we doubt the Top Rank would host another 'Cocks gig, but never mentioned the town itself. We still enjoy it there, and had enjoyed some of the gig in question. I would have liked to do an encore, but such decisions are made collectively, with more than the group having an option.

STEVE DIGGLE

> Our 'legendary' uncaring attitude, seems to me largely
> mythical – the stuff dreams are made of. We've been caring a
> lot longer than I care to remember – and we've learned more
> than we could ever forget.
> *STEVE DIGGLE,*
> *BUZZCOCKS, Manchester*

More annoying than any reputation damage was the theft of our gear.
Once the carnage had subsided, the crew told us we'd lost Pete's amp
– one of our beloved H/H 'robots' – and some of John's cymbals. We
assumed they'd been looted by the rioters. But perhaps not.

Brighton was the penultimate gig of the tour before the final night in
Guildford, so we had to replace our missing gear quickly. Early the next
day, John went to Henrit's drum shop on Wardour Street to buy new
cymbals. He told the bloke at the counter the bits he wanted.

'You're in luck,' the guy said. 'We've just had those exact cymbals
come in this morning. Some bloke from Subway Sect.'

Our support band in Brighton.

IN 2009, BOB DYLAN had his own radio show called *Theme Time Hour*
where he'd play an eclectic bunch of records on the same topic. One episode was about happiness. Here's how Bob introduced one of the tracks.

'Seems like everybody's happy nowadays, least according to the
Buzzcocks. They're a group from England. The first time they ever
performed, they opened for the Sex Pistols in 1976. Their record label
gave them creative control and the first single under that deal was
banned by the BBC. Sounds like they knew what they were doin'. . .'

For me, a lifelong Dylan fan ever since I heard Linda James play his
first album when I was 7, that was like getting a thumbs-up from God.

The record that got us on Bob's show took its title from Aldous
Huxley's *Brave New World*, the famous dystopian sci-fi novel about a
future society brainwashed into a state of permanent bliss by the drug
soma. As someone says in the book, 'Everybody's happy nowadays.'

Pete's song, as he presented it, was very simple, just a few chords
with his high vocal melody on top. As we began knocking it around,

and because I couldn't quite hear what Pete was playing, I found this little descending melody that seemed to fit perfectly. *Ding! Ding! Ding! Ding!* Those four notes were mine. Not being funny, but without that there's hardly any tune. Or at least Altered Images must have thought so as they later nicked my 'Everybody's Happy Nowadays' riff for 'I Could Be Happy'. Seeing how they named themselves after one of Malcolm Garrett's pseudonyms on the back of a Buzzcocks sleeve, I don't think they'd be in any position to deny this. Imitation, flattery, et cetera.

It very obviously had the makings of another strong Buzzcocks single – the only song we ever did twice on *Top of the Pops*, the second time with Pete cheekily flashing his money. When Dylan played it in 2009, he also joked about the song's bizarre afterlife.

'That was the Buzzcocks, "Everybody's Happy Nowadays", and just to show you that the wheels keep turning and time marches on, that was considered kind of a punk rock record when it came out. But in January 2007, the AARP, that's the American Association of Retired People, released a new TV commercial that celebrates the ageing process. And what they used as a soundtrack? You've guessed it. The Buzzcocks.'

Great as that single is, the B-side was always much more important. To date, it's also the Buzzcocks song that's been used on more film soundtracks than any other. I'm glad it's had that recognition because, for me, 'Why Can't I Touch It?' is as good a record as we ever made.

The tune germinated from my love of the last track on the Stones' *It's Only Rock'n'Roll* album, 'Fingerprint File'. It's a funky Seventies groove with Keith playing these beautiful loose, swiping chords. I wasn't trying to copy the same chords, just the vibe of how he was playing them, these little static bursts of energy with spaces between. All great players understand space. You don't need to play the whole time and fill every second with flash noodling rubbish. Like morse code, the silences between the dots and the dashes are what gives it meaning. So I took the idea of 'Fingerprint File' and came up with my own chords, a different tune, but with the same attitude. Once I started playing it, John and Paddy fell in behind me, finding their own groove with that great dub-style bass line. Pete was late that particular day, so by the time he arrived for rehearsal the three of us were playing this cool slow dubby thing, none of us sure what it was other than it sounded fucking fantastic.

Then he joined in, adding the words and his own beautiful melody on top. Effortless. It wasn't until many, many years later I learned he'd modelled his lyrics on a Captain Beefheart song, 'Kandy Korn'. He never told me, just as I never told him the music came via the Stones. It might sound weird, but we never discussed our songs. It was, 'OK. That's done. Next.' We'd never compliment each other either. 'Oh, I really like that one, Pete.' 'Why, thank you, Steve.' Not in a million years! It wouldn't have been cool and just wasn't in our nature.

Both sides were recorded in Strawberry Studios, 10cc's place in Stockport, the first single we'd made up north since *Spiral Scratch*. (Funnily enough, after we went to Strawberry, Joy Division started going there; it was like they had sniffer dogs on us.) There was a Greek restaurant nearby where we piled in one lunchtime for a slap-up meal, all dipping into the hummus and taramasalata, knocking back the ouzo and retsina. So by the time we returned to Strawberry that afternoon to do 'Why Can't I Touch It?' we were flying. Far from hindering us, it added to the exotic mystique of that track, an extra psychedelic wooziness in the vibe between me and Pete flickering off each other. We were stood face to face, headphones on, his guitar in one ear, mine in the other. We hadn't planned how long the track would last so as it got to the instrumental break we both went off script. It was like a conversation. He'd look at me and go *durnur-nur-nur* on his guitar. I'd look at him and go *dur-nur-durnur-nur* on mine. The pair of us still tripping on ouzo, we just kept it going and going, which is what you hear on record. That's me and Pete at our best, this beautiful telepathic riffing back and forth. Siamese Buzzcocks. Everything about that track, the music, the melody, Rushent's production, is just sublime. It's why making the two sides of that single is one of my fondest studio memories. 'Everybody's Happy Nowadays' soundtracked its own mood. It felt, to me, like we all were. Even Pete. At least until the ouzo wore off.

18 / *EVERYTHING IS WRONG*

WHO *WAS* PETE SHELLEY? I don't think he knew anymore. There was a distance creeping in between the private Pete, a closed book, and 'Buzzcocks Pete', the person he felt he had to be in public. It was getting to the point where we'd play a gig, all of us giving it our best except for him, going through the motions like someone who couldn't hide the fact they didn't enjoy it anymore. A strange apathetic nonchalance. If I could see it, so could the audience. He was not only starting to short-change them, but us as a band.

The tragedy was we'd been on this glorious ascent all through 1978, so everything was set up for '79 to be even bigger for us, as it would be for the rest of our old punk peers. The Pistols were finished, but that year Lydon released PiL's *Metal Box*. The Clash made *London Calling*. The Jam made *Setting Sons*. Buzzcocks should have done the same, made our permanent mark and bade goodbye to the Seventies with the album that would define us for generations to come.

We didn't. The reason we didn't was because when our time came we just didn't have the goods. Pete's muse was in the dustbin. The guy who wrote all those great Buzzcocks songs on our first two albums had disappeared. It felt like, 'Has anybody seen Pete Shelley recently?' The band were expanding outwards, but he was shrinking inwards. The only new songs he seemed capable of writing were negative, insular and depressing. The titles told their own story: 'I Don't Know What To Do

With My Life', 'Hollow Inside', 'Something's Gone Wrong Again'. Not so much songs as cries for help. The sad thing is nobody could. Pete was going through his own psychological meltdown and he wouldn't let any of us in. He never did.

There was no question of taking time out either. Given the strike rate we'd been working to, our label automatically expected a new single every three months. Except this time, once 'Everybody's Happy Nowadays' had been and gone, the cupboard was bare. None of his new songs sounded like singles. The only one that did was mine. That's the only positive that came out of Pete's songwriting doldrums: the fact I stepped up to fill the void with 'Harmony In My Head'.

That song was my *Ulysses*. Punk meets modernism. I set out to do on record what Joyce had done on the page, except he was writing about one day in Dublin in 1904 – I was writing about one day in Manchester in 1979. By then it was no longer the city I'd grown up with. The people were the same, but the centre of town had been gutted by redevelopers to make way for the Arndale Centre, this cold impersonal gulag of commerce like something from Orwell's *Nineteen Eighty-Four*, the Ministry of Plenty, where my Joycean epiphany struck me one afternoon, boggling at the crowds of normal everyday human beings struggling to pay their bills. It was like Dante's Inferno on the high street. I felt overwhelmed, seeing so much humanity surrounded by so much inhumanity. These people, their faces, the neon shop signs, the clatter of their feet. The same way Joyce saw heroism in mundane everyday existence, I could see it in the desperate masses squeezing themselves down Market Street into the Arndale Centre. *This* was life, the sound of the percolation of the crowd. That was the harmony in my head. Life can be shit, life can be difficult, but it still has its own harmony. That's what the song's about.

The words and music came hand in hand. I sat strumming a few chords and the first thing I sang was, *'Whenever I'm in doubt . . .'* It all kind of fell out at once. I made a rough home demo, which I played back through my mum's telly with a DIN plug lead so I could hear how it sounded in mono through one speaker. Even with just my voice and one guitar I could tell I was onto something pretty catchy. Consciously, I also wanted to write a steamroller of a song, something hard and angry like an antidote to the sort of love songs Pete had been writing. It wasn't like I was sick of them, but I was sick of us becoming typecast *because* of them. People needed to be reminded that there was always that other layer to Buzzcocks, the 'Boredom' layer, the 'Autonomy' layer, the 'Pulse Beat' layer. It wasn't all Mills & Boon with fast guitars, and it wasn't all Pete. He was the golden blue-eyed choirboy, but there was another writer in the band. The shifty bloke to the side playing the shovel with strings. Me. And what I had to sing was just as important as anything he had to.

If anything, I did Pete a favour on that single by taking the pressure off when he was clearly struggling. He never voiced any objections, though I'd stop short of saying he was pleased. You can see how pissed off he looks when we did it on *Top of the Pops* (our final appearance in July '79 – cursed to end our time on the show just as we began it, introduced by Jimmy Savile). I'm snarling at the front while Pete's behind me, staring at the floor, turning his back to the audience. He couldn't even be arsed shaving for the cameras, like he wanted the viewers to think I'd been holding him hostage in my basement all week so I could sing lead for a change. You can see him just about bring himself to mime backing vocals at the end, which must have killed him. The irony is Pete's not even on the record.

The biggest objection to 'Harmony In My Head' came from Rushent. I'm not sure if it was the song he didn't like or the subject. He was a Tory, remember, so I don't think he appreciated the working-class lyrics – probably why he eventually ended up running off and making lift music with the Human League – though his main problem was the way I sang, or rather shouted, the verses. 'Go back and *sing it* properly!' He hated it, but I refused to redo it. I knew it needed a rough rock'n'roll voice, like a Little Richard, or a Joe Strummer-type delivery, the voice of a man who'd just chain-smoked 20 fags, which is pretty much how I did it. It might have sold more and been more of a mainstream hit if I'd toned it down, but then it wouldn't have been as honest.

That's why I'm so proud of 'Harmony In My Head'. It's a raw shout from the streets of Manchester, reminding the world who Buzzcocks were and where we came from (i.e. not Bolton). It was obviously a huge moment for me as a songwriter as until then I'd only sung backing *'oh-oh'*s and the odd album track. Taking the lead on a single was a small step into the limelight but a giant leap cementing my public identity in the group thereafter, almost like a personal anthem, which I suppose it is. If 'Ever Fallen In Love' was the millstone around Pete's neck, I'm happy for 'Harmony In My Head' to be mine. If that's the song that gets played on the radio when I die, then I'm fine with that. Just be sure to whack the volume up full.

Pete still got to do the B-side, 'Something's Gone Wrong Again'. If you were being polite, you'd call it 'a homage' to Iggy and the Stooges' 'I Wanna Be Your Dog'. A harsher person might say 'rip-off': the same chords, the same stabbing piano all the way through. Flat and linear. I did what I could to add a bit of variety with the higher chord change (the *'again and again'* bit), but there wasn't a lot of inspiration happening with Pete on that track. A warning shot of worse things to come.

'**THE YELLOW ALBUM.**' That's what I've always called it. Yellow, the colour of jaundice. All these years later, I still don't like it. I've never liked it. I have to respect any fans who tell me they do, but I still think they need their ears syringing. No one can convince me that the third Buzzcocks album is a good Buzzcocks album. It isn't, and I should know. I'm one of the guilty parties responsible.

There was a jinx on that record from the very start. We were supposed to record in our usual home, Olympic, except when we turned up on the first day our guitars were missing. The roadies, whose job it was to deliver our gear to the studio in time, had forgotten. It was downhill from there.

Instead, we ended up recording in Eden, a smaller studio on a residential street in Acton where we'd made 'Harmony In My Head' a month or so earlier. So, already, we'd fucked with the feng shui of our tried-and-tested album formula. It was still us and Rushent, only by then Martin was stumbling down his own weird path with alcohol, having some sort of personal crisis. And before anyone accuses me of being a hypocritical pisshead, for all our shenanigans on tour, when it came to the studio we were always sober, workmanlike and on the clock.

Whatever Rushent's problems, it probably explains why he ditched our previous live-takes-then-overdubs method in favour of a laborious jigsaw process cutting and pasting bits of different takes together like he was building Lego. So we're in the wrong place with the right bloke in the wrong headspace arsing around with our usual working practices. This is before we even get to the songs. And for that we only had ourselves to blame.

When your main songwriter is in a negative frame of mind it's impossible not to end up with a negative record. That's the main reason I don't like the yellow album. I can handle heaviness and intensity, but there has to be light and shade. There's none on that record. It's mostly all shade because that's where Pete's head was. In a cave. It's not so much a Buzzcocks album as a Pete-Shelley-exorcising-his-demons album. Cold and brutal.

The only two good songs he wrote for it are the only two anyone mentions. The single, 'You Say You Don't Love Me', was a glimpse of the old Pete otherwise missing in action. Hats off, that was all him: the riffs, the solo, everything. Indisputably a really great song, but then he had a really great source: 'Rain' by the Beatles (if you compare the vocal melodies, you'll see where he got it from). So was the closer, 'I Believe'. That still had the old Buzzcocks sparkle about it, very simple and great lyrics, but it's all about building up for the power finale. Taken literally, no love in this world anymore, it's as bleak a song as Pete ever wrote, but he took the bit between his teeth and sang it with a fire you don't hear anywhere else on that album. The more it repeats, the more intense it overloads, which is why 'I Believe' was always a killer live. The only other runner-up, for me, is 'Hollow Inside', which had a beautiful melancholic jangling riff, but it's basically Pete having a nervous breakdown repeating the same words over and over, banging his head off the walls of his padded cell. Which pretty much set the tone for the rest of it.

I don't have anything to say about his others. They were either boring uninspired Buzzcocks-by-numbers or dismal sobs from the psychiatrist couch. And I'm not saying my three were any better either. The significant difference was my contributions were purely reactive to his. From what he'd been demoing and rehearsing I could see which way the third album was tipping so my response was to do the opposite. He went dark, I went light. He went slow, I went fast. He wept, I laughed. 'Sitting Round At Home' was about being numbed by TV, but it's more about the musical dynamic, that schizophrenic quiet/loud punk thing as I wanted to inject some much needed life and energy. 'You Know You Can't Help It' was me deliberately trying to invert a typical Pete song about *not* getting the girl (or guy). Lyrically, not my finest hour, but I was doing what I could to lighten the mood with whatever means necessary: if Pete had written better songs to begin with, you'd never have had to suffer it, trust me.

The best of my slim pickings was probably 'Mad Mad Judy'. The title came from a book of Thomas Hardy poems I'd had since I was 17. His was called 'Mad Judy' so I just added another 'Mad'. Because my girlfriend was called Judith people assumed it was about her. It wasn't. Firstly, I'd never have done that to her, and secondly, Judith wasn't the mad one: *I* was the nutter. So the song's not based on anyone. It's just about a girl with paranoia, so in a funny way I'm adding to the album's list of mental illnesses, only it's an outward look at this Judy character, not me bleating on about feeling paranoid myself. At least there was nothing down about the tune, like a blast of ECT with a pinch of Ray Charles's 'What'd I Say' in there to up the tempo even further.

The sum of all these parts made a pretty poor whole. We messed about with different studio effects, flangers and vocoders, all very interesting to do at the time, but I never had any idea where that record was going. I still don't. There was no direction, just Pete with all his Germanic misery and a load of confusion. We'd let ourselves down, never mind our fans. I can't imagine how it must have felt for them running to the shops, bringing it home and playing it for the first time. If I'd been them, I'd have been bitterly disappointed.

Calling it *A Different Kind Of Tension* was another mistake. Very lazy. It was confusingly too much like the title of our first album, even if it was the name of one of the tracks. It actually came from something I said via Jon Savage's *Sounds* review of *Love Bites*, headlined 'Another Kind Of Tension'. Jon's same review became this needless conceptual catalyst for the naming of the two sides, 'The Rose On The Chocolate Box' and 'The Thorn Beneath The Rose'. The running order was chosen so my songs were all mixed within side one (the Rose) leaving the whole of side two to Pete's existential angst (the Thorn). Which to me only highlighted the self-indulgence of it all. Bedsit music for depressives.

At least the album got the cover it deserved. A shit one. Yellow, with the four of us inside this triangle. Malcolm Garrett had been on his own personal gimmick where each of our albums had a different geometric shape in his design – square, circle, triangle, like he was copying the windows on fucking *Play School*. The stupidest thing was you couldn't even tell it was *us* on the front as the picture was so dark. It deliberately obscured who we were. Even though we'd had hits and were sufficiently known, I never thought we were big enough yet to do that. It's OK to do a *White Album* after you've put the Beatles on the front of the eight before it. This was only our third. It was like a graphic exercise in making the whole thing look as unappetising as possible, another reason it ended up selling less than either of our first two albums. So mission accomplished.

Me and Pete sat in on the mixing of it, but from that day to this I must have listened back to it once maximum. I don't need to. I know the very little that's good about it and I'd sooner forget the bad. The best thing I can say about *A Different Kind Of Tension* is that we finished it.

That same cheerless late summer of '79 I also lost my grandad. He was overweight with heart problems and had taken ill, but when they got him into the hospital he went a bit nuts. I don't know if it was the drugs they were giving him, but he started hallucinating. 'They don't like me in here cos I'm a trade union man! They're doing all these tests on me!' He was always a very private man who didn't even like anyone looking in the bathroom if he was having a wash. So someone like him in hospital with nurses poking things up his arse was too much for him. 'Get me out of here!' Maybe I could have, and I really regret that I didn't do more, but it all happened at the worst possible time. At the very point he needed me, I was on the other side of the Atlantic.

IT WAS ALL TRUE. That's what freaked me out the first time I went to America. Everything you've seen on TV. It's all fucking true. You saw the Manhattan skyline approaching through the cab windscreen. Next thing you're flying across the Brooklyn Bridge. The steam coming out of the ground and the yellow cabs, just like *Kojak*. The red fire hydrants, the blue mail boxes, just like in Huckleberry Hound and Quick Draw McGraw cartoons. And the money, the green crinkly dollars, just like the ones you used to get in packs of chewing gum as a kid. It was like being on acid. Except this bus I never wanted to get off.

The Technicolor culture shock was irresistible. Even Pete came back to life, if only briefly. As soon as we arrived, the pair of us dropped off our bags and settled in the hotel bar. The foam had barely touched our lips when these two women latched onto us. I don't know if they were professional groupies who knew we were coming, but after a few drinks and a couple of cheeky lines they escorted us into the ladies' loo. I got busy with one over in one corner while Pete took the other into a cubicle; considering how depressed he'd been for the past few months, it was nice to hear him rediscover the meaning of 'Everybody's Happy Nowadays'. Once we'd done our bit for transatlantic relations, as we were zipping up our flies someone came up with the great idea to swap clothes. Which is how me and Pete came to be staggering out of the toilets, still in our trousers but wearing these two women's blouses.

'Pete? Steve?'

And straight into Miles Copeland, our new US label boss. Even better, he'd brought some bigwig from A&M with him and another mate, this Hollywood director. All tans, teeth, shirts and cufflinks, staring at me and Pete in these blouses, looking like the wrong New York Dolls, pissed and coked up with these two dishevelled women giggling behind us wearing our shirts, both with daft grins on our faces.

Welcome to America!

We'd been putting off going there for two years. Not because we didn't want to, we just had too many commitments trapping us at home. As part of our new deal over there with Miles's label, IRS, to tie in with our first US tour they put out a 16-track compilation so American audiences could play catch-up on the story so far: *Singles Going Steady*. That's the only reason it happened, otherwise we'd never have thought of putting it out in the UK. Eventually we did, and eventually it became this mythical celebrated singles collection, like our *Meaty, Beaty, Big & Bouncy* or *High Tide And Green Grass*. But at the time none of us ever gave it much thought. 'The Yanks want to stick this out? OK, go on then.' It was no big deal.

They always say that the first time you visit New York feels like being in a film, which it did. It's just that in 1979 that film was still *Taxi Driver*. The day we arrived, someone got shot across the street from our hotel, the Gramercy Park, 2 Lexington Avenue. As I was checking in I could have sworn I heard a loud bang but assumed it was someone's car backfiring. Later, I was flicking around the TV channels in my room and it was on the news. 'A man was shot today near the bottom of Lexington Avenue, Gramercy Park.' It was all either wonderfully glamorous or unbelievably dangerous.

I did my best to block out the danger and focus on the glamour instead. The day of our gig, on a drunken spur of the moment, I looked in the phone directory. There it was. 'The Dakota'. To me, it was entirely logical. My first time in New York, I'm in a band – why *wouldn't* I invite John Lennon to our gig?

'Hello? Is that the Dakota?'

'Yes.'

'Is John there?'

'John?'

'John Lennon.'

'Are you a friend of his?'

'Yeah. I'm just down the road from him, in Manchester.'

'What's the name, please?'

'It's Steve from Buzzcocks. We're playing tonight in the East Village, Club 57. I thought maybe John might like to come down and see us.'

'Steve, you said?'

'That's right. From Buzzcocks. Manchester, North of England. He'll know.'

'Hold the line, please.'

I held the line. *This is it! Even if he tells me 'Fuck off, kid!' that'd be enough. In fact that'd be even better. Being told to fuck off by John Lennon? I'd have that carved on my gravestone! Jesus, this is nuts! The next voice I hear is going to be his!*

'Hello?'

The next voice I heard wasn't his. It was the Dakota reception bloke again.

'I've just spoken to John . . .'

That'll do!

'. . . and he said ring back in an hour.'

And so one hour passed. I got more pissed. Too pissed. I never rang back.

Idiot!

The truth is I was so giddy just imagining him in his glasses, puffing on a joint, sat next to Yoko, being told, 'There's a Steve from Buzzcocks wants to speak to you,' that I left it at that. I sometimes do wish I'd rung him back, but at least I picked up the phone once and gave it a go. And, if nothing else, I know for a fact John Lennon got to hear the name Buzzcocks.

HE MISSED A CRACKING GIG. All our American audiences were phenomenal but especially New York where the appetite for British punk was still rabid. The Club 57 show was sponsored by a local radio station, one of those WXZKY-type names you get all over America that all sound alike. Between the crowd going bananas and being an English band with a lot to prove we all got a bit carried away, especially John. A few months earlier, I'd taken him to the pictures to see the new Who documentary, *The Kids Are Alright*, which must have planted some seed of Moonish chaos in him. Come the very end, as we finished the encore, he kicked over his drums and tore down the giant sponsor's banner for WXWhatever that had been hanging behind us the whole gig. As he was thrashing about, cymbal stands falling all over the place, a woman from the radio station came on stage to present us with a bouquet of flowers. We all took one look at her. 'Leave it out, luv!' Then calmly walked off to the dressing room.

I don't think they could have been any more offended had we all dropped our trousers and shat on the stage. (Funnily enough, our last number was 'Oh Shit' too.) As we were cooling down in the dressing room, out in the corridor all we could hear was shouting and argy-bargy.

'HOW FUCKING DARE THEY!'

The people from the radio station were up in arms, particularly one bloke.

'LEMME AT 'EM! LEMME GET MY HANDS ON THOSE GUYS!'

Luckily for us, there was a barricade of people outside blocking their path. Amongst them was a photographer we'd brought over with us who we called 'the Man in the White Suit', like the Alec Guinness film. He'd flown over in this pristine white suit only to be told when he landed that his baggage has been mislaid. So for three days in New York all he had to wear was this white suit. By day three it was like a tramp's hankie, all grey and shabby, which probably didn't help his mood. As our mate, the Man in the White Suit waded into the argument with the radio people by doing us what he thought a big favour. Belting one of them right across the chops.

Next thing, our tour manager pokes his head round the door.

'Right. We all need to get the fuck out of here, NOW!'

While the punches were flying down one end of the corridor, we sneaked out and legged it towards the back stairs. Which is when we ran into the Ramones.

'Hey! *LOVED* you guys!'

We loved them too. It's just that at that precise moment our only thought was getting the fuck out of there as quickly as possible. If you've ever seen the shaking hands bit after the Royal Variety Performance, just imagine that at about 50 times the speed. That was us 'meeting' the Ramones, all four of them in a row backed against the wall while we hurried along – 'Hi! Hi! Hi! Hi!' – before flying out of the door. They must have thought we were either whizzing our tits off or the rudest cunts who ever lived.

Once outside, our troubles still weren't over.

'YOU LIMEY BASTARDS!'

The radio people were now thundering after us down the street. It's nighttime New York, sirens wailing, junkies rolling about on the sidewalk, and there's us, four skinny Mancs running along, waving our arms, frantically trying to hail the nearest cab like something out of the Keystone Cops. More's the pity that I hadn't dragged Lennon down to see it. I reckon the Northern shitkicker in him would have laughed his head off.

THAT FIRST VISIT TO AMERICA was like being in our own *The Kids Are Alright*. In Washington D.C. I went the full Townshend and smashed the most expensive guitar I had, a 1954 Les Paul that cost the best part of a grand. It was partly an accident – I threw it across the stage, not expecting to break the neck off – but once I knew I'd bust it I turned it into a philosophical statement. As I told a reporter at the time, 'It's just a piece of wood with strings on.' What I meant by that was, to kids who have nothing who want to play guitar, a vintage Les Paul is like the Holy Grail, the Rolls-Royce of instruments, but it's not the be all and end all. Once you get to the top of the mountain and can afford these things you realise they're worthless. Don't invest your hopes in materialism. It's a beautiful guitar but it *is* just a piece of fucking wood with strings. Like my wheelbarrow-of-burning-money idea. What's it really worth? Nothing.

After playing the East and Midwest, including a hop over the border to Toronto, the tour wound up in Los Angeles at the Santa Monica Civic Auditorium. As advance promotion, Miles had ordered stickers printed up – 'The Buzzcocks are coming' – and plastered them all around LA. Before the gig I met a girl who drove me out to the beach. We sat in her car smoking a joint and watching the sun set across the Pacific before giving the shock absorbers a vigorous stress test. Then we smoked another. She drove me straight back to the venue where I drank champagne, took cocaine, went on stage and played to a sold-out audience of 3,000 cheering kids who went so nuts one of them smashed a glass door.

Pete's famous line was, 'Reality's a dream'. For me, the dream was now a reality. Sex, drugs, rock'n'roll. I was a 24-year-old guy from Manchester having the time of his life. I couldn't understand how anyone else in that position wouldn't feel the same. But Pete didn't. He gorged himself on sex and drugs just as much as I did, only he'd lost all interest in rock'n'roll. The only bit that actually mattered.

IN ALL THE MADNESS AND EXCITEMENT of America I'd almost forgotten the yellow album. But as soon as we came home, there it was, our newly released dead horse waiting for us to flog it.

As if the prospect of touring it around the UK wasn't gloomy enough, we decided to invite our unshakeable understudies Joy Division as support. Years later, they'd dine out on the stories of the jolly practical wheezes they played on us, like chucking maggots on our sound desk and squashing live mice through the windows of our tour bus. Personally, I think it's really nice that having spent so long copying our every move they finally found their true calling as Manchester's answer to Jeremy Beadle.

I only got to speak to Ian Curtis properly at an afterparty towards the end of the tour. Amidst the usual drinks and coke flying around, the pair of us ended up having a little one-to-one in the corner. He seemed a really nice lad, quite quiet, down to earth, but visibly troubled.

'I've got a bit of a problem,' he said. 'I've just met this lovely Belgian girl.'

'Great,' I told him, thinking he was about to tap me up for spare johnnies.

'No, no,' he said. 'The problem is I'm married. I've got a wife back home in Macclesfield. I don't know what to do about it.'

I can only think he must have opened up to me knowing my reputation at the time as an incorrigible shagger. Like he thought, *Steve's got no moral scruples. Maybe* he'll *know?*

'Listen, Ian,' I said. 'I hear what you're saying, but if it helps you feel any better, we're all playing away from home. It's not just you, it's the way it is for all of us. Don't overthink it or beat yourself up about it, mate. Just try and enjoy yourself.'

This would have been early November 1979. Six months later, Ian hanged himself. It's the last marital pep talk I ever gave.

19 / *SENSES OUT OF CONTROL*

WE MADE IT TO THE EIGHTIES. Just about. Two American tours at the end of '79 had good as fried us to a crisp. The yellow album had done as badly as expected and 'You Say You Don't Love Me' was the first Buzzcocks single in two years not to make the charts. Pete was never more than a few tablets away from his next nervous breakdown and I was bouncing from one party to the next for as long as the drugs would last. What we all needed now, more than ever, was somebody to restore some peace and calm to the band.

Instead, we did what only a stark raving insane person would have thought the perfect fix for the fragile burned-out Buzzcocks of 1980. Put us back in a studio with the certifiable headcase known as Martin Hannett.

It all came together like a perfect storm. We knew we weren't in any fit state to start another album, but the idea of recording a few singles upfront in a oner to stretch out over the rest of the year seemed reasonable enough. Between us, me and Pete had just enough songs for three As and Bs. All we had to do was get down to business as usual and book a studio with Rushent.

That was the spanner in the works. Rushent wasn't available. He was out of the country, recording in New York, meaning we'd have to carry on and do our best without him. Possibly it was the thought of having to deal with untrusted outsiders that put us off trying anybody new. I wish I could remember. More than anything I just wish I could remember who decided bringing Hannett back into the fold was a good idea. Because they wanted sectioning just as much as he did.

In the three years since we made *Spiral Scratch*, Hannett had made a name for himself as the in-house producer for Tony Wilson's Factory Records, recording everything Joy Division ever did. He'd also had a Top 10 hit with Jilted John so his reputation was that of the musical Midas of Manchester. A lot of it was true. Everything he touched did seem to turn to gold, including *Spiral Scratch*, which had also belatedly made the Top 40 when it was re-released in '79. In the studio, Hannett really *could* be an alchemist. But he was first and foremost a chemist. As in the kind who cooks up crystal meth.

None of it being around back then, that was the one drug Hannett *didn't* do. Every other one you can think of was his breakfast, lunch and dinner. This was the heavily signposted disaster we were now hurtling towards like a car over a cliff edge. Because if we seriously thought we'd seen and done too may drugs on the road in America, it was nothing compared to a month in the studio with Hannett.

When I say 'we', I have to specify me and Pete. Poor John and Paddy were always the straight ones, so if anything, it was twice as bad for them, having to deal with all the lunacy cold without any of the mind-bending benefits. My take on it was, naïvely perhaps, that we'd entered some new *Sgt. Pepper* phase. For the first time ever, because Hannett couldn't function without them, we were going to bring drugs into the studio. It worked for the Beatles, so, who knew, maybe our own 'I Am The Walrus' was just around the corner?

Big mistake. The difference was the Beatles could get as trashed as they liked because they always had sober old George Martin behind the desk to sort them out. We had the actual fucking Eggman.

I can't remember how many weeks exactly it took us. It felt like years. All I know is we ended up using four different studios to record just six songs. We started off in Manchester making demos in Pluto, the studio the Clash had just used to make 'Bankrobber'. That was the easy bit. It was when we shifted operations to Advision in London, near the Post Office Tower, that the madness kicked in. It started off where nothing could happen until someone delivered the weed. Next thing, the spliffs are done but nothing happened until someone delivered the coke. Before you know it, the coke's all gone so nothing happened until someone delivered the acid. It was 'No Moët – no show-ay' taken to the next narcotic level.

Not surprisingly, after one week of this non-stop drugfest we still hadn't finished the job. On Rushent's clock we'd have made a whole album by now. With Hannett everything took at least twice as long, which is why we ended up moving studios again, this time to the Town House in Shepherd's Bush. That's where the 'Rolfisms' started. It was part drugs, part stir craziness, but me and Pete were so off our nuts we'd start banging things and singing 'Sun Arise' by Rolf Harris. Then all four of us – including John and Paddy, who didn't even have the excuse of being out of it – would form a conga line and dance out into the corridor between the other studios, still bashing away and singing, all the way to the dining area, where we'd conga round the tables of whoever else was there – including the Psychedelic Furs who we completely freaked out – chanting *'Sun ariiiiiise!'* like some satanic Hare Krishna cult. Meantime, Hannett never left his chair. He'd just let us get on with our Rolfisms and rack out the next lines ready for when we got back.

As if all this wasn't silly enough, we subjected a revolving door of guest musicians to witness our idiocy. I'd bend down to snort a line off the top of a monitor, come back up and see some bloke with a viola case. I'd bend down to take another one, come up again and they'd be gone, but there'd be a jazz trumpeter blinking at me instead. It'd be: *'Sniff!* Who are you again? *Sniff!* Cello? *Sniff!* OK, luv. *Sniff!* Just go in there and play summat. *Sniff!'* We had some great players, like Georgie Born, the cellist from Henry Cow, having to contend with these coked-up clowns, only for Hannett to bury them so deep in his sludgy mix they might as well have not even been there. I dread to think how many tracks Martin used per song. At one point we were dropping spoons on piano strings and setting off fire extinguishers. He even had me and Pete do a whole vocal track for 'Are Everything' quacking along to the main riff in Donald Duck voices. With enough echo, it actually sounded great. Or it did to anyone as off their tits as we were.

After the Town House, we prayed that would be *it*. In total, we'd recorded seven songs – six for three singles and a spare, Pete's 'I Look Alone', which we eventually gave away on the NME's *C81* compilation. Except the 'finished' mixes Hannett first sent us were all swirly and mushy-sounding. I had to tell him. 'Martin, this doesn't sound like Buzzcocks, it sounds like fucking Hawkwind!' Meaning we'd have to mix them again. Meaning going back with him into *another* studio.

It was a bit like the war film *A Bridge Too Far*. Strawberry Studios in Stockport, where we'd previously made 'Everybody's Happy Nowadays' with Rushent. That was the studio too far.

The plan was for me and Pete to spend a few days there with Hannett just to clean up his mixes. But it was the same old same old just as in London. Wait for the weed, wait for the coke, wait for the acid. Sometime during the first day, Hannett wandered off, presumably for a piss. Me and Pete sat at the mixing desk waiting for him to come back for what seemed like forever. Eventually I'd had enough so went to check where he'd got to. I found him in the lounge area watching porn on VHS, eating a peanut butter sandwich.

Not long after that, Pete stopped coming. It was just me, Hannett, drugs, porn and peanut butter. Another time he did his disappearing act, I went looking for him and found his legs sticking out of a cupboard. For a second I thought he was dead. 'Martin!' Then he pulled himself out of it, clutching an old echo box. 'I haven't seen one of these things in years.' He was a hopeless case, lost in his own mad professor's world of mental abstraction.

Hannett never did finish the job. He managed to mix the first two singles OK, but by the third we had to go back to Rushent on our hands and knees after he came back from America. God bless him, we spent a few days down at his new home studio complex in Berkshire, Genetic, where he added the brass section to 'What Do You Know?' – which is why you can hear them so clearly compared to the Hannett mixes – and did as good a repair job as anyone could. Had circumstances been different, Rushent would've done them all in the first place. It would have taken us barely one week in one studio, there'd have been no drugs, no Rolfisms, no porn, no nonsense. And Buzzcocks might actually have survived to make another record.

*

THE SAD IRONY is that those three singles – as fate decreed, the last three original Buzzcocks singles – were a bounce back to form after the yellow album. Making life as unnecessarily complicated as ever, we told the label we didn't want to do straight A- and B-sides. Each single would be labelled 'Part 1', 'Part 2', 'Part 3'. None would specify which was the main A-side but they'd be marked by symbols; the second and third singles even had P- and Q- and R- and S-sides instead. When we first played the tracks to the label they complained. 'We can't hear a single.' But we stuck to our guns. 'They all are.'

Each one was a strong coupling, one of Pete's, one of mine. Typically, his songs were emotional, mine more political. I loved that juxtaposition, that people literally got the two sides of Buzzcocks on one single. All of Pete's had good melodies. 'Are Everything' was a simple looping chord sequence, very hypnotic, almost in the 'ESP' way; even mine and Pete's quacking (still in there somewhere) didn't spoil it. 'Strange Thing' was Pete writing about depression, but unlike the yellow album it had a fantastic spirit and energy about it with our two guitars chopping back and forth, pop but still unconventional. And 'What Do You Know?' was just a great song, again very simple but very catchy, especially with Rushent's brass polish on top.

My own 'Why She's A Girl From The Chainstore' was the only one we made a video for. And when I say video I mean *video*. It was filmed on one of those clunky old Ferguson Videostar cameras, so more like an episode of *Crossroads* than a fancy Duran Duran job. It took us a couple of days in John Lewis's in Manchester, me doing my bad miming with guest cameos from Pete's dad and Linder playing a zombified sales assistant. We filmed it in normal shop hours so you had all these confused customers looking at Linder going, 'What the hell's wrong with her?' One bloke stopped me and said, 'What's all this about, then?' I told him, 'Don't worry, mate, it's just a soap powder advert.'

The song was partly inspired by Henry Miller's *Black Spring*, which begins by saying the only real heroes are the ones you meet in the street, not in books or films. So I wanted to make a heroine of the chainstore girl; subconsciously, it might also have had something to do with my mam who spent most of her life working in shops. It also asks why working-class people become conditioned and trapped by their environment, even by how they speak. The lyrics reference the sociologist Basil Bernstein and his codes of language: how the way people talk in the classroom is different from the way people talk at home. The girl from the chainstore is a victim of her own social circumstance, *'facing Bernstein's barrier'.*

After all the shouty vocals I'd been doing on 'Harmony In My Head' and 'Mad Mad Judy' I was determined to try harder this time when it came to singing. 'Chainstore' was definitely my best vocal across those singles. Of the others, 'Airwaves Dream' turned out OK, basically me trying to do a bit of a Brian Eno using a cheap keyboard I got from Johnny Roadhouse Music in Manchester. But my biggest regret is my singing on 'Running Free'. The best of my three songs had my shittest vocal. I blame Hannett entirely. It had been a typically mad druggy night in the studio, up until about 5 or 6 a.m., by which point I was completely fucked and just needed to go to my bed. But Hannett persuaded me to stay and lay down a vocal. I told him I was too knackered. 'Don't worry,' he said. 'We'll just put down a guide vocal for now. We'll redo it later.' So I went in and didn't so much sing it as groan it. But for whatever reason *that* became the final vocal. Even when Rushent did his emergency patch-up of the mix I pleaded to try another one. But, like the song says – the best bloody harmony line which I gave Pete to sing – *'no, no, no, no time'*. It bothers me to this day because that was like my entire life philosophy in song – I *do* just want to spend my time running free – and I never did it justice.

None of those last three singles made the Top 40, but then we never did try and write for the charts. What I loved about that little triptych was that none of them were formulaic; they all took the sound of Buzzcocks somewhere new. If we'd only been able to harness that creativity and dispense with all the chaotic bullshit in between, we could've made an amazing fourth album.

But it took us to actually try it to realise we were finished.

20 / *NOTHING LEFT*

THE END, WHEN IT CAME, was more whimper than bang. There were no tears or tantrums or flying fists. Maybe that was the problem. Not enough honest emotions being expressed. On the surface we were all still getting on, still gigging at home and abroad, but by the end of 1980 everyone was slowly splintering off. Pete had his ongoing thing with his boyfriend Francis under the Tiller Boys name, Paddy had been playing with ex-members of the Fall in another group, the Teardrops, and even John had started playing drums with his own band, the Things, as well as recording with Pauline Murray and the Invisible Girls. I never wanted to do anything outside Buzzcocks, but it got to the point where I thought, if I can't beat 'em, I may as well join 'em. That summer I made my first solo three-track EP, *50 Years Of Comparative Wealth*, with Paddy on bass and John on drums. Essentially a Buzzcocks record, minus Pete: in different circumstances, one or two of those tracks could have easily ended up Buzzcocks songs. Unfortunately, the six-month-delayed timing of its release couldn't have been more awkward. The rumours of our split were in the papers one week, then my EP came out the next. To the press, and the fans, it gave the impression I was the one who wanted to go solo, which was never the case. I never ever wanted Buzzcocks to stop. Nor was I the one who pulled the final trigger.

It was Pete. If you want to be blunt about it, he broke up the band. But whether it was entirely his own decision or outside forces twisting his arm is a much greyer area.

By that point, me and Pete were in two different camps: he was in Pontins and I was in Butlin's. Pontins being a house in Gorton he shared with Francis and a few other student types. I used to hate going round there, not because of Pete but because of his flatmates who reminded me of the winged monkeys in *The Wizard of Oz*. They'd all sit in a row on his sofa, gawping down their noses at me like I was some uncouth vulgarian he had the misfortune to be stuck in a group with, all believing they were his real friends when anyone could see they were just sycophants there to make up the rent. I could only imagine the conversations as soon as I'd left the room. 'Oh, you don't need *them*, Pete. Everyone knows *you're* the star. You'd be *much* better off going solo.' Et cetera, et cetera, even though none of them had the faintest idea about the reality of Buzzcocks, all the hell and high water me and Pete had been through together since '76. But these were the people who now had his ear, steering his ego. So that was Pontins.

Butlin's was the same terraced house on Granby Street in Chadderton that I'd bought with the money after our first album. Because Judith studied design, she helped me fix the place up and sorted all the furnishings while I was away on tour. The plan was that she'd move in with me when I got back. Only at exactly the same time, my brother Phil and his equally eccentric mate Dave – a sculptor from Dudley who permanently dressed in a gasman's coat and cap like he'd come to read the meter – had both finished art college in Hull and needed somewhere to live. I said they could crash at my house for two weeks. They stayed two years.

Once they turned up, Judith left. We never broke up over it; she just knew it wasn't the domestic bliss she'd envisaged: three drunk nutcases turning her home into some bonkers *Coronation Street* version of Andy Warhol's Factory. I'd be doing my music in one room, Phil would be flinging paint in another and Dave would be dragging some massive chunk of marble from a demolished fishmonger's into the backyard to hack into a sculpture, still in his gasman's coat, cap and goggles. Occasionally we'd all swap. They'd be making noises with hoovers and cardboard boxes, and I'd have a go at chiselling an old tree trunk, usually to a soundtrack of Faust who we listened to all the time (their 'It's A Rainy Day, Sunshine Girl' was the musical inspiration for the title song off my solo EP, '50 Years Of Comparative Wealth'). Every night we'd go through this ritual charade in the kitchen where one of us would have to find the pepper pot while blindfolded. The rule was we could only go to the pub and get pissed if the pepper pot was found. I never remember a night when it wasn't.

To anyone looking in, it must have seemed like a madhouse. I saw it as a beautifully bohemian arthouse, the three of us weirdos carving out this little commune on the edge of Oldham. Every day at the kitchen table we'd have fascinating conversations about life, painting, literature, war or philosophy, like some late-night arts discussion on Channel 4. Meantime, round at Pete's, him and his minions would probably be discussing that year's Eurovision Song Contest (a lifelong fan, he never missed it).

So we were both living in our separate microcosms: him with his gargoyles, me with van Gogh and the gasman. We now only really saw each other at rehearsals and gigs. The days of me and Pete spending long hours together in the pub drinking, laughing and arguing about all sorts of nonsense like an old married couple were long gone.

As we were drifting apart as a band, the management around Buzzcocks was also coming loose at the seams. It was a bit like the situation with the Beatles ploughing all their money into the Apple empire. Ours was ploughing into Richard Boon's New Hormones, not so much an empire as a small constituency with outstanding accountancy issues. Nothing sinister, just amateur. Myself and John both received letters from the Inland Revenue demanding unpaid monies. It turned out there'd been an audit or some official paperwork which we were supposed to sign off but nobody at our office had asked us. We both said, 'What signatures?' So someone else's incompetence very nearly got us fined for tax dodging. The way cash was flowing in and spilling out of New Hormones, this wasn't surprising. I only wish I'd asked more questions at the time. Like, why is Buzzcocks' income being used to fund demos by the Fall? Why are we dishing money out to any old roadie who stumbles into the office waving a receipt for fuck knows what? And why is the New Hormones record label now a vanity project for Richard's friends, like Pete with his Tiller Boys, or Linder's band, Ludus? Maybe some of them were interesting records in their obscure arty way, but they must have sold about three copies each. And, ultimately, as the company cash cow, Buzzcocks were paying for them. This was the crux of the problem. We were a Top 40 band signed to a major label being managed with a parochial indie mentality.

The real shame was had New Hormones got their act together they could have given Factory Records a decent run for their money. Instead, they had a knack for handing Tony Wilson a load of good ideas on a plate so he could nick them for himself. Like starting an independent record label in Manchester with its own nightclub.

When the Haçienda opened in 1982, the moment I walked in I realised Factory had taken their whole SS thing with Joy Division and New Order too far. *Jesus, now they've gone and built the bloody Reichstag!* But whether he admitted it or not, Wilson's inspiration for it was our earlier New Hormones multimedia night the Beach Club, held in a split-level nightspot called Oozits near Manchester Victoria Station. On one floor we had bands like Frank Sidebottom's first group, the Freshies, on another we'd screen films like *Eraserhead*. I remember seeing Wilson there once, for some reason dressed in a combat suit like a Vietnam vet, looking around, drinking it all in, mentally joining the dots. Two years later, the Haçienda opened. It was just the Beach Club with reinforced concrete. Even the design of the place with the silver and orange and yellows and blacks was a rip-off of Malcolm Garrett's colour palette for early Buzzcocks artwork. Peter Saville even went to the same college as him. It was conspicuous fraud on an industrial scale.

None of these things were the sole individual cause behind Buzzcocks' break-up, just all part of the context. As I said, Pete pulled the trigger. But it wasn't so much the why that hurt. It was the how.

THE DAYS OF OUR LABEL bankrolling us to make albums in a lovely studio down in London like Olympic were well and truly over. Our lack of recent commercial success coupled with changes at the top in EMI meant we'd been reduced to the barrel scrapings of any company budget. When it came to start the fourth album they could just about spare enough dough to put us back in Pluto in Manchester. Like money, inspiration was also in short supply. It was assumed that, as the two main writers, me and Pete would both submit a batch of songs and take it from there. Ever since the dreaded yellow album I'd been contributing a lot more ideas. Some never got further than the demo stage, though they'd later be officially released as 'lost' rarities, like 'The Drive System' and 'Jesus Made Me Feel Guilty', and a really silly one me and John did mucking about on piano called 'Mother Of Turds' like George Formby meets Bertolt Brecht. But the big revolution for me and Pete was when Portastudios came out. Until then we'd had to put our ideas down on clunky reel-to-reel machines. With a Portastudio you could record four-track demos on a standard cassette, a hell of a lot quicker and easier. So going into the fourth album I had maybe half a dozen songs I'd already put on tape. Paddy was also writing more, including one about his dad, 'No Friend Of Mine', which we managed to demo with him singing lead vocal.

Pete turned up with next to nothing. Two songs. I can't remember the second one, but the first was called 'Homosapien', which, as I've since found out, was yet another old one he'd written long before the band. He played it to me on acoustic guitar. Immediately, I thought it sounded like a good Buzzcocks song with a simple catchy melody. But, as I told him, we were still shy of an album's worth. 'Pete, we need more songs. You've got to get some ideas together.'

Which is when the plot thickened and the shenanigans started. The ordinarily reliable Martin Rushent stepped in to help by suggesting Pete come down to his studio in Berkshire and work on some demos. The deal, as everyone else in the band understood it, was that Pete would go away, write some songs, make demos of them with Martin, then return to Manchester and finish the album with us. We were getting nowhere fast just kicking our heels in Pluto, smoking too much dope and waiting for the pub to open. It seemed a positive step forward.

Pete had been down at Rushent's place a week when I rang up to see how things were going. I spoke to Martin. 'Yeah, great,' he said. 'Everything's going fine.' So I left it at that.

Another week passed. Still no word from Pete. So I rang again. This time it was a studio assistant who answered. I asked to speak to Pete or Martin. They said nobody was around so I left a message to call me back when they got the chance. Nobody did.

A few more days passed and I rang again. The same thing. 'Sorry, they're not here just now.' I left another message and, again, nobody rang back. I was naïve enough not to be suspicious, just increasingly annoyed.

That's when the trigger pulled.

The gunshot that killed Buzzcocks wasn't a loud ricochet. It was the soft sound of a letterbox flapping and an envelope falling noiselessly to the doormat. Three letters, one sent to each member of the band, received the same day. The sender wasn't Pete. It was his lawyer, who in dry formal language spelled out that his client, one Pete Shelley, was no longer a member of the band known as Buzzcocks.

This was how Pete split up the band. By paying a lawyer to tell us he didn't want to carry on anymore.

Spineless cunt.

That's what I thought at the time. The ultimate insult to injury, taking the coward's way out. It was the very worst of Pete Shelley. That coldness within him, that he could do that to all of us, his mates. To not have the bottle to tell us to our faces, but by letter, and not even a letter in his own hand but typed on his behalf by some overpaid legal prick. That I should have to learn Pete wanted to end it from a complete fucking stranger. I was frothing.

Now, looking back, it's not anger I feel. It's sadness.

Pete, you silly bastard – why couldn't you have talked *to me?*

If he had, I'd have understood. If he'd said at the time, 'Steve, I'm tired. I can't do this anymore,' at first, knowing me, I'd have definitely tried to talk him out of it. But if he'd explained that he wanted to try something on his own instead, ultimately I'd have backed him. 'OK, man, you've got to do what's best for you in the end.' Because, being honest, we probably were all frazzled and needed to stop. All he had to do was tell us all, face to face, the way Howard had when he'd decided he didn't want to carry on. After everything me and Pete had been through, he owed me that at the very least.

The sadness I feel is because he couldn't. Not physically. Pete couldn't have brought himself to say it out loud. If he had, it would probably have broken his heart. He didn't want to be the bad guy causing any problems and always ran away from confrontation. If I ever made a mistake, I'd always own up to it. Pete never could. It would simply destroy him to admit he'd ever done anything wrong. This was the whole crux of the matter with Pete, that the bloke who famously sang about spurning natural emotions wasn't actually able to express them. That's why he'd retreat into the unfeeling frozen wasteland, hiding behind lawyers, sending letters to say the simple thing he couldn't. I don't suspect for one minute he was proud of himself. But that's the only way Pete knew how to operate.

I didn't contact him. The damage was done, and anything I'd have said in the heat of that moment would only have made it worse. But I don't remember any discussion of us continuing as a trio either. Now that we'd all been poking other irons in the fire we took it as the cue to knock Buzzcocks on the head. It also came as no big surprise that the 'band demos' he was supposed to be making with Martin ended up as the Pete Shelley solo album *Homosapien*. Et tu, Rushent?

From beginning to end, the story of the original Buzzcocks lasted not quite five years. I'd first met Pete in June 1976. I received the letter from his lawyer in March 1981, just as the Thatcher government announced the latest rising unemployment figures: 2,400,000 out of work.

Make that 2,400,001.

21 / *I DON'T KNOW WHAT TO DO WITH MY LIFE*

VERY EARLY ON, I realised that me and the Eighties were never gonna work. I had a mate at Virgin Music Publishing named Jumbo. Not long after Buzzcocks split, I went to see him to pick his brains about what I should do next. 'Steve,' he tutted, 'guitar groups are over. These days it's all kids making music at home playing keyboards with one finger.' In 1981 you only had to switch on *Top of the Pops* to see Jumbo was right. The punk rock wars were over and the machines had taken over. Everything was synths. The big album that year was *Dare* by the Human League, produced by Martin Rushent straight after he finished Pete's *Homosapien* album; the irony, as Pete would later insist, was that he'd paid for the drum machine Rushent ended up using on all of Human League's hits.

I'd made one EP as Steve Diggle, but I didn't suddenly want to go solo. I still needed a band around me, except this was the Eighties. Bands weren't called the Clash or the Jam anymore; they had names like A Flock of Seagulls and Classix Nouveau. At least that's my excuse for spending the rest of the decade making records under the umbrella of Flag of Convenience.

It was my brother's suggestion. A shipping term for merchant vessels which aren't affiliated to any owner so instead fly a flag of convenience for whatever country they choose to register in. As a name, it sounded very Eighties. We even looked very Eighties: boiler suits, shades and, like everyone else's, at one point my hair even crept dangerously close to a Chris Waddle mullet. Later, I tried to simplify and abbreviate it to F.O.C., thinking of Orchestral Manoeuvres in the Dark being O.M.D., which was a pretty terrible idea. The line-up was never static, so in a way it was a Mark E. Smith and the Fall situation – I was Mark, F.O.C. were my Fall. But at least for the first few years I had the pleasure of playing with John again. He was the best drummer I knew so he was always going to be my first choice, even if it gave the false impression two ex-Buzzcocks had broken away to form a new band together, when really it was a case of me asking John if he fancied joining my new project. The flipside of that was Paddy ended up playing bass for Pete on tour in the US. A bit like a divorce, everyone has to decide whether to stay friends with the husband or the wife.

Stylistically, the F.O.C. blueprint was somewhere between early Roxy Music and the Plastic Ono Band, quite arty, but heavy. Lyrically, I was reading a lot of post-war plays, stuff like Harold Pinter's *The Dumb Waiter*, and John Osborne. He was another big influence as his autobiography, *A Better Class of Person*, had just been published and I had *The Entertainer* on video, which I must have worn out. So in my head, or rather in my songs, I was trying to combine Eno, Ono and Archie Rice. Possibly why nobody got us. As the years went on it was obvious F.O.C. were fish out of water. Or rather we were fish *in* water, only somebody had drained the sea from around us.

I likened it to one of my favourite films ever, *Rocky II*. That's like a metaphor for me in the Eighties, and another VHS tape I played to death both at home and on the tour bus. Critical consensus is that the best Rocky film is the first one. That's great too, and I'm not knocking it, but for me it's all about *Rocky II*. The comeback! Rocky's done it once, but can he do it again? Now that he's famous and he's being exploited making those awful aftershave ads, can he get himself in shape and back in the ring and this time *beat* Apollo? It's a simple story, which is why I love it. The moral is: never give up. That's how I felt throughout that decade. Buzzcocks was like my first *Rocky*, the story of how I came from nowhere and made it to the final bell of the big fight. But now I'd done it once, could this Manchester Stallion do it again?

One person who believed I might was the head of Sire Records, Seymour Stein, who had enough faith in Flag of Convenience to put out the first single. Because I now had the same manager as Gerry Rafferty – Michael Gray, a former journalist and Dylan aficionado who'd worked as a publicist for United Artists – we used Gerry's producer, Hugh Murphy. 'Life On The Telephone' couldn't have been more Eighties-sounding had it tried: guitars with chorus pedals, droning keyboards and floaty backing vocals. It was a deliberately poppy sweetener so Sire would stump up money for an album, as I tried to convince Seymour when I met him in the café of Fortnum & Mason's to discuss ideas. I began by explaining how our album had to be a lot darker and heavier.

Seymour raised an eyebrow. 'Heavy how?'

'Heavy like the Stooges,' I said. 'And it's going to be called *The Accused*.'

He didn't look convinced. 'That all sounds a bit ominous, Steve.'

So he changed the subject by spelling out the musical lay of the land as he saw it. 'I've just signed this girl singer back in New York. I think she's going to be *really* big.'

If Seymour wasn't interested in me, I didn't see why I should listen to anything else he had to say. The only reason I remember the conversation so well is because it's the first time I heard the name.

'She's called Madonna.'

This was 1982. The Eighties had already set sail without me.

FROM A COMMERCIAL POINT OF VIEW, I was in no man's land. Sire only ever put out that one single. I tried knocking on other doors, including Rough Trade. Richard Boon was now working for them, so I passed on a demo tape to play to Geoff Travis. His verdict: 'Ooh, I'm not sure about *this*.' I don't know how hard Richard tried to persuade him otherwise, but that was a tough one to swallow.

As a tenacious last resort, I set up my own independent – MCM Records, as in the roman numerals for 1990 – and put out the majority of

F.O.C.'s records myself. None of them troubled the charts, or even the indie charts for that, but artistically those seven years were an invaluable learning curve for me, both as a writer and a singer. And even if a lot of it was banging my head against a brick wall, the bruises did me good.

Things weren't really going that much better for Pete, other than cosmetically. Ever the press's golden boy, he was being swamped with praise for his new electronic solo records. I'd be lying if I said it didn't bother me, not because I wanted Pete to fail but because by comparison nobody seemed to want me to succeed. That's what irked me most about Richard's Rough Trade rejection. I started to feel like the Man in the Iron Mask – the wrong brother locked up in the tower while the other one gets to be king. But though Pete had great reviews, his solo UK sales figures told their own story. I realised why when a girl played me his album at a house party in Warrington. She wanted to know what I thought, so I told her. 'It sounds lonely.' Because it did. Pete was only a brilliant frontman so long as he had a band behind him. Without one he sounded desolate. Admittedly, I was probably still smarting from the split and the whole lawyer business, but that was my honest opinion.

I wasn't alone. Throughout the Eighties, Buzzcocks fans were forever coming up to me and asking, 'When are you getting back together?' Even though I was as bloody-minded about F.O.C. as Pete was about his solo career, at the back of my mind I knew they had a point. But as time went on it felt less and less likely.

Manchester wasn't so big that our paths never crossed. Inevitably, me and Pete saw each other out and about in town. Not wishing to rob this story of a dramatic showdown moment, the first time we did we were both alarmingly civil. But he'd always be with his crowd, I'd be with mine. Sometimes I'd get the cold shoulder. Other times it'd be a cursory nod. 'Alright.' There were no big discussions picking over the past. Pete being Pete, he never wanted to talk about Buzzcocks. A few times I tried and he always shut it down.

This made for a pretty uncomfortable piece of television when three of us were reunited on the sofas of the BBC's revamped *Whistle Test* in February 1985. They had a regular slot called 'Hindsight' where they'd play an old clip from the original *Old Grey Whistle Test*. This week it was Buzzcocks playing 'Sixteen Again' from 1978. Me and John, representing

F.O.C., had to watch it together with Pete, promoting his latest solo single, before a brief interview with Andy Kershaw about what we were up to now. Me and John ended up doing most of the talking as Pete was in one of his weird moods, like he felt embarrassed. I don't know if it was because he was being reminded of who he used to be or because he had to sit beside us, but he was definitely casting an atmosphere. At the end, Kershaw wrapped up by asking if the rumours Buzzcocks might reform were untrue.

'There's rumours about the Beatles too,' said Pete. Then he added, 'We're just waiting for Steve to get shot.' Not one of his better jokes.

Unfortunately for him, I didn't. Worse luck, one year later, we even had to share the same bill. It was comically poignant. The Festival of the Tenth Summer, a one-day show at Manchester's G-Mex to mark ten years since the Sex Pistols played the Lesser Free Trade Hall in June '76 – the very gig me and Pete first met. It was organised by Factory Records with New Order and the Smiths headlining a who's who of Manchester music including the Fall, John Cooper Clarke, Frank Sidebottom, the usual suspects. I only got on there thanks to Tony Wilson's ally and promoter, the late great Dr Alan Wise, who told me, 'You should be in this, Steve.' And, bless him, he crowbarred me into the line-up, not as F.O.C. but plain Steve Diggle. The best thing for me was getting to play John Cale's piano (no idea what the connection was with him being on the bill), which was pretty bold considering I'd never played one in front of an audience before. The whole event felt a bit like Factory does Live Aid, but the most surreal thing about it, apart from Pete also being on the bill, was the fact Howard was too. All three of us doing our own solo slots. As the most important band of the bloody lot, the occasion lent itself to an obvious celebratory Buzzcocks get-together, had anybody thought to ask. Or maybe they had. And maybe someone had already refused.

AWAY FROM THE FEW SPOTLIGHTS that wanted me, at home I'd become a reluctant country squire. On the strictest proviso that my mad brother and his mate the gasman didn't join us, Judith found us a house way up in the Pennines in a little village called Belmont, near the Winter Hill

TV mast. A beautiful place, strangely, with the worst telly reception I ever had. For a lot of people it would have been the idyllic rural dream, my 'mansion on the hill' as I'd jokingly call it. I'd sit in my music room looking out over fields of cows and sheep and panoramic views across the moors, watching the clouds roll by. And it killed me.

It was the isolation. Being stuck away up in the hills, outside the city, with nothing around for miles. It took me to pull back the curtains on a Sunday morning and see ramblers in red knee socks traipsing past my window to realise I'm a city kid, born and raised. I got so bored that when anyone came canvassing round the door and asked what I did, I'd tell them I was a Russian spy. I felt like a flower not being watered. *If I stay here the rest of my life, I'm going to die.* Genuinely.

I'd wanted to make it work for Judith's sake, but we'd only been living there three weeks when she first moved out back to her parents. I didn't blame her. The grim truth, for her, was that I couldn't be domesticated. I was nervous about losing my freedom, still taking too many drugs, snorting tons of coke, smoking a bit of heroin, drinking too much and doing all the things a bloke in a steady relationship shouldn't be doing. I always thought I was careful, never leaving any footprints in any flowerbeds so to speak, but my absence spoke for itself. I'd joined Buzzcocks when I was 21 and spent the rest of my twenties in the firing line of rock'n'roll. I now understand why soldiers can't adjust to normal life after years of tours of duty in Afghanistan. Your body gets used to a certain level of adrenaline and you can't readjust, which is where the spiral of booze and drugs begins. I was now 30, but moving to the countryside wasn't ever going to turn me into James Herriot overnight. If anything, it made me even worse. The fact Manchester was over twenty miles away didn't stop me staying out partying anywhere that served booze after the pubs shut. Often the Haçienda, which before acid house was the only reason people ever went there, to get a pint after last orders – otherwise it was just twenty sad bastards shivering in a warehouse the size of B&Q watching a porn film projected in the corner. Or some dodgy Chinese restaurant where they'd only let you drink with food, so I'd sit there getting sloshed with my mates till six in the morning over a plate of fried duck's feet. Then I'd cab home to Belmont to face the music from Judith as the sun was rising. She'd be crying, 'What time do you call this?' I'd be so out of my head that I could barely speak, slurring, 'I'm off to my bed,' and wrestling with what I thought was the bedroom door handle before collapsing into the airing cupboard. It must have looked like a sitcom. Except I was the only one who found it funny.

Looking back, I was lost. Not unhappy – the amount of drugs I was taking, happiness was the least of my problems – just adrift. Like being back on page one of *The History of Mr Polly*, a man trying to find his place in the world all over again.

Culturally, the Eighties had little that interested me musically, apart from the Smiths. If you didn't get them, you didn't get life. It was the funniness of Morrissey I loved, and the jangle of Johnny Marr, the fact they kept guitars to the fore when everyone else was pissing about on keyboards. You could hear the Buzzcocks influence – I remember seeing Morrissey out in Manchester in the very early days, cutting an enigmatic figure even then, hovering in the corner of the Electric Circus – but it was more a shared aesthetic, not a fuzzy rip-off like a lot of the little indie bands John Peel used to play who were just yodelling poor imitations of 'What Do I Get?'. But the rest of the stuff in the charts left me cold. The sickly icing on the cake was when Fine Young Cannibals had a Top 10 hit giving it all their silly rickets legs to a cover of 'Ever Fallen In Love'. Of all Buzzcocks songs, they would have to choose that one. As if the Eighties weren't bad enough, now they were deliberately goading me from every quarter.

The love for Buzzcocks had never died, but it never did me any favours in terms of F.O.C. whose fortunes remained mixed at best. I'm still very proud of a lot of the records, especially the album *Northwest Skyline*, which had a bit of jangle and a Sixties kitchen-sink influence, including the sleeve, so in a funny roundabout way it was a return salute to what the Smiths were up to, especially 'Pictures In My Mind': I'd helped inspire them, now they were inspiring me. But F.O.C. weren't seen as indie enough to be an indie band and weren't mainstream enough to be a chart band. So we fell between two stools and straight under the floorboards beneath. On stage we always had loads of energy (something I think we captured on the live B-side 'Keep On Pushing') and put new records out whenever we could, but the schedule wasn't enough to occupy my time as it had in Buzzcocks. And we all know what Morrissey says about the devil and idle hands.

Looking for any excuse to get out of the mansion on the hill, I'd often go into town to meet my mate Mike Richardson, a graphic designer who worked for Granada TV. There was a pub over the road from the studios, the Stables, where all the *Coronation Street* actors used to drink. None of them had a clue about Buzzcocks or who I was, so they assumed I was some bloke who worked at Granada, same as Mike. It got to the point where I'd pop in to the studio canteen after a night on the piss to get some breakfast and nobody batted an eyelid. But the *Corrie* crowd were great. Mike Baldwin would buy me the odd whisky while Ivy Tilsley would ask me to hold the fruit machine for her while she nipped to the bar. 'Can you look after this, luvvie? I've got two lemons.' I'd pop to the toilets and do coke with some of the younger actors, but I better not name any names in case they're still in it: last time I looked, one of them was.

It wasn't that I'd given up on music, but I enjoyed being in the company of people who had nothing to do with it – actors especially, and the pubs of Manchester were full of them. Another favourite haunt was Corbières Bar, a subterranean pub next door to the Royal Exchange Theatre where I got to know members of the company and crew. One drunken conversation led to another, and the next thing I knew I was on the stage of the Royal Exchange every night for six weeks as an extra in a crowd scene of Ben Jonson's *The Alchemist*. Stood holding a lance in the centre of a Jacobean drama, I did wonder whether *this* was Mrs Shaughnessy's prophecy all along.

More through boredom and curiosity than thespian ambition, I applied for an Equity Card, mainly because a lot of my new mates got by working as extras. I ended up tagging along for the jolly. Soon I was being not so much cast as shepherded in the background of a couple of TV things myself. One was a bloke at the bar ordering a pint in an episode of *Making Out*. Another was as a rocker in a BBC film drama set in early Sixties Blackpool called *Angel Voices*, where I wore a leather biker jacket and scored pills off this other rocker woman in a club scene. Talk about typecast: either getting pissed or buying drugs. I made a few more uncredited blink-and-miss walk-ons and I enjoyed the whole process of being on set, watching and learning how films were made, but it was only ever a fun distraction.* I still had a day job – and no intention of giving it up.

THE SUMMER OF '88, everything suddenly changed. Manchester, music and drugs. One night I got a call from one of my mates telling me I had to come down the Haçienda. 'You won't believe it! It's packed!' I didn't, so I went to see for myself. He was right. Packed – with bank managers with their shirts off flapping their arms about to bleeps and blips. I didn't understand it. Then someone gave me an ecstasy pill. I waited. I still didn't understand it. Then I took a handful of the bastards. I waited a bit longer. *Then* I understood it.

That was the problem. It was like *Brave New World* and soma. It only made sense if you were out of your fucking mind. And there was just as much of an Orwellian *Nineteen Eighty-Four* element. Gather everyone in the Reichstag for the Two-Minute Rave, like automated morons all shouting the same thing. *'Take me higher!'* That's all fine and well at 2 a.m. when you're pumped full of drugs, but what good is that lying in bed on a Sunday morning? I'd still rather have Simon and Garfunkel, thanks. Don't get me wrong, the whole rave scene had a great spirit and was a lot of fun *if* you were there sharing that moment, but there was no nourishment on any level. Not lyrically, not musically, perhaps only physically because it made you sweat so much. But then so did *Shape Up & Dance with Felicity Kendall*.

No music should ever come with a 'drugs not included' label, but acid house did. Like a toy for Christmas that only worked with the right batteries. You don't have to be stoned to get Hendrix. OK, he sounds fucking *amazing* if you are, but he's still amazing if you listen to him sober. Take away the drugs, and acid house music was, well, shit,

---

* Many years later, in 2012 I had my only credited cameo in a rock'n'roll comedy film starring Phil Daniels and Keith Allen called *Vinyl*. I have one scene with Phil near the beginning, at a funeral, playing myself standing at the graveside of his character's dead bandmate. Anybody who's seen it will know the fact I never gave up music to become an actor definitely wasn't the film and TV world's loss.

basically. I also didn't like the way it turned the DJ into the Elvis of the day. Some lanky wretch chewing gum and playing records over in the corner thinking they're a rock'n'roll star just because they know how to work a bloody turntable? I knew that when I was 7.

The only thing I liked about acid house, apart from the drugs, was the psychedelic element. It was also irresistibly infectious. I could slag off the music all day long – and still do – but it changed the landscape, certainly in Manchester. In the early Eighties, when everything seemed bleak with unemployment and Thatcherism and the miners' strike, it was all people taking smack in council high-rises. That was still going on in 1988, but at least there was a visible optimism about the city with kids coming out of the estates, into the clubs, taking happier drugs. This was their punk rock. Even an old git of 33 like me appreciated that much.

Whatever my misgivings about the Haçienda and Factory, I never had any problems with Tony Wilson. He was always very good to me, and my brother Phil, who by the late Eighties was starting to make a name for himself as an abstract painter. Wilson was a big fan of Phil's work so he invited him onto his new Sunday late-night show for Granada, *The Other Side of Midnight*. Phil asked me if I'd appear with him in a piece of performance art, the idea being he'd be action painting on a canvas on the floor while I stood nearby playing guitar, which is what we did. Somebody had just given me an acid house mixtape which I ran through a speaker with me improvising over the top with a wah-wah pedal. While Phil was Pollocking I was wah-wahing over bleeps and blips. Uncannily enough, this was October 1988, just as the Stone Roses brought out 'Elephant Stone'. Pollock and wah-wah were very much in season that month.

But fate is weird. What they say about the butterfly effect is all true. A seemingly small and insignificant act can set off a chain of events culminating in something disproportionately momentous. If the letter from Pete's lawyer in '81 was the gunshot that killed the group, seven years later that bizarre Diggle brothers' performance on *The Other Side of Midnight* pulled a different kind of trigger. The firing of the starting pistol towards Buzzcocks' reunion.

22 / *WHEN LOVE TURNS AROUND*

IT HAPPENED LIKE THIS. After the Wilson TV show, me and Phil were invited to repeat the same action-painting and wah-wah act in Paris as part of a week of gigs promoted by the Haçienda at a club next to the Moulin Rouge, La Locomotive. While over there, I met a promoter who asked if I wanted to come back and play my own gig with F.O.C. 'Oui! Merci beaucoup!' A date was sorted, and everything seemed fine until the day of reckoning when our van pulled up in Pigalle and I saw the poster for the gig outside the door.

'BUZZCOCKS F.O.C.'

Merde.

I asked the promoter what the hell he was playing at.

'You're Steve from ze Buzzcocks,' he said, a bit sheepish. 'But zis is F.O.C., oui? So!'

'So?'

'So we 'ave to get ze people in somehow.'

'Yeah, I know, mate, but it's not the same band, is it? I don't even play any Buzzcocks songs. It's all my own new stuff. You're just conning people.'

'Mais non, Steve! C'est bien. Don't worry.'

I had a choice. Either tell him to fuck off, turn around, go home, cancel the gig and not get paid. Or just go along with it and pray we didn't get bottled off by however many French Buzzcocks fans fell for it.

Obviously, I stayed. The promoter made sure of it by taking us out for a slap-up meal before the gig, no centimes spared. Food of the gods, a lovely piece of Dover sole with lemon, bottle after bottle of the best French wine, topped off with several large malt whiskies. By the time I stood up to leave I was handsomely full and twice as pissed. As I was staggering back down the street towards the venue I could see a giant crowd of at least a thousand people. In my drunkenness I thought they were queuing to gawp at the can-can girls flashing their bloomers in the Moulin Rouge next door. Only as I got nearer, I realised this was *our* crowd.

'Shiiiiiit!'

The shock only sobered me up so much. When I got to the dressing room I still had to stick my head in a sink of cold water, desperately trying to sort myself out. But we played the gig and, against the odds, it went without a hitch. The Parisians aren't exactly shy when it comes to starting a riot, so the fact they didn't when they never heard a single Buzzcocks song all night was a minor miracle. The takings were good, the promoter was happy and afterwards we all celebrated by getting off our heads on ecstasy. Being 'Buzzcocks F.O.C.' for one night hadn't been such a bad idea after all.

And so it continued. We did another gig under the same name in Berlin. I knew it wasn't right, but as this was all happening in mainland Europe and not Britain I felt I could justify it. Or at least we were getting away with it, pulling in foreign audiences who might not ordinarily come and see F.O.C. because they'd never heard of us.

When we got back home, a new offer was waiting from Howard Jones: not the cockatoo with the keyboard but the manager of the Haçienda, nicknamed 'Ginger'. I was already getting a bit tired of releasing F.O.C. records on my own MCM label that weren't getting any attention, so when Ginger offered to put out a 12-inch on his own label, Thin Line, it seemed perfect timing. He'd done the same a few years before for the Stone Roses with their very first single, 'So Young', and by coincidence we now had one of the original Roses, Andy Couzens, on guitar in F.O.C. This would only be the second record on

Ginger's label and, like the first, would be produced by his business partner.

Martin Hannett.

Somewhere along the line I must have pissed off the karma gods. Because here I was, back in the studio with the lunatic who'd all but broken up Buzzcocks nine years earlier.

Hannett hadn't changed. He was still the same lovable madman, only ever so slightly worse. We already had a good song we'd recorded at Drone in Chorlton, 'Tomorrow's Sunset', a psychedelic guitar tune that had a bit of a ravey vibe, so very of its time. All Hannett had to do was mix it and add a few overdubs, which is why Ginger booked three days at Amazon studios in Liverpool for that very purpose. Why there and not in Manchester I've no idea, but getting Hannett as far as Liverpool was a disaster in itself. The day we were due to start work, me and Andy went to pick him up, but he refused to set off until we'd taken him to some pub where he'd arranged to meet his dealer, who never showed. As the minutes ticked by, Martin grew more and more fidgety. So did I.

'Come on, Martin? We can't be hanging around. The studio's booked, we've got work to do.'

So off we flew to Liverpool, and I mean flew, as Andy had a vintage Plymouth Barracuda that ran on nitrous gas so it felt like being in a jet plane. But, soon as we arrived at the studio, Hannett cracked.

'It's no good. We've got to go back.'

He was desperate. Heroin addicts usually are. Andy reluctantly agreed to drive him back to Manchester to score his gear while I stayed with the engineer and got on with laying some guitar effects down. Many hours later, a happier Hannett returned. So happy he wanted to go straight to the pub. And so the same old cycle of insanity began. From drink to spliff to coke and whatever else he was doing. Hannett spent most of the session completely out of it, lying on the sofa while me and the engineer fiddled away on 'Tomorrow's Sunset'. Only very occasionally would Martin wake up and say his piece.

'It's the end of the world! It's space invaders! Just turn the bass up!'

This was what 'produced by Martin Hannett' meant by 1989.

I still wasn't sure about putting the 12-inch out under the name 'Buzzcocks F.O.C.', but Ginger persuaded me. 'You've got to do it,

Steve.' It was his label after all, and he wanted the single to sell. So the chain was now complete. Because me and Phil had been on Wilson's TV show, because we'd then done the same in Paris, because F.O.C. were then invited to Paris and promoted as 'Buzzcocks F.O.C.' without our knowledge, because it worked and because we did it again, because we then decided to put out a single under the name of Buzzcocks F.O.C., the gauntlet was thrown down.

The one who picked it up was our old US promoter, Ian Copeland, brother of our former label boss, Miles. When it came to Ian's attention I'd been gigging and recording as Buzzcocks F.O.C., he put the feelers out in America. Sadly for my own band, it wasn't the F.O.C. half of the equation he was interested in. He only wanted Buzzcocks.

In the meantime, Pete had broken his silence and got back in touch. True to his old ways, through my letterbox via a third party. I was half expecting it. A legal cease-and-desist threat now that I'd resurrected the name 'Buzzcocks', from his manager, someone named Raf Edmonds. Which I ignored, until a few weeks later when my phone rang and the same Raf Edmonds was on the other end of the line. I braced myself, thinking the conversation was probably going to get ugly. Instead, Raf told me about Ian Copeland's proposition.

'He wants Buzzcocks to reform for a three-week tour of America.'

I knew what was coming. Not only was Raf going to tell me it was never going to happen, he was about to lay some heavy manners that if I tried to hijack it for my own Buzzcocks F.O.C. tour, him and Pete's lawyers would take me to the cleaners.

'Pete says he would.'

Eh?

'In principle.'

Fucking hell!

'What about John Maher and Paddy Garvey?'

'Yes, in principle, too. They will if everyone else will.'

It was that unbelievably simple. Eight years after Pete split us up at the beginning of the Eighties, I was the one who'd inadvertently brought us back together at the end of it. Buzzcocks reformed in the autumn of 1989. From that day to this, they haven't broken up since.

*

TIME REALLY IS A HEALER. Once the reunion tour contracts were sorted, the four of us met up for our first band rehearsal in eight years at Easy Hire on Brewery Road, just north of London's King's Cross. We were all a bit nervous, but as soon as we saw one another it just became funny, looking each other up and down, seeing how we'd all changed. Age aside, none of us had much, apart from Paddy, who somewhere between 1981 and moving to New York had lost his Prestwich accent. It was now a fully Americanised 'Hey, guys!'

The biggest relief was Pete. He wasn't anything like the spiky Pete I'd last sat beside on *Whistle Test*. He was the old Pete again. The one I'd missed. Between us, we'd both had to swallow enough pride to be there in terms of any future prospects he'd had for his solo career and wherever I thought I was going with F.O.C. But he had the familiar twinkle in his eye, like he'd finally got over himself. He wasn't Pete Shelley solo star anymore. He was my old bandmate. The two of us just looked at each other – 'Fancy a pint?' – and to the chagrin of John and Paddy went straight to the Easy Hire bar before we'd opened our guitar cases.

Over the years that followed, as in the past, many of our happiest moments together were spent in our cups. We'd both missed our comic drunken bickering. He'd wind me up for wanting to write political songs. 'You want to be Ralph McTell singing "The Streets Of London".' I'd take the piss back. 'Better that than your lovey-dovey Mills & Boon crap.' Anyone looking in might be mistaken into thinking we actually hated each other, but then nobody understood me and Pete the way only we did. We wound each other up as no one else could and we made each other laugh as no one else could. We were two sides of one coin and we both genuinely loved it. The drinks, the jokes, the philosophising, the verbal fencing. One time we were doing a radio interview in Chester, went to the pub afterwards and got so pissed we missed the last train back to Manchester and had to get a hotel for the night. We carried on drinking in the bar, then took nightcaps up to our room, lying on twin beds, pints of Guinness on our bedside cabinets, still arguing as we fell asleep. A proper *Likely Lads* scene. There was also the time we were supposed to spend a week making demos round my house but instead spent every day in the pub up the road. Eventually, after another skinful, I said, 'Come on, Pete, we've got to get something down.' So back we wobbled to mine where Pete plugged in and recorded a perfect guitar solo, finished the last note, grinned at me, hiccupped, then fell backwards, out for the count.

Ever gone to the pub with someone you shouldn't've?

But much as I was glad we were friends again, those eight years out of Buzzcocks had toughened me up in terms of fending for myself and learning not to rely on anyone else. Initially, we'd only agreed to reunite for three weeks in America and a fourth week of gigs in the UK when we got back. If that had been it, I'd have still carried on doing what I was doing before so I wasn't going to start being overly sentimental about it.

Uncharacteristically, Pete was the one who did. One night in New York, he turned to me and said, 'I'm so glad we're back together.' There were tears brimming in his eyes. Call me cynical, but coming from someone who four years earlier had said on national TV he was waiting for me to be assassinated, this was a bit tough to take. But then at least he'd said it aloud. For Pete, that was huge. The Eighties had been a little kinder to him than they had to me, but at the end of it he'd come full circle. The Leigh grammar-school boy still needed the toerag from the Manchester comp.

The reunion tour itself was amazing, on stage and off. On, the four of us had the same incredible chemistry. Off, I threw myself into more incredible chemistry. I never had the chance to tour F.O.C. in the States so I made up for lost time however, whatever and with whoever I could. Until I found myself lying in my bed in the Chateau Marmont hotel in LA, coked-up to the gills, a girl grinding on top of me, one hand steadying her, the other holding a phone receiver while I was supposed to be conducting an interview.

Journalist: 'Say, Steve, how's it feel to be back on tour in America?'

Me, short of breath: *'Great, mate!'*

The Chateau Marmont was the famous Hollywood hotel where John Belushi died of a cocaine overdose. Knowing this didn't stop me tempting fate. Nothing could. I was living for, and in, the moment and prepared to pay any price for it. My mindset at the time, had I gone the way of Belushi and died of a heart attack there and then, on drugs, having sex in Hollywood at the age of 34 I'd have thought it a beautiful way to go. The maybe pathetic but stark honest truth.

Once those first US and UK reunion dates were done, John bailed. Both as the best drummer I've ever known, and as a mate, I'd have loved him to stay, but at the age of 29 he'd already seen and done enough in music and was now building up a business customising cars and drag racing. Never one to suffer fools gladly, he moved to the Isle of Harris in the Outer Hebrides.

His departure marked the end of the original Buzzcocks dynamic. From then on, and for the next 28 years, it would remain the core of me and Pete plus a changing rhythm section. First to fill John's drum stool was, aptly enough, his biggest fan. As a teenager, Mike Joyce from the Smiths used to tap out John's beats on the back of his mum's sofa. Buzzcocks were his favourite band, so it was a dream-come-true *Jim'll Fix It* situation when I asked him to join, thanks to a recommendation from our mutual mate, Gary Rostock from Easterhouse. Mike slotted in perfectly, both as a tight drummer and someone not shy of partying, and stuck with us for the best part of two years before he left to drum for Public Image Ltd. From us to an ex-Pistol, it was like he was making a career moving up the bill of the Lesser Free Trade Hall.

Not long after Mike left, in early '92 Paddy retired. Still living in New York, he found the constant travelling back and forth to the UK to rehearse and record tough, especially being married with two young kids. Always quite sensible, he chose family over Buzzcocks. A crunch decision I, too, couldn't avoid any longer.

BACK IN THE MANSION ON THE HILL, my home life was falling apart. It was all me. I fucked up. I have no hesitation in saying that. I did genuinely love and adore Judith. She created this domestic paradise where everything was right, and I was the one who fucked it up. I blame nobody but myself. I chose music, drugs and chaos over love, home and stability. But then I always have.

Judith was the one who always tried. She'd move out, move back, I'd be the same, she'd move out again, but she always wanted it to work. But you make your bed, you lie in it, you ride bareback after ten pints of Guinness and the next two words you hear change your entire universe.

'I'm pregnant.'

We weren't married and had never discussed kids. At least I hadn't as I never wanted them. I couldn't handle the responsibility of a fucking library card so a tiny gurgling human being needing its nappy changing every ten minutes was way beyond my capabilities. But at some point between hangovers, the airing cupboard and kissing and making up, I became the father of a beautiful baby boy. I wanted to call him James, as in Joyce, but Judith wanted to name him after her dad, Jack, so he became Jack James. I absolutely loved him, and still do, even if I was never there for him. But I just couldn't make the same sacrifice Paddy had made.

Instead, I did what every selfish bastard does. I upped and left. I tried to justify it to myself by thinking, *Well, Lennon left Cynthia holding Julian, so maybe it's OK?* It wasn't OK. All it meant was Lennon had been a cunt and now I was being a cunt. It was one of the most horrible scenes of my entire life, walking out the door to my car, Judith crying on the doorstep holding our boy. 'Don't go.' That was the worst of it. I'd been seeing a girl down south, which was partly the catalyst, but Judith didn't even tell me to fuck off. She wanted me to stay. I was so messed up, partly through drugs, but also psychologically with the stress of it, even I wasn't sure if leaving was the right thing. At first I checked myself into the Britannia Hotel in Manchester to try and sort my head out. I sat in my room, making a list of pros and cons. Then I drove down to London and did the same thing again in the Columbia Hotel. I don't think I finished the list. All I know is I never went back. The thing with the girl I was seeing fizzled out soon afterwards, but I stayed and eventually bought a house up in the hilly North, within walking distance of Hampstead Heath and the cinematic views over the ever-changing city skyline. I've never regretted moving. Manchester is my birthplace, but London is my home.

All I'd ever wanted was freedom. I'd hurt the people I loved most to get it, and I'll always regret having to do that, but for me there's never been any other choice. Heading towards 40, I was still the same 20-year-old who wrote and believed in 'Autonomy'. The older I got, the more obvious it became. Give me that. Or give me death.

23 / *TIME'S UP*

LIVING ON MY OWN AGAIN meant I could do what I liked. Living in London as Britpop was kicking in, what I liked most was drugs. They were everywhere. The Nineties were probably the druggiest decade I've ever known. Good drugs, bad drugs, fun drugs, dirty drugs. I made a Woolies pick'n'mix of the lot of them.

I never saw it as a problem. Not even when I moved into my new house and ended up living in one upstairs room with a mattress on the floor, a kettle and an empty petrol canister: the mattress for lying on while I smoked crack and heroin, the kettle for the rare pangs of hunger when I fancied a Pot Noodle, the petrol canister to piss in to save me having to walk to the toilet. Only when the day came when I went to piss and realised the canister was almost full did I pause to take stock of what I was doing.

Deluded as it may sound, I've never considered myself a drug addict. I've sailed very close, especially in the Nineties. Drugs have taken me to the edge of the precipice more than once or twice. I've stood on the ledge and peered over into the abyss. I've felt the ground loosen beneath my feet. But I've never fallen. Not even after being awake for eleven days straight on crystal meth, which I wouldn't recommend to anyone who cherishes the ability to move their limbs of their own free will. For the record, I wouldn't advocate *any* drugs to anyone. Most people shouldn't do them because most people aren't like me, a spiritual wanderer and sexual adventurer, the main reasons I've ever taken them. That I've survived without too much damage is as much luck as constitution, and I say this with neither pride nor shame, just honesty. Even when I got lost *in* them, I never lost myself *to* them because I've always had a purpose. Music always came first.

THESE DAYS BAND REUNIONS ARE BIG BUSINESS because nostalgia is big business. Probably because today's music is so useless everyone's listening to the music of the past. This wasn't the case when Buzzcocks reformed. Because we'd only been out of the game for eight or nine years it wasn't such a big deal, and because between baggy, grunge and Britpop there was an onslaught of exciting new guitar bands in the Nineties, be it the Stone Roses, Nirvana or Oasis. By comparison, me and Pete, now geriatrics in our late thirties, found ourselves as 'the old guard' pitted against kids the same age as we were when we started.

After being back nearly four years, in 1993 we finally released a new album, *Trade Test Transmissions*: our first since the dreaded yellow one in 1979, and the first with new bassist Tony Barber and his mate Phil Barker on drums. That consolidated our line-up for the next decade. Maybe it was an omen, but the whole time we were making that album, our none-more-German producer Ralph P. Ruppert complained of toothache. But it was vital both for me and Pete that between us we kept writing new music. Neither of us wanted Buzzcocks to become a touring museum piece just churning out the old hits, much as we loved playing them. And even if, sales-wise, *Trade Test Transmissions* never set the world alight, it gave us another good excuse to tour it.

It's strange the places where rock'n'roll can take you. Going on the road, your life is mapped out like a military manoeuvre, a typed schedule of dates and cities and hotels and flight numbers that don't really mean anything until you get there. *Sunday: Munich.* Then you turn up and realise your gig is in the actual old airport building next to where the 1958 Manchester United disaster happened. That really affected me. Having flashbacks to being a kid, over the road in Grandad's house, him showing me his old Busby Babes programmes with Duncan Edwards, telling me all about the crash, who died and who survived. And now here I was, at the scene of the tragedy. We'd been travelling in a people carrier so I asked to be driven down the old runway. I sat quietly looking through the windscreen at the stretching tarmac, feeling the vibes, thinking of those lost sons of Manchester, thinking of Grandad, almost like a conversation with him in my head. *Can you hear me, Grandad? You won't believe this, but I'm here in the old Munich airport. I'm doing this for you and the Busby Babes. 'Forever, and ever, we'll follow the boys!'*

Just as intense, as we had plenty of time before the next gig, the following morning we decided to go and visit the nearby remains of Dachau. Only we would have to turn up the one day of the week when the place was closed. Pete was all for driving on, but I wasn't going to be cheated. I'd come that far and knew I was probably never going to have the chance to be there again. And so I found myself breaking into a Nazi concentration camp.

Pete, having none of it, stayed grumbling in the car while me, Tony and Phil walked round the perimeter and found a spot to clamber in over the barbed wire. It was like *The Great Escape* in reverse. The camp felt even more eerie than the old airport, thinking about what had gone on there just half a century before, imagining the Jerries with their machine guns, seeing the watchtowers and the crematoriums where they burned the bodies. A profoundly sobering moment. I picked an acorn off the ground – I still have it – clenched it tight in my fist and closed my eyes. Same as the airport runway, like I was trying to tune into something. The lost frequencies of the dead.

We crept around the camp a bit more until we suddenly spotted staff moving around inside the museum shop. Our cue to leave. We thought maybe the safest thing to do would be to walk to the front entrance where the staff were bound to see us, maybe give us a bollocking, then let us out. So we waited, but nobody came. Thinking, 'Sod this', I started climbing up by the main gate. I was halfway over the top when into the car park pulled a coachful of Israeli tourists whose first sight of Dachau was a frantic bloke wearing an army parka trying to clamber free. The coach door was flung open and a fat little Jewish guy with a beard ran over shouting, 'Are you alright, boy? Do you need any help?' I was trying not to laugh. 'Nah, thanks, I'm OK, mate.' There's the crazy spectrum of life right there. In the space of a few minutes I'd gone from a sombre reflection on the evils of the Holocaust to something from an episode of *'Allo 'Allo!*

*

STEVE DIGGLE

AMERICA HAD A DIFFERENT ATTITUDE to the reformed Buzzcocks than at home. In many ways a healthier one. They were more accepting and less judgemental in terms of comparing the then and now. It helped that the big alternative American bands of the early Nineties were a lot more conspicuously influenced by British punk, and us in particular. Green Day very audibly loved Buzzcocks and always cited us as an influence. So did my good pal Eddie Vedder, who hung out with us during our first US reunion tour before he'd even joined Pearl Jam; many years later, we'd support them at Madison Square Garden where they played 'Why Can't I Touch It?' and I joined them on stage for a cover of the Who's 'Baba O'Reilly' while Meg Ryan bopped in the wings. But the most meaningful endorsement we ever received from American shores came from a brilliant blue-eyed Jesus lookalike from Washington State.

I first met Kurt Cobain in November '93 on the *Trade Test* tour in Boston. Nirvana were also on the road in Massachusetts and, with a day off between gigs, came to see us at the Paradise club. The first thing Kurt said to me was, 'I love the way you smash TVs, man.' To tie in with our new album title, our staging involved a collage of flickering images on banks of cheap old TV sets our roadies would pick up from junk shops. At the end of each gig I'd usually smash one with my mic stand. An acquired skill, as I'd learned the hard way, having electrocuted myself a few weeks earlier in Germany. I'd plunged the metal stand through the TV screen when it must have hit some live component. Because I was still holding onto it, the shock went through my body, my muscles tensed and I couldn't let go. It must only have been the adrenaline of the gig that somehow gave me the strength to release my grip, otherwise I'd have been toast. That's when I realised the knack is to throw the stand but let go at the same time, like a harpoon. With enough practice and enough cheap TVs I perfected it, striking it bullseye in the middle so the screen implodes and you get a dramatic puff of smoke from the gas of the old cathode tubes inside. You couldn't do it with today's boring flat-screen tellies. It's a lost art, like penny-farthings and spud guns.

When I told Kurt this electrocution story he was fascinated. He said, 'I've only ever smashed *one* TV in my life!' Dave Grohl and Krist Novoselic were also there, both friendly guys and incredibly enthusiastic about us. The upshot being Nirvana asked if we'd support them in Europe the following spring. At that point they were pretty much the biggest, or certainly most important, rock band on the planet. We didn't have to think twice.

The next time I saw Kurt he was chopping out lines of cocaine on Nirvana's double-decker tour bus. This was on the first date in Portugal, at a huge indoor arena in Cascais, near Lisbon. Kurt invited me in, pointed to the coke, said 'Help yourself,' then popped upstairs. I'm guessing, knowing what I do now, that he'd gone to take heroin in private. So I stayed downstairs, snorting the lines he'd racked out, chatting to Dave, Krist and their other guitarist, Pat, when sometime later Kurt returned. He looked at the empty table with a few flecks of white powder on it. 'Where's it gone?' Silly bastard that I am, he'd cut out two grams for the pair of us and I'd absentmindedly snorted the lot. At least he saw the funny side.

The Kurt I got to know for the two weeks we toured with them *was* funny. Not exactly Tommy Cooper, granted, but he wasn't some pained manic depressive. There's backstage video footage of Nirvana and Buzzcocks hanging around on that tour where you can see he's no tortured soul. Dishevelled, yes – he always looked like he'd fallen out of a doorway in Camden – but in no way disturbed. It wasn't like with Ian Curtis, who you could say showed some warning signs by taking me aside to discuss his marriage crisis. There was none of that with Kurt. Courtney wasn't around, and we never got that personal. The deepest conversation me and him ever had was about the struggle of keeping a band together. He wanted to know why I thought Buzzcocks had managed to last so long. 'A sense of humour,' I said. 'You need to have one to survive. Especially early on, it's important when you're a band stuck in the same Transit van that you can all laugh together. Maybe it's a bit easier for us coming from the North. But without a sense of humour, you're fucked.'

Obviously I'd heard Nirvana before we met them, but I hadn't fully appreciated what an incredible band they were until that tour, witnessing them live every night. Like a cross between the Pistols and Led Zeppelin, punk rock plus sheer heavy metal power. They had it all. Balls, attitude and killer tunes. And they couldn't have been nicer people. No egos or any of the usual American rock star bullshit considering how many millions of CDs they must have been selling. Even after we left the tour, Kurt wore a Buzzcocks beanie hat on stage in Milan before a crowd of 8,000. Back home we were still getting snidey reviews in the *NME* for being too old and uncool. Now, here was the coolest frontman from the coolest band in the world at that moment proudly flying our flag. Kurt was the 'mean it, man' real deal.

There's only one image which, with tragic hindsight, does stick out in my mind when I think of him. We played the Zenith in Paris, and the dressing room had a window where you could look down outside over the crowd below. The image that haunts me is of Kurt waving a plastic gun, pointing it through the window pretending to shoot people. A few nights later, we said our goodbyes after our last scheduled gig with them in Grenoble, leaving them to head on to Italy and Northern Europe before coming over to the UK where Buzzcocks were due to support them again at Brixton Academy on 5 April 1994. The day Kurt shot himself.

Not long after we left the tour, Kurt fell sick in Munich. By creepy coincidence, the last gig Nirvana ever played was that same old airport terminal, scene of the Busby Babes air disaster. A few days later, he was hospitalised in Rome after taking an overdose. The rest of the dates, including Brixton, were cancelled. Kurt recovered, then flew home to Seattle. The rest, we know. He'd been lying dead a couple of days before they discovered his body.

I was stunned. Only seven weeks ago I'd seen him in the flesh. Now I'm looking at my TV and there's a newsreader telling me he's dead. It just didn't make any sense. Down the years I've often told the story about accidentally taking his share of coke on the tour bus. My usual line is that I'd like to be buried with the gram I owe so I can give it back to him in heaven. Me being me, joking about it is my way of dealing with it. But there's nothing funny about what happened to Kurt.

That September, Nirvana won the 'Best Alternative Video' category at the MTV Awards. Dave Grohl, wearing a Buzzcocks sweatshirt, collected the trophy. 'I'm not the most vocal person in the world,' he said, 'but it'd be silly to say that it doesn't feel like there's something missing.'

A broken man in a Buzzcocks top, talking of loss. I had no idea what a prophetic moment that would be.

*

THE NINETIES WAS A DECADE OF EXTREMES. Extreme tragedy. Extreme farce. The worst thing ever to happen to Buzzcocks, at least in name, started with a phone call from the BBC to our manager, Raf, sometime around the deflated post-Euros autumn of '96. They were filming the pilot episode of a new comedy panel show about pop music. The working title was a pun on the Pistols' *Never Mind The Bollocks* album: *Never Mind the Buzzcocks*. They asked him if it was OK to use our name. Assured it was only a one-off pilot, Raf said yes.

As everyone knows, the supposed pilot became a successful long-running programme which still gets repeated on free-to-air TV. The original host, Mark Lamarr, was a genuine fan of ours who used to tell me it was meant as a compliment and great publicity. Was it fuck. All it did was cheapen the name of Buzzcocks, which is why I've always loathed it. Nor did the BBC ever pay us a penny. I'm sure if they'd had a long-running panel show called *Never Mind the Coca-Cola*, they'd be up to their ears in lawsuits. For a while I thought about it and went as far as contacting the Musicians' Union to see about using their lawyers. A few people told me we had a strong case in terms of intellectual property and misuse of brand name, but, typical Pete, he didn't want to cause any fuss. Then he did the stupidest thing of all and went on it as a panellist, making a fool of himself, and of us, by killing any last chance we had of compensation. I wouldn't have minded if the show was any good, but the few times I looked in, it was dreadful. Unfunny comedians desperate for attention and loser musicians suffocating in their last gasps of fame sat tapping out a Right Said Fred song or haw-hawing trying to pick out some poor bastard from Mud in an identity parade. The worst of it being that because the whole programme title is a bit of a mouthful, everyone called it 'Buzzcocks' for short, which drove me mental.

Fortunately, despite all the old repeats and new reboots, as culture marches on fewer and fewer people seem to give a toss about it. I'm glad but not surprised. Compared to the musical legacy of me and Pete, not to mention Howard, John and Paddy, it'll take more than a few shit jokes by some student comedians to wipe the real meaning of Buzzcocks from history.

*

UNLIKE MYSELF, by the Noughties Pete had finally settled down, at least on the surface. He got married to a Japanese fan, Miniko, who gave birth to his only son. Miniko didn't particularly like me. For that matter neither did Pete's second wife, Greta. It was a bit like when I used to go round his house in Gorton and get evil looks off his gargoyle flatmates. Both of Pete's wives saw me as a bad influence, as if I used to drag him to the pub against his will, tie him to a chair and pour alcohol down his throat through a funnel until he couldn't walk. If anything, he'd be the one dragging *me* to the pub. Because he'd moved to Camden, a few miles down the hill from where I lived, and because he knew I was always out and about in the Britpop pubs like the Good Mixer, he'd say to me, 'How come you never ask *me* to go drinking in Camden?' So I did, and we'd get slaughtered, and he loved it. The strangest thing was the first time I went to call on him – feeling a bit like a kid, 'Can Pete come out to play?' – I walked in his living room and there he was sat on his sofa, smiling, hand in hand with some bloke. I didn't ask. Perhaps marriage hadn't straightened him out as much as everyone thought. Whether that had any bearing on the eventual break-up of him and Miniko, who eventually went back to Japan with their son, I've no idea. That was their business. But that was typical Pete. Inscrutable to the end.

The extraordinary thing after the band reformed was that me and Pete never fell out. We'd do the drunken bickering routine, but that was our private sitcom for our own enjoyment. It never got heavy, apart from just the once. Even then it wasn't his doing, nor mine, but someone else in our orbit driving a wedge between us for their own gain. I don't want to name names or point fingers as it was all silly inter-band power-struggle business best buried in the past. But it got to the point where, just for a second, me and Pete almost came to blows while on tour in France. I almost had my hands on him when I suddenly stopped. 'What the fuck are we *doing*?' I could never hit Pete. But that was the end of it, and neither of us ever let things get that far again. The beauty of it was nobody *could* come between me and Pete, which explains why his wives were never my greatest fans. It was like a secret language only we could speak. You couldn't begin to try and convey it all to anybody else. It'd take too long. Too many nuances, too many in-jokes, too much telepathy for anyone else to ever grasp. Like trying to teach Russian, in Arabic, to a native Chinese speaker.

Without ever vocalising it, we learned to appreciate what we had together, which as we grew into our forties and fifties was a great livelihood. As the years went by and the music industry changed, inevitably the pace of Buzzcocks became less intense. We made three albums in the Nineties, two in the Noughties and just one in the decade after. The times they had a-changed, and not necessarily for the better. Physical sales slumped and digital streaming took over. Great if you're a kid on a smartphone with the whole history of recorded music at your fingertips for free. Not so great if you're a musician used to making a living from record sales and airplay royalties.

But Buzzcocks' saving grace has always been the gigs. The demand to see us live never stopped, and not a year passed when we didn't tour, whether long jaunts across Europe and America or a few months of festivals over the summer. It gave both of us the time and space to live our own lives in between, without the band ever becoming the all-consuming pressure cooker that split us up the first time round. I definitely missed the intensity of constant recording and gigging a lot more than Pete so used my downtime away from Buzzcocks to work on a succession of solo albums and play my own shows. Whereas Pete lost interest in maintaining a parallel solo career, preferring the quiet and comfort of his new home with Greta in Estonia. Which was one way of ensuring I wouldn't be rapping on his door every night inviting him out for a pint.

By the end, I think Pete saw Buzzcocks as a bit of a school holiday. A few months out of the house to have fun, see a bit of the world, play his songs and get pissed with me every night before he flew back to whatever version of reality he'd made for himself in Tallinn. Every tour he seemed to bring a new hobby with him, like a professional telescope when he suddenly got big into astronomy. Sometimes he'd set it up after gigs and point stars and planets out. 'Have a look at this. There's Mars . . . there's Uranus.' Beautiful memories, just me and Pete, staring up at the unfathomable universe twinkling above us. But then the next tour it'd be gone. It's why we were always joking about what the next fad would be that he'd end up shoving under his stairs.

He still wrote songs when needed for the next album, but as time went on I'm not sure how much his heart was in it anymore. I think Pete reached a stage where he regarded his role in Buzzcocks as creating to formula. He could write a great punchy pop song in his sleep, so that's what he did, being Mr Safety, thinking that's all people expected. Whereas I was always trying to push the experimentation, that avant-garde quality that had set us apart from everyone else. Being our own harshest critic, that's what's missing from a lot of those later records. Too often we went for familiarity over originality.

As I've grown older, the vanity of my inner mod has meant I've always tried to make sure I'm still recognisably the same Steve Diggle from Buzzcocks as much as I can be. My dad's genes luckily meant I wasn't going to go bald, but I really couldn't live with myself being a fat bastard on stage singing 'Harmony In My Head' looking like a Weeble Man.

Pete had no such hang-ups. By the time he reached 60, his love of food, and beer, caught up with him until his physique wasn't far off an Eighties darts player: a ballooning gut and a scraggly beard to match. We now had a great younger rhythm section with Chris Remington on bass and Danny Farrant on drums, both cool skinny lads. Then me, the oldest mod in town still with the same (admittedly dyed) haircut, throwing my best Townshend shapes. None of which made much difference because centre stage in the spotlight there's Jocky Wilson singing 'Ever Fallen In Love'. No two ways about it, Pete was unhealthy. That probably sounds rich coming from me after all my years of bodily abuse, but regardless of whatever illegal poisons I've ingested, I'm all for healthy eating. It's maybe one of the things that's saved me. I'm mainly vegetarian and eat as much organic as I can, especially beetroot, my elixir of life; and, these days, the only thing I snort on a daily basis is a bowl of steam from a fresh kettle every morning to clear my sinuses. Pete, ever the gastronome, ate what he wanted and never considered what fatbergs might be building up in his arteries. He couldn't care less, as long as he was happy. But all happiness has its price.

IN THE SUMMER OF 2018, Buzzcocks were playing a festival in Sunderland and staying at a hotel in nearby Newcastle. That day Pete came to see me in my room.

'I've been thinking,' he said. 'Maybe it's time for me to retire . . .'

For a second I froze. *Hang on! Is he saying he wants us to stop again? And is he actually telling me to my face this time, which would be a bloody first?*

'. . . but I'd understand if you wanted to carry on. That's fine. If you, Chris and Danny want to keep the band going, you have my blessing.'

He looked and sounded quite serious.

'Nah!' I shook my head, laughing. 'You're going nowhere, mate! You can't call it quits. No way. You and I have got a lot more to do, yet.'

Pete rolled his eyes and smiled. The subject was dropped.

Two weeks later, we played our last festival of the summer in Belfast, a one-day open-air punk spectacular with Stiff Little Fingers and the Damned. Pete made another strange comment before the gig along similar lines to our conversation in Newcastle. I gave him the same reply. 'Don't start that again. Come on, Pete. You don't mean it.' Nothing more was said.

The festival itself was the 'great craic' Irish crowds both sides of the border invariably are – and always have been since we first toured there during the Troubles way back in '78. The penultimate song of our set was 'Ever Fallen In Love', sung by Pete. The last was 'Harmony In My Head', sung by me. The last song Pete ever played with Buzzcocks.

The next morning, we didn't bother with breakfast. Instead, me, Pete and our tour manager, Pablo, went to the pub round the corner from our hotel for Irish stew and Guinness. (Even though I'm mainly vegetarian, it was another of those when-in-Rome situations.) Pete was in his element. This is what he loved most, a hearty rustic meal of meat, veg and gravy and several pints of *proper* Guinness, smooth as nectar. As it turned out, the Last Supper.

He flew home to Estonia and I flew back to London. We weren't due to see each other again until our next gig in the Netherlands just before Christmas. Then, one Thursday evening in early December, as I was heading out to meet my girlfriend, my phone rang. It was Raf.

Half an hour later, I was alone, drinking outside a pub in the freezing cold unable to think beyond the one question pounding inside my skull.

What the fuck *was* I going to do now?

24 / *AUTONOMY*

NO MOËT – NO SHOW-AY. No Chandon – no band on.

It was there. Just the one bottle on my dressing-room table. Unopened.

I'd been sober all week. A conscious decision because I knew how important this was and I knew I had to keep it together. Ordinarily I'd be guzzling it, pouring it in a plastic pint glass ready to take on stage. But there was nothing ordinary about this. Sat backstage in the Royal Albert Hall, watching an expectant capacity crowd on closed-circuit TV. This was supposed to have been Buzzcocks' special gig celebrating 40 years of *Singles Going Steady*. Now it was the same date, the same venue, but a tribute concert to Pete Shelley instead. The remaining Buzzcocks (me, Chris and Danny), the surviving original Buzzcocks (me, John and Paddy), plus special guests: the Damned's Dave Vanian and Captain Sensible, Thurston Moore, Tim Burgess, Pete Perrett from the Only Ones, plus Richard Jobson from Skids and Pauline Murray from Penetration, our two support acts. We also had a video message from Howard, Paul Morley as emcee and Pete's widow, Greta, in the building. I'd be up on stage the whole time, both as singer and ringmaster. The pressure squarely on my shoulders, tonight I needed all my wits about me.

Of all the bloody ironies, though. All those years, all those bottles me and Pete must have drained. 'No Moët – no show-ay!' And here I was on my own, not touching a drop. I could imagine him up there looking down, laughing, egging me on to pop the cork. And for a second I thought about it, staring at the full bottle in its ice bucket with condensation running down the neck. But I'd come this far.

We all gave him a fittingly ramshackle send-off. One stuffy broadsheet critic with his head very firmly up his arse called it 'rowdy' and 'tuneless': maybe he'd got his diary mixed up and come on the wrong night expecting an Elgar recital? But for me, and for the fans I spoke to afterwards, it captured the true spirit of punk, which is who we were and why we'd all come. As the last chord of 'Ever Fallen In Love' rang out, all I could see was people on their feet up in the boxes, all round the balconies, the entire Albert Hall cheering and clapping. I stood at the front of the stage, hands over my head, applauding them back. Then, with a saluting gesture, I spoke into the mic.

'God bless you, Peter.'

What else was there to say? That night was the closing of a chapter, like the great wake after the funeral most of us never attended.* But for me it was also a necessary rite of passage. The mourning before the morning.

FROM THE MOMENT I took Raf's phone call on 6 December 2018 I was never in any denial about Pete. I already knew the mechanics of death. I know what it is and what it does because it's been there my whole life, ever since the night my mate Alan died, the night I nearly died. I'd seen it enough times since then that Pete dying all of a sudden wasn't going to destroy me.

I didn't even fall to pieces after losing my dad, at least not straight away. It was the fags that got him in the end. He died of an embolism, aged 75, though he still looked well laid out in his coffin with a suntan, his best suit on and his Man City scarf. Even the undertaker said, 'Your dad looks healthy.' I felt like nudging him. 'OK, Dad, joke's over. Get up now, stop messing about.' But it wasn't until about six months later while I was driving that it hit me like a ton of bricks my dad was really *gone*. When I finally shed a tear for him.

---

* Pete was laid to rest in a private family service in Tallinn, Estonia, on 13 December 2018.

Losing Pete wasn't going to be any worse. You either crumble, metaphysically, or you become philosophical. With my dad, I coped by thinking about Darwin's theory of evolution. Like a swan that dies, and then another swan will come along and take a different shape, the subtle changes from generation to generation. Or maybe part of me was thinking of Yeats' poem 'The Wild Swans at Coole'.

'I have looked upon those brilliant creatures . . .'

That's how I dealt with my dad, so with Pete I adopted the same frame of mind. Without death there is no evolution. Plus, with all the books I'd read when I was younger, I was always well equipped with the understanding that we're all born to die. That's the thing about death. It's very democratic.

But I still had that question hanging over my head: what the fuck *was* I going to do now?

I discussed it at length with Raf. Always a very practical man, he didn't put me under any pressure. 'Look, we're still in the land of the living,' he said. 'But it's entirely up to you whether you want to carry on as Buzzcocks or not.'

With Pete gone, that left me as the last link to the band's origins, all the way back to Howard and that first Free Trade Hall gig. One thing a lot of people possibly didn't fully appreciate was that I'd been the only one who'd never quit the band at any point in our history. Howard quit first, then Pete quit, which forced us to split the first time round. After we reformed, both John and Paddy quit in turn. So I was the only one who'd *never* left Buzzcocks. If I suddenly gave it all up now, it would feel like surrender. And surrendering for what? Because Pete was dead? I don't give in to death that easily.

In the First World War they used to tell the troops going over the top that if a man goes down beside you, don't stop, carry on across the battlefield. In the aftermath of Pete, I thought about Buzzcocks the same way. There was also one other very important factor. Because of the conversations we'd had during the festivals last summer, I knew in my heart that Pete had been happy for me to carry on without him. 'You have my blessing.'

And so I came to my decision. For myself, for Pete's memory, for the fans, for the love of the music and everything we'd ever done together,

I couldn't stand back and let it die without at the very least *trying* to soldier on. Because the sound of Buzzcocks has always been the sound of life. I wasn't going to be the one to switch that off. I was ready to turn it up.

IN OUR LATE SEVENTIES HEYDAY, it took a lot of effort to be hateful. If you didn't like anyone in a band and wanted to get it off your chest, you'd have to put pen to paper, buy a stamp, stick it in an envelope and walk to the nearest post box. Then you'd have to wait a few weeks and see if your bile was deemed worthy enough or funny enough to print in the letters pages of the *NME* or one of the other music papers. And only if it was, could you then pat yourself on the back knowing that the band or person you'd slagged off would probably also read it, and your name, calling them all the wankers under the sun.

It took a lot less effort in 2019. Some of the online abuse I received for continuing Buzzcocks, you'd think I'd killed Pete Shelley myself. It was a sad eye-opener to how the minds of some so-called 'fans' worked. Maybe they'd have been happier if I *had* crumbled? Amidst all their venom and negativity I wonder if those people stopped for a second to consider how I was actually feeling. You know, Pete's actual *mate*, the one who knew and played with him for the best part of 42 fucking years? That carrying on as Buzzcocks was my own way of trying to turn the ultimate negative – death – into a positive? Because I still had that same old Rocky mentality. I still had hope.

By 2019 I'd lost count of the various stages of my life in terms of Rocky analogies. If my Eighties wilderness years were *Rocky II*, then I must have been on at least *IV* or *V* by then. Or probably *Rocky Balboa*, the one where he's older and nobody thinks he can still do it. That'd be about right for post-Pete Buzzcocks.

That's partly why the first gig we played without Pete we walked out to the *Rocky* theme, 'Gonna Fly Now'. The comeback *after* the comeback. It was a tentative period, those first gigs with me moving over to centre stage as lead singer. I had no idea what people's expectations were: whether they'd accept us playing Pete's songs without him, whether they'd accept me singing them instead of him or whether they'd accept us playing brand-new material at all.

I had to be honest with myself when it came to the choice of old songs. Some of Pete's fitted me better than others. I tried 'Sixteen Again', a great song, but singing it felt weird because I didn't particularly want to be 16 again. I also wasn't about to change my voice and become a Pete Shelley impressionist for every other song, then switch back out of it again. Like Mike Yarwood – 'And this is me!' It was only going to work if I sang them in my own voice. At the same time, I'd written enough of my own through the years that I didn't have to rely on Pete's for an entire set. So it was a delicate balance between being neither The Steve Diggle Band nor The Pete Shelley Memorial Band while still staying true to the sacred spirit of Buzzcocks.

As the message-board weasels loved to point out, *of course* it wasn't going to be 'the same'. But it wasn't 'the same' when Howard left either. Without him, Buzzcocks became something else. That also applied to Pete. I got so sick of journalists asking me 'Why are you carrying on?' that the only way I could make them understand was to compare the history of Buzzcocks to vases from the great dynasties of ancient China. Just as you had your Yuan vase, your Ming vase, then your Qing vase, with us you had your Howard Devoto vase, then your Pete Shelley vase and now it was my turn to make the next one. The Steve Diggle vase. Because they're all Buzzcocks. And they're all priceless.

THE BIGGEST TEST OF ALL was writing the first new Buzzcocks album without Pete. By 2020, I felt ready for it. Just as well, since soon I'd have no excuse for not trying. The pandemic brought any other plans for the year to a halt, while the onset of lockdown restrictions meant we spent the best part of two years off the road. It was just like being back on the dole again, sitting round the house all day, not going anywhere. So I gave myself a purpose. If all I had was me, my guitar and a means to record, I'd make the best use of my time I could and write the album of my life. No point being half-arsed about these things. That was my aim.

In the past, I'd write a song and I'd know instinctively whether it felt like something for Buzzcocks or something best done solo. Sometimes it was obvious, sometimes it was a thin line, sometimes they were interchangeable. A year after Pete died, we released our first single without him, 'Gotta Get Better', a re-recording of a solo track I'd made a few years earlier. The sentiment seemed very apt, but it was more because we were about to go on tour and I was keen to put something new out, just as a statement that this was a new beginning for all of us. So that song, 'Gotta Get Better', was already there, ready and waiting.

This was different. I was consciously writing a Buzzcocks album, only I had to be my own sounding board. Talk about autonomy: by dictionary definition *'the ability to make your own decisions without being controlled by anyone else'*. I didn't have any alternative. There was nobody else to bounce off. In the past me and Pete would both contribute songs and pick the ones that balanced each other out. The yin and the yang of Shelley and Diggle is what made our best albums tick. Now it was all yang. So I had to force myself to be more objective about myself than I had in the past, almost like being my own boxing trainer. I had to be Rocky and Mickey at the same time. 'Do that!' 'No, not like that! Do that instead!' I took it very seriously, and I had to because I knew, whatever I did, there'd be people gunning for me, willing me to fail. I needed to catch them off guard with some serious knockout punches.

So that's how I spent lockdown. Shadow boxing at home, waking up at 3 a.m. with ideas in my head, making demos, trying to write an album from scratch, in sequence. I'd never done that before. I'd always written songs and then jumbled them up whichever way I thought best. Doing it sequentially actually made it more exciting. Coming up with a great opener, 'Senses Out Of Control', then thinking, OK, so where do we go after this? Same as I would planning a setlist. By the end of lockdown I had a dozen tracks with more hooks than a fishing-tackle shop that I knew were good enough to be the next Buzzcocks album. And a title for it: *Sonics In The Soul.*

I'm very proud of it. As our New Chapter album, it does everything I wanted: honour the legacy of the past while pointing towards the future. They say you shouldn't believe everything you read in the papers, but I'd like to make an exception for Garry Bushell's glowing review in the *Daily Express*: 'As good as anything the band wrote in their golden years'. After all the shit I'd had flung at me when I announced I was carrying on, it was nice to be vindicated by an old punk like Garry. Better still was the reaction in concert from fans – as in *proper* fans, not anonymous internet trolls. Had they rejected it, and the band without Pete, I'd probably have had to knock it all on the head, but the love and energy of the gigs, playing the new stuff live, has been genuinely humbling. I could say a lot more about it, but ultimately the album speaks for itself. These days it's never been easier to check out music for free. If you've not heard it, but you've still been bothered enough to read this book, all I ask is that you google it – *Sonics In The Soul* – and give it a listen.

THE ONE SUBJECT *everybody* expected me to write a song about, of course, was Pete, like it was my duty to come back with the punk 'Candle In The Wind'. (Though if it was about the real Pete, it'd be more like 'Three Sheets In The Wind'.) Because it was the first Buzzcocks single since he died, those who didn't know 'Gotta Get Better' was one of my older solo songs thought I was singing about struggling to cope with his death. Others reached the same wrong conclusion about the album track 'You've Changed Everything Now', but it doesn't bother me. People are free to put any interpretation on any song they want. In music, meaning is all in the ear of the beholder. The funny thing is that I actually *did* write a song for Pete. They were just looking for it in the wrong place.

It was a song I wasn't sure about, and because I wasn't sure I didn't want it on *Sonics In The Soul*. Only because, musically, it didn't feel that Buzzcocksy. It was one of those borderline ones where I thought maybe I'd be better saving it for a solo record. I was also a bit self-conscious about the subject. Was it too cheesy? I didn't want to be like Brian May making a huge song and dance because his mate Freddie was dead, weeping and a-wailing with pianos and orchestras and fuck knows what else. But I'd been having these odd emotional flashbacks to me and Pete. These rushes of memory when I least expected it, when it hit me. *Fuck! He's* gone. *I'm never going to see him again.* The more I was forced to think about him, the more I kept coming back to the psychology of his personality, how his whole life all he ever wanted was to be loved, difficult as he sometimes made it for anyone who tried. That's when it came to me, almost like saying it out loud. 'Hope heaven loves you, Pete.'

That became the song. 'Hope Heaven Loves You'.

The words and melody were very simple. Just a couple of verses describing Pete as I knew him. A loner who never stood a chance until punk rock came along, playing two-note solos with his broken guitar.

It ended up as one of two 10-inch B-sides to the album's first single, 'Senses Out Of Control'. I was happy for it to slip under the radar a bit, not to overegg it, which I easily could have for cheap publicity, to just leave it there as my little epitaph for the fans to find in their own time.

Hope heaven loves you,
Heaven loves you,
The stars above you,
Over your dead soul

From the heart, Pete. Hope heaven loves you.

If it does half as much as I did, I know he'll be alright.

EPILOGUE / *HARMONY IN MY HEAD*

FORTY-SEVEN YEARS in the business, and we're finally given the recognition of a permanent monument to Buzzcocks' legacy. And it would have to be the week I break a fucking rib.

Not the first time I'd come a cropper on holiday scootering around the mountain roads of Greece. A previous accident twenty years earlier nearly put an end to my career when I smashed my wrist; for a brief and very frightening period it looked unlikely I'd ever play guitar again. This time I'd merely fallen off and cracked my ribcage. No major damage done, except I was due to play a festival back in London to mark Buzzcocks' inauguration into the Camden Music Walk of Fame. My doctor advised against it, but then my doctor's not from Manchester. Where I come from, Man City goalkeeper Bert Trautmann once won an FA Cup final with a broken neck. In the same spirit, it'd take more than a bandaged torso to keep this United fan from his hour of glory.

But it's true, in nearly 50 years, we'd received fuck all. Not a Brit, not a Grammy, not an Ivor Novello, nothing. Until this. A stone in the pavement of Camden High Street joining those for Amy Winehouse, the Who, David Bowie and dozens of others added each year. Our place in the pantheon of greats. To be trodden on for eternity by cybergoths.

The honour was bittersweet, coming nearly five years after Pete died and less than a year since our dear manager, Raf, died of a heart attack at the wheel of his car while driving home from a Buzzcocks gig in Coventry. The lightning strikes just keep on coming. Raf was 79 and spent the last 33 of those years doing as much, if not more, for us as a band than anybody I can think of. But then, by 2023, so many other players in our story were long gone: Martin Hannett, aged 42; Joe Strummer, 50; Tony Wilson, 57; Malcolm McLaren, 64; Martin Rushent, 62; not forgetting Ian Curtis, 23, and Kurt Cobain, 27. Yet here I was, a daft old 68-year-old moaning about a broken rib, having miraculously outlived the lot of them. Fate really is a picky bastard.

The inauguration ceremony took place on a sunny Friday morning in early September, in a roped-off section of Camden High Street in front of a small audience of invited media, friends and guest speakers including my great mate Gary Crowley, one of the best broadcasters in the business who never gets the recognition he deserves. Ever the fan's fan, he brought along his original cassette copy of *Singles Going Steady*. How can you not love Crowley?

As proceedings began, myself, Chris, Danny, our new guitarist Mani Perazzoli and our tour manager Pablo took our seats in the front row just as the host stepped up to the podium: a lanky bloke with glasses and a ponytail wearing a Ben Sherman shirt named Phil Alexander who used to edit *Mojo* – funnily enough, the only magazine that ever did give Buzzcocks an award, in 2006, for 'Inspiration'. He started off by talking about our punk origins.

'Obviously, the early line-up of Steve Shelley . . .'

Eh? Who's he?

'. . . Howard Devoto, obviously, and Steve Diggle and John Mayer . . .'

Mayer? It's Maher, mate. Or maybe he's thinking of John Major?

'. . . opened for the Pistols in '76 . . .'

At least he got that one right.

'Then there's the incredible albums. To be honest with you, that run of three. *Another Music In A Different Kitchen* . . .'

Yep. Great album.

'. . . *Love Bites* . . .'

That one too, yep.

'. . . and *A Different Kind Of Tension . . .*'
The yellow one? Are you fucking serious?
'. . . they're just stone-cold classics without a doubt.'
The last one isn't. You heard it, mate? Stone cold, maybe, but no classic. Where's he getting this all from, Wikipedia?
'Following Steve's passing in 2018 . . .'
JESUS CHRIST!

At that point I thought I must be hallucinating. That it had to be the painkillers for my ribs playing tricks with my hearing. But then I could see everyone around me, Chris, Danny, Pablo, all staring at me giving it the 'eh?' face. I still wouldn't have believed it had someone not taped the whole thing and played it back. But he definitely said it. 'Following Steve's passing.'

That just about summed up my career. Forty-seven years of nobody giving a shit, and when the day finally comes to be honoured for my life's service to Buzzcocks they're already talking about me like I'm dead. You could balls it up, but you really couldn't make it up.

At least everyone else who got near the podium gave a lovely testimonial: Lee Bennett, the founder of the Music Walk of Fame, good old Crowley who, bless him, even quoted 'No Moët – no show-ay', and Carl Barât from the Libertines, another band we'd actively inspired. Then it came to my turn.

I hadn't prepared anything as I just wanted to speak off the cuff, in the moment. Had I been a bit quicker, I should've started with, 'Reports of my death have been greatly exaggerated.' Instead, I waffled on a bit, not expecting it to feel as emotional as it did. Now I understood, if only a little, how Dave Grohl must have felt at the MTV Awards all those years ago.

'We've got to remember my dear, dear brother Pete Shelley today. Without him, y'know . . .'

When I said that everyone started clapping. *Bloody typical! Never mind hope heaven loves you, Pete, you're still stealing my thunder down here!*

Finally, once all the speeches were done, the moment came for the unveiling of our stone. A black circle in a beautiful blue granite surround, laid in the pavement beside the New Rock leather and boot store. Better that than KFC. It's a very simple marker, spelling out everything it needs in just a few words: 'BUZZCOCKS', 'ICON', '2023'. But my favourite thing of all is what it says directly under our name.

'MANCHESTER, ENGLAND'.

Take that, Bolton. The true birthplace of Buzzcocks, there for all the world to see. Literally written in stone.

THERE ARE A THOUSAND MORE TALES I could tell. Crazy rock'n'roll war stories from 40 years on the road, of endless sex and drugs, dealers with guns, falling off stage, comic run-ins with other musicians, the sort of yarns I'd share holding court in the pub that land best when the listener is a few drinks in. I could probably make a night of them and sell tickets – 'An Audience with Steve Diggle' – and sit there on my stool with a pint and a microphone, brushing my trousers like *Dave Allen at Large*, raconteuring for hours. It'd be funny, and people would laugh. But the thing is, they'd just be silly stories. Punchlines with no meaning. Not *the* story.

The same goes for my friends. There are a great many important people in my life, best mates I've known for decades, who I've not written about, all probably reaching this point in the book and screaming, 'Almost the last page, and that wanker's still not mentioned me!' I hope they know who they are, and how much I love them. But this is my book, not Eamonn Andrews' red book. They're all important characters in my life – just not in the story I've chosen to tell.

So what *is* my story?

I came from nothing. I'm scrapheap Northern factory-fodder class. I had no hope or prospects in life. Then punk rock saved me, same as it did Pete. It made my childhood rock'n'roll dream come true. To this day, I've never taken it for granted.

It's a bit like another favourite novel, *Martin Eden* by Jack London. Most people only know him for his books about wolves, but *Martin Eden* is the one to read. It's semi-autobiographical, about a poor bloke from the gutter who doesn't even know how to hold a knife and fork but who's obsessed with becoming a writer and bettering himself in middle-class society. Eventually, after a lot of hardship and rejection, he does, only by the time he becomes a hugely successful author he's so disillusioned he realises that fame and money and status is all a load of bollocks. The thing that he wished for turns out to be a soulless existence. And so poor Martin Eden goes the way of Curtis and Cobain and commits suicide by drowning himself in the sea. The powerful ending always stuck with me because, unless it was a freak printing error in my copy, the last sentence deliberately has no full stop.

Obviously, I'm nothing like Martin Eden, psychologically. My mantra still remains 'life's too serious to be taken seriously'. But the coming from nothing and suddenly getting the thing you always thought impossible I totally understand. The difference is Martin Eden made the mistake of thinking it would make him a better person. I never have. I've played on stage at Madison Square Garden, but I'm no better and no different from when I used to queue for a bus in Manchester Piccadilly Gardens. Success is nice, and so is a comfortable income, but that's not what drives me. What drives me is music and freedom, same as it did when I was 18, living at home on the dole. I'm still the same Steve Diggle. Snap me in half and you'll find 'Autonomy' running through me like a stick of rock.

I always thought that when I got to 65 I'd retire and become a lollipop man. But that milestone's already passed and I'm still here. The moment I ever do get sick of playing, I'll have no qualms about stopping. It's just that I can't see it happening. Not unless I fall off a scooter and break my wrist again, this time permanently. Until then, I still believe in the holy church of rock'n'roll. Standing on stage, looking out at the crowd, I see it all. God, the devil and the gas bill. Good or bad, it's all still one harmony in my head.

Actually, that's the one song that's now become a bit of a monster live as I've gone a bit Dylan with the arrangement. Not changing the tune, just extending it by adding an extra spoken bit. My punk soliloquy, as I call it.

'Tall glass corporate buildings are making you feel that small,
Take your library books back – if there is a fucking library,
Take your feet off the table!
No parking!
You talking to me? Am I talking to you?

I don't want to be a soldier, I don't want to kill no one,
I don't want to see some fucker diiiiiiiiiiiiie!'

Ian Brown saw me play it and told me afterwards, 'Steve, you've got to stop doing that new bit in "Harmony In My Head"!' He didn't get that for me to still stand up there I've got to keep the paint wet. I'm not trying to recreate the past, I'm trying to create the future. I don't want to be permanently trapped in the bell jar of back then. I need to be free in the here and now, for as long as I've got left.

As long as I've got left?

I don't think about it. What's the point?

We can't control the lightning strikes. Mine's coming one day, I know. There's a bolt with my name on it, same as there was for Pete. Between drugs, car crashes, electric shocks and child murderers, I've already dodged more than my share for one lifetime. Knowing my luck, it'll probably get me on a dull Thursday morning when I'm crossing the road to buy some cigarettes. But that's out of my hands. Every day I wake up is another day I'm not dead, and until I am I'll live each one to the full. Freedom, music, friends. Take it from one who's already lost too many: we're lucky bastards, all of us, who are still here. Because when the house lights rise at the end of the gig, life is the only harmony that matters. That's why I refuse to give mine a full stop

THE BUZZCOCKS SONGS OF STEVE DIGGLE

All listed by first year of release; where appropriate, any demos and rarities issued at a much later date are included in their original year of recording.

1978
'Fast Cars' (*Another Music In A Different Kitchen* LP; title and music by Diggle, words by Shelley and Devoto)

'Autonomy' (*Another Music In A Different Kitchen* LP; also B-side of 'I Don't Mind')

'I Need' (*Another Music In A Different Kitchen* LP; music by Diggle, words by Shelley)

'Love Is Lies' (*Love Bites* LP)

'Late For The Train' (*Love Bites* LP; music by Diggle, Garvey, Maher and Shelley)

'Promises' (A-side; music by Diggle, words by Shelley; original words also by Diggle as heard on the working demo titled 'Children' available on various reissues)

1979
'Why Can't I Touch It?' (B-side of 'Everybody's Happy Nowadays'; music by Diggle, Garvey, Maher and Shelley; words by Shelley)

'Harmony In My Head' (A-side)

'Sitting Round At Home' (*A Different Kind Of Tension* LP)
'You Know You Can't Help It' (*A Different Kind Of Tension* LP)
'Mad Mad Judy' (*A Different Kind Of Tension* LP)
'The Drive System' (demoed 1979; released on the 1997 rarities compilation *Chronology*)
'Jesus Made Me Feel Guilty' (demoed 1979; released on the 1997 rarities compilation *Chronology*)

1980
'Why She's A Girl From The Chainstore' (AA-side of 'Are Everything')
'Airwaves Dream' (AA-side of 'Strange Thing')
'Running Free' (A-side)

1991
'Alive Tonight' (A-side; later re-recorded for *Trade Test Transmissions* LP)
'Successful Street' (12-inch B-side of above)
'Wallpaper World' (recorded 1991; released in 2020 on *The 1991 Demo Album*)
'Searching For Your Love' (recorded 1991; released in 2020 on *The 1991 Demo Album*)
'Tranquillizer' (recorded 1991; released in 2020 on *The 1991 Demo Album*)

1993
'Isolation' (*Trade Test Transmissions* LP)
'When Love Turns Around' (*Trade Test Transmissions* LP)
'Energy' (*Trade Test Transmissions* LP)
'Unthinkable' (*Trade Test Transmissions* LP)
'Trash Away' (B-side of 'Do It' single from *Trade Test Transmissions* LP)
'Inside' (B-side of 'Innocent' single from *Trade Test Transmissions* LP)

1994
'Roll It Over' (B-side of 'Libertine Angel' single)

STEVE DIGGLE

1996
'What Am I Supposed To Do' (*All Set* LP)
'Playing For Time' (*All Set* LP)
'Back With You' (*All Set* LP)
'Holding Me Down' (*All Set* LP, Japanese edition bonus track; alternative version featured as B-side of 'Reconciliation' single, 2006)
'Television World' (*All Set* LP, Japanese edition bonus track)
'Everyday Sky' (*All Set* LP, Japanese edition bonus track)
'Every Day And Every Night' (demoed 1996; released as B-side of 'Sell You Everything' single, 2006)

1999
'Speed Of Life' (*Modern* LP)
'Don't Let The Car Crash' (*Modern* LP)
'Doesn't Mean Anything' (*Modern* LP)
'Turn Of The Screw' (*Modern* LP)
'Stranger In Your Town' (*Modern* LP)

2003
'Sick City Sometimes' (single from *Buzzcocks* LP)
'Wake Up Call' (*Buzzcocks* LP)
'Driving You Insane' (*Buzzcocks* LP)
'Certain Move' (*Buzzcocks* LP)
'Up For The Crack' (*Buzzcocks* LP)
'Don't Come Back' (B-side of 'Jerk' single from *Buzzcocks* LP)

2006
'Sell You Everything' (single from *Flat-Pack Philosophy* LP)
'Soul Survivor' (*Flat-Pack Philosophy* LP)
'Big Brother Wheels' (*Flat-Pack Philosophy* LP)
'Sound Of A Gun' (*Flat-Pack Philosophy* LP)
'Between Heaven And Hell' (*Flat-Pack Philosophy* LP)
'Don't Matter What You Say' (B-side of 'Wish I Never Loved You' single from *Flat-Pack Philosophy* LP)
'See Through You' (B-side of 'Reconciliation' CD single from *Flat-Pack Philosophy* LP)

2014

'People Are Strange Machines' (*The Way* LP)

'In The Back' (single from *The Way* LP)

'Third Dimension' (*The Way* LP)

'Changing Rainbows/Modern Times' (*The Way* LP)

'Saving Yourself' (*The Way* LP)

'Generation Suicide' (B-side of 'It's Not You' single from *The Way* LP)

'Dream On Baby' (B-side of 'The Way' single from *The Way* LP)

2020

'Gotta Get Better' (A-side)

'Destination Zero' (B-side of above)

2022

'Senses Out Of Control' (10-inch single from *Sonics In The Soul* LP)

'Carnival Of Illusion' (from 'Senses Out Of Control' 10-inch single)

'Hope Heaven Loves You' (from 'Senses Out Of Control' 10-inch single)

'Manchester Rain' (*Sonics In The Soul* LP)

'You've Changed Everything Now' (*Sonics In The Soul* LP)

'Bad Dreams' (*Sonics In The Soul* LP)

'Nothingless World' (*Sonics In The Soul* LP)

'Don't Mess With My Brain' (*Sonics In The Soul* LP)

'Just Got To Let It Go' (*Sonics In The Soul* LP)

'Everything Is Wrong' (*Sonics In The Soul* LP)

'Experimental Farm' (*Sonics In The Soul* LP)

'Can You Hear Tomorrow' (*Sonics In The Soul* LP)

'Venus Eyes' (*Sonics In The Soul* LP)

STEVE DIGGLE NON-BUZZCOCKS DISCOGRAPHY

1981 / STEVE DIGGLE
50 Years Of Comparative Wealth *(IRS Records, 7-inch EP)*
'Shut Out The Light (Rothko)', '50 Years Of Comparative Wealth', 'Here Comes The Fire Brigade'

1982 / FLAG OF CONVENIENCE
'Life On The Telephone'/'The Other Man's Sin' *(Sire, 7-inch single)*
+ 'Picking Up On Audio Sound' *(PVC Records, 12-inch single version)*

1984 / FLAG OF CONVENIENCE
'Change'/'Longest Life' *(Weird Sisters, 7-inch single)*

The Big Secret *(Self-released cassette album)*
'Change', 'The Arrow Has Come', 'Drift Away', 'Picking Up', 'Life On The Telephone', 'Longest Life', 'Men From The City', 'Who Is Innocent', 'Both Hands In The Fire'

1986 / FLAG OF CONVENIENCE
'New House'/'Keep On Pushing (Live)' *(MCM Records, 7-inch single)*

1987 / F.O.C.
Northwest Skyline *(MCM Records, LP)*
'Northwest Skyline', 'Pictures In My Mind',* 'Just Like Mr Trendy Said', 'Hell Is Other People', 'Should I Ever Go Deaf',* 'Drowned In Your Heartache',* 'The Destructor', 'Gaol Of Love', 'The Greatest Sin',* 'From Day To Day (And Other Days)', 'Mirror Of The World'
*(Tracks marked * also released separately on 'Should I Ever Go Deaf', MCM Records, 12-inch EP.)*

'Last Train To Safety'/'The Rain In England', 'Human Jungle' *(MCM Records, 12-inch single listed as THE F.O.C.)*

1988 / F.O.C.
Exiles *(MCM Records, 12-inch EP)*
'Exiles', 'Can't Stop The World', 'Shot Down With Your Gun', 'Tragedy In Market Street'

War On The Wireless Set *(MCM America, US LP)*
'Heartbreak Story', 'In The Back', 'Danger Time', 'New House', 'Scene Of The Crime', 'Graduate Of Pain', 'No Escape', 'Show Boy', 'One Hundred Tears', 'Drift Away'

1989 / BUZZCOCKS F.O.C.
'Tomorrow's Sunset', 'Life With The Lions'/'Sunset 12-inch Bat Mix'
(Thin Line, 12-inch and CD single)

1993 / STEVE DIGGLE
Heated & Rising *(3.30 Records, CD EP)*
'Heated & Rising', 'Over & Out', 'Terminal', 'Wednesday's Flowers'

2000 / STEVE DIGGLE
Some Reality *(3.30 Records, CD album)*
'Just Because', 'Playing With Fire', 'Where You're From', 'Time Of Your Life', 'Blowing Hot', 'Three Sheets To The Wind', 'What Else Can You Do', 'Something In Your Mind', 'Heavy Hammer', 'All Around Your Face', 'Turning Point'

STEVE DIGGLE

2005 / STEVE DIGGLE
Serious Contender *(3.30 Records, CD album)*
'Serious Contender', 'Lie In Bed', 'Hard Highway', 'Wallpaper World', 'See Through You', 'Starbucks Around The World', 'Across The Sun', 'Round And Round', 'Terminal', 'If I Never Get To Heaven', 'Jet Fighter', 'Shake The System', 'Early Grave'

2010 / STEVE DIGGLE & THE REVOLUTION OF SOUND
Air Conditioning *(3.30 Records, CD album)*
'In The Air', 'Hey Maria', 'Planet Star', 'World Spinning Round', 'Listen To Your Tambourine', 'Rock Revolution Punk', 'Yeah Man Yeah', 'Victory Road', 'Altitude High', 'Plastic Kisses', 'Changing Of Your Guard', 'Sparkle Of The Sun', 'Rock Revolution Punk (Acoustic Version)'

2014 / STEVE DIGGLE
'Gotta Get Better' *(3.30 Records, digital single)*

2016 / STEVE DIGGLE
Inner Space Times *(3.30 Records, CD album)*
'Sound Of The Soul (Intro)', 'Wake Up The Dream', 'Bang Apocalypse', 'Way Too Far', 'Kaleidoscope Girl', 'Sick City Sometimes (Piano Version)', 'Bullet In Your Heart', 'Desolation Rainbow', 'The Weatherman Said', 'Holding On', 'I Can't Promise Anything Today', 'Inner Space Times', 'Sound Of The Soul (Outro)'

Wheels Of Time *(3.30 Records, 4-CD box set)*
Boxed collection of the albums *Some Reality*, *Serious Contender*, *Air Conditioning* and *Inner Space Times*.

For further information visit www.stevediggle.co.uk

ACKNOWLEDGEMENTS

Steve Diggle would like to thank

Jack Wrightson-Diggle, Dale, Judith Wrightson
Janet, Eric, Wendy, Sandra, Philip Diggle
George, Philip, Natalie, Terry Lavin, Nicholas, Steve Fletcher
Gia Barbera (lawyer) and Sally
Eleni Zachou, Nikolaos Zachou, Aikaterini Paparizou
Tomo Nomuk, Sonia Garcia, Justin and Yuka Dickens
Rock Pete, Pete Jones, Alan Parker, Terry Rawlings
James Russell, Chalki, Westi, Paul Andrew Bedford
Katie Taty, Joe, Sophie Nobbs and Rob
Chris Remington, Mani Perazzoli, Danny Farrant
Ollie Slaney and Sophie
Liam, Debbie, Katie, Paul, Wilko
Kayleigh, Paul Prince of Wales, Eon Ballinger
Jim Sturman KC for pending legal services
Kevin Pocklington at the North Literary Agency
Simon Goddard, Alison Rae
David 'Baz' Barraclough and everyone at Omnibus Press